☐ A History of Small Business in America

TWAYNE'S EVOLUTION OF AMERICAN BUSINESS SERIES

Industries Institutions, and Entrepreneurs

Edwin J. Perkins
SERIES EDITOR
UNIVERSITY OF SOUTHERN CALIFORNIA

OTHER TITLES

The American Automobile Industry
    John B. Rae

DuPont and the International Chemical Industry
    Graham D. Taylor and Patricia E. Sudnik

E. H. Harriman: Master Railroader
    Lloyd J. Mercer

The Credit Card Industry
    Lewis Mandell

American Commercial Banking
    Benjamin J. Klebaner

The United States Tire Industry
    Michael J. French

The Amusement Park Industry
    Judith A. Adams

America's Search for Economic Stability
    Kenneth Weiher

☐ A HISTORY OF SMALL BUSINESS IN AMERICA

Mansel G. Blackford

TWAYNE PUBLISHERS ☐ NEW YORK
Maxwell Macmillan Canada Toronto
Maxwell Macmillan International
New York Oxford Singapore Sydney

A History of Small Business in America
Mansel G. Blackford

Copyright © 1991 by Twayne Publishers

Twayne Publishers   Maxwell Macmillan Canada, Inc.
Macmillan Publishing Company   1200 Eglinton Avenue East
866 Third Avenue   Suite 200
New York, New York 10022   Don Mills, Ontario M3C 3N1

Macmillan Publishing Company is part of the Maxwell Communication Group
of Companies.

Library of Congress Cataloging-in-Publication Data

Blackford, Mansel G., 1944–
    A history of small business in America / Mansel G. Blackford.
        p.   cm. — (Twayne's evolution of American business series)
    Includes bibliographical references (p.   ) and index.
    ISBN 0-8057-9824-2 (hc : alk. paper). — ISBN 0-8057-9825-0 (pb :
alk. paper)
    1. Small business—United States—History. 2. Small business—
Government policy—United States—History. I. Title. II. Series:
Twayne's evolution of American business series : no. 10.
HD2346.U5B56 1991
338.6′42′0973—dc20   91-41983
                                                              CIP

10 9 8 7 6 5 4 3 2 1

Printed in the United States of America

For K. Austin Kerr, a friend and colleague

CONTENTS

Preface   ix

Introduction: Americans, Scholars, and
Small Business   xi

1   The Traditional Business System: Small
    Firms before 1880   1

2   Small Business in the Age of Giant
    Enterprise, 1880–1920   27

3   Government Policies for Small Business,
    1921–1971   63

4   Small Business in a Maturing National
    Economy, 1921–1971   82

5   Small Business in Modern America,
    1972–1990   106

    Conclusion: Future Research Needs   121
    Chronology   126
    Notes and References   129
    Selected Bibliography   163
    Index   173

PREFACE

IN LIGHT OF BOTH THE EXPANDING INTER-
est in small business in general and our growing understanding of small
firms, the time is ripe for a study that pulls together and makes sense of the
history of small businesses in America. This volume presents a comprehensive, chronological account of the history of small business in the United
States, focusing on two interrelated issues: (a) the changing place of small
business in America's business system, including an examination of managerial strategies and the institutional growth of small firms, and (b) the
evolution of public attitudes and public policies toward small businesses.
This book describes and analyzes the changing fortunes of small businesses
in farming, manufacturing, sales, and services from colonial times to the
present. While always focusing on small business, this study of necessity
examines the evolving relationship between big business and small business
after 1880, when big business began developing in a major way.

The Introduction presents an overview of small business, examining
the definition and importance of such firms. Chapter 1 looks at small
business development prior to 1880, when big businesses first began
emerging in manufacturing in large numbers. In these early years small
businesses were the norm in nearly all fields, and a small business ideology began developing. Chapter 2 examines how small businesses coped
with the rise of big businesses through 1920. Chapters 3 and 4 analyze
small business development as a part of America's maturing business
system between 1921 and 1971. During these years small firms faced
growing competition from big businesses in sales as well as in manufacturing and responded by trying to protect themselves through state and
national legislation. Chapter 5 examines small business from 1972 to
1990, a time marked by growing foreign competition for American firms
and by the occurrence of significant changes in relations between large and
small firms. Finally, the Conclusion suggests possible avenues for future
research concerning small business in America.

I have long been interested in the history of small business in America, both personally and professionally. My father was involved in the formation of several small businesses, one of them quite successful and another not. His work—for there was lots of work—in these small firms intrigued me as I grew up and made me wonder just what motivated him and others of his ilk. My field of research and teaching has been business history. I chose to work in this field because examining the development of business institutions in the United States has always seemed to me a fruitful way to understand the country's cultural, political, and social, as well as economic, evolution. More than most nations, the United States has possessed a business culture. Yet that culture and those business institutions have been only partly explored. Business historians and other scholars have focused their energies mainly on trying to unravel the development of big business in America, to the neglect of small enterprises. I hope this study will help redress that imbalance and thereby add to our understanding of both business institutions and broader matters of culture and politics in the United States.

I have incurred many intellectual debts in the preparation of this volume, and I would like to take this opportunity to thank those who have helped me. Particular thanks are owed Professor Edwin Perkins for encouraging me to undertake this daunting project and for providing useful comments and suggestions on my work as it progressed. Carol C. Chin, a senior editor for Twayne Publishers, also provided valuable advice. I would like to thank, too, Professors John Ingham and Philip Scranton for their comments and ideas on parts of my study. Professor Thomas Dicke read and commented on the entire manuscript, and his suggestions improved it in numerous ways. My colleagues in American business history at Ohio State University—Professors K. Austin Kerr, William Childs, and Monys Hagen (a postdoctoral fellow for 1989–90)—have been most supportive, frequently sharing with me their thoughts on small business development. Marjorie Haffner provided very helpful secretarial services, and Dr. and Mrs. A. M. Fulton read and commented on the manuscript in its entirety, providing useful suggestions on how it might be improved for general readers. I remain, of course, responsible for any errors of fact or interpretation this study may contain.

INTRODUCTION
Americans, Scholars, and Small Business

OBSERVING THE AMERICAN SCENE IN THE early 1830s, the French writer and social commentator Alexis de Tocqueville noted, "What astonishes me in the United States is not so much the marvelous grandeur of some undertakings as the innumerable multitude of small ones."[1] Some 150 years later, President Ronald Reagan asserted that a "strong small business record" should be "a national priority," for only through the continued development of small enterprises could "all Americans who wish . . . turn ideas and dreams into businesses and jobs."[2] As these statements suggest, small businesses have long been central to American life. In fact, from the founding of the first colonies in the 1600s to the present day, small businesses have been integral to the economic, political, and cultural development of the United States.

Despite their importance, small businesses have until quite recently attracted less attention from scholars than larger enterprises have. "That scholars know far too little about the history of small enterprise is a truism," observed the business historian Ralph Hidy in 1970.[3] Over the past two decades, however, there has been an awakening of interest in small businesses on the part of historians, social scientists, and faculty members at business schools. As big businesses have faltered as engines of economic growth in America, some observers have come to see smaller firms as likely sources for economic rejuvenation. This introduction provides historical context for that growing interest by briefly surveying the changing roles small businesses have played in America and by looking in more detail at how scholars have dealt with small firms.

□ What Is Small?

Despite the progress being made in scholarly understanding of small business, there exists no agreement on what is meant by "small." As the head of the Small Business Administration (SBA) noted in 1988, "There is no standard size definition of a small business."[4] The law setting up the SBA in 1953 stated that a small business is a firm "independently owned and operated . . . and not dominant in its field of operation."[5] Since its establishment, the SBA has defined small businesses in different ways. In the late 1950s, the agency viewed as small industrial establishments with fewer than 250 employees, wholesalers whose annual sales amounted to $5 million or less, and retail and service businesses with yearly sales of $1 million or less.[6] Thirty years later, reflecting the growing sizes of businesses in the United States, the SBA was defining any firm with 500 or fewer employees as small, though the acceptable maximum number of employees might vary by industry group. For instance, in retail sales only those firms with 100 or fewer employees were considered small, "since most retail establishments have only a few employees, and most retail firms have few establishments." A more precise breakdown of the size categories in use by the SBA in 1988 was as follows: under 20 employees, very small; 20–99, small; 100–499, medium-size; and over 500, large.[7]

Scholars have differed in their delineation of small businesses. While many have accepted the definitions of the SBA, others have focused on functional characteristics, rather than on absolute measures of size. Thus, in a 1955 study the economist Harold Vatter differentiated between large and small firms in the butter, flour, automobile, and glass container industries by noting that small businesses were more likely to (a) rely on local sources for raw materials, (b) have higher total unit costs of production, (c) be one-plant establishments, and (d) be dependent on larger firms.[8] By the same token, the economic historian Ross Robertson observed, "It seems best to define 'small' business in relative terms. A business remains 'small' as long as its guiding venturer and chief operating officer maintains direct and firm lines of communication with his operating managers and keeps personal ties with a large proportion of his work force, including all key personnel."[9]

To me the functional approach makes sense, for most small businesses seem to share several characteristics. Their management arrangements are usually simple. The chief executive officer, who is often also the owner, runs the business personally. He or she knows the other managers and most of the workers. In a small company I have studied, one of the directors recalled that in the firm's formative years its management setup consisted simply of "a gang" of friends fighting for their lives.[10] In small companies the elaborate hierarchies of top, middle, and lower management that normally exist in big businesses are not present. Moreover, most small businesses are single-unit enterprises. They do not have plants or offices in more than one locality. As locally oriented companies, small businesses commonly recruit their work forces from their communities and are deeply involved in community affairs. They are also more apt than larger firms to purchase their raw materials locally and to produce for local rather than national or international markets.[11]

Nonetheless, the question of just what constitutes a small firm must be approached with caution. It is important to recognize that (a) neither large nor small firms constitute entirely homogeneous groups and (b) a "gray," intermediate area exists between the two groups. Certainly, conceptions of small businesses have varied from one period to the next, as demonstrated by the shifting definitions offered by the SBA in just the post–World War II period. Firms with 100 employees that are today seen as small businesses by the SBA would in the mid-1800s have been viewed as large by most Americans. Finally, it is important to understand that what is regarded as small in one field of endeavor may be seen as large in another.[12]

Wherever possible, I have taken the functional approach in defining small businesses in this study; however, my work is a synthesizing study, relying largely on the studies of other scholars and the investigations of federal government agencies. Since others have often taken approaches based on absolute measures of size—most commonly, the number of employees in a firm—I have had to be eclectic in my approach to definitions of the nature of businesses.

☐ The Importance of Small Business in America

Small businesses have always played significant roles in America's economic evolution. As is now well known through the writings of Alfred D. Chandler, Jr., and other business historians, prior to the mid-1800s small businesses were the norm in the United States.[13] Thousands of small firms handled the production and distribution of goods and services in the American economy. Only from the middle nineteenth century did many big businesses emerge in fields where new technologies permitted economies of scale in the production and/or distribution of goods. When they did develop, first in railroads and then in certain industrial fields, big businesses came to dominate those sectors of the economy in which they arose and were sustained. Small businesses did not, however, disappear. They adjusted to the presence of big businesses. While their relative share of America's industrial output declined, small businesses continued to grow in absolute numbers, even in manufacturing. By developing market niches ignored by large manufacturers or by becoming the suppliers of intermediate goods to larger industrial firms, small businesses persisted in the industrial segment of America's business system. Only in farming did small businesses dramatically decrease in significance. In most other fields—in the sales and service sectors, especially—small firms, while losing market shares to larger concerns, remained important.

The years after World War II witnessed fluctuations in the fortunes of small businesses. The 1950s and 1960s were a period of decline for most types of small firms. While the aggregate number of businesses, nearly all of which were small enterprises, rose in the United States from about 11 million in 1958 to nearly 17 million in 1980, the relative importance of small businesses fell. Something of a resurgence in small business occurred in the late 1970s and the 1980s. Particularly noticeable was the growing role of small business in manufacturing. In a reversal of its previous decline relative to big business, small business increased its share of America's total manufacturing output from 33 to 37% between 1976 and 1986. As the head of the Office of Advocacy of the SBA noted in 1988, "Small businesses have done exceptionally well during the 1980s."[14]

If small businesses have been vital to America's economic development, they have perhaps been even more important as a component of American culture. More so than in other nations, culture in the United States has developed as a business culture. As early as 1837, a German immigrant to America, Francis J. Grund, observed, "Business is the very soul of an American; he pursues it . . . as the fountain of all human felicity."[15] The love affair of most Americans with business has focused especially on small business. From the time of Thomas Jefferson to the present, many Americans have seen the owners of small businesses as epitomizing all that is best about the American way of life.

Even as they embraced what they viewed as the superior efficiency and productivity of big businesses, Americans continued to revere small business people. For many, as the historian Rowland Berthoff has observed, they symbolized "self-reliant personal independence," and by their continued existence small businesses seemed to offer a chance of "upward[ly]-mobile, dynamic entrepreneurship."[16] Twentieth-century Americans, however, have frequently differentiated between small businesses, which they have seen as inefficient and backward, and small business people, whom they have continued to admire. Following World War II, the small business owner was often pictured as a bastion of political as well as economic democracy in the cold war between the United States and the Soviet Union. In his study of small business, the political scientist John Bunzel captured well the enduring symbolic importance of small business people to Americans: "He [the small business person] appears to have few enemies and is, in fact, something of a national hero. In his own way he represents the independence, freedom, and perseverance that have long been identified with the American way of doing things. . . . The small businessman has managed to be a symbol of success even in times when he has not, in point of fact, been financially successful. If the myth is sometimes stronger than the reality, it is only because it reinforces the tradition of individualism upon which so much in American life has been dependent."[17]

The importance of small business to the development of America's business system and cultural values has carried over into the political realm as well. Small businesses have often received special treatment in state and national legislation. A major reason for the enactment of America's first antitrust laws, the Sherman Act in 1890 and the Clayton Act in 1914, was a generalized desire to protect small firms from the perceived "unfair" encroachments of larger companies, even though the larger businesses were usually much more efficient in their production and distribution of goods to consumers.[18] In the 1920s and 1930s, large chain store operations extended their reach throughout the United States. Competing with smaller mom-and-pop grocery stores and drugstores, the chains frequently benefited from economies of scale and were able to sell at prices lower than those of their smaller rivals. Responding to this threat to small businesses, a number of states passed legislation heavily taxing chain stores, and Congress enacted the Robinson-Patman Act of 1936 and the Miller-Tydings Act of 1937 to shield small retailers from the competition of larger firms.[19] More recently, Congress created the SBA in 1953 as a federal government agency charged with the goal of encouraging small business development in the United States and, through the Regulatory Flexibility Act of 1980 and other measures, exempted small firms from many aspects of federal government regulation of business.

Nevertheless, the expressed desires of Congress and the state legislatures have not usually succeeded. In fact, some of the legislation—the Sherman Act and perhaps the Robinson-Patman Act—have aided larger concerns at the expense of smaller ones, and other pieces of legislation designed to help small firms have been largely ineffective. Moreover, actions of the federal government, such as its defense procurement policies, have often favored large over small businesses.[20] Thus, a paradox has existed. Whereas Americans have generally admired the owners of small businesses and desired the preservation of small enterprises, even at the expense of economic efficiency, governmental policies nonetheless have often directly or indirectly furthered the development of big businesses in the United States. A discrepancy has existed between political rhetoric and reality, one that continues to the present day.

□ Scholarship Dealing with Small Business

Until recently, most historians have neglected the evolution of small business in favor of examining the development of big business. Although lamentable, this emphasis on the study of big business by historians is understandable. The rise of big businesses *did* transform parts of the business systems of the United States and the world. Change did occur most rapidly in the realm of big business, and so historians, generally more interested in chronicling change than in recording continuity, have focused on the larger companies and the executives who have run them. Then too, those wanting to study small businesses have faced practical difficulties: most small firms last for only a few years and fail to preserve the types of records historians need for their work.[21] Nonetheless, historians, while generally most interested in big businesses, have on occasion been concerned with the development of small businesses.

Retailing, a field long dominated by small firms, attracted much of the early attention given to small business. In the 1930s and 1940s, Lewis Atherton explored the evolution of retailing in a series of studies stressing the importance of small country stores to the development of America's marketing system.[22] A complex web bound the country stores to wholesalers and manufacturers in the United States and abroad. Atherton's works and the studies of other scholars showed the significance of these stores not simply as retail outlets but also as sources of credit and business information for people in their localities.[23]

Small business in manufacturing initially attracted less attention from historians, but two early case studies pointed to directions that later historians would follow. Martha Taber prepared a history of the companies, all small businesses, involved in the development of America's leading cutlery-making region, the Connecticut Valley, in 1955.[24] Taber showed that the same set of firms dominated the industry from its establishment in the 1830s through World War II. A year later Theodore Marburg published an account of the Smith and Griggs Company as a small business in the brass-fabricating industry. The development of specialty products, management by hard-driving entrepreneurs eager to pioneer in new production technologies, and maintenance of friendly personal relations with wholesalers brought growth and prosperity to Smith and Griggs between the time of its founding, in 1865, and about 1908. Conversely, the erosion of those factors led to a decline in the company's fortunes in the twentieth century, and it went out of existence in 1936.[25]

Going beyond these two studies, the economic and business historian James H. Soltow, in a path-breaking work published in 1965, examined the evolution of small metal-fabricating and machine-making companies in New England between 1890 and 1957.[26] Like Taber and Marburg, Soltow found in their ability to carve out market niches for their products a leading reason for the persistence of successful small businesses over several generations. Widely reprinted, this extended essay showed that small businesses, even in manufacturing, could successfully adjust to the rise of big businesses in the United States.

Historians' interest in small businesses heightened in the 1970s and early 1980s, as it became apparent that America's big businesses were having increasing trouble with foreign competition. The 17 essays composing *Small Business in American Life*, edited by Stuart Bruchey and appearing in 1980, illustrated the wide variety of social and economic roles played by small business owners in the development of the United States. Rich in the diversity of its offerings, this volume pointed out the need for additional work on the history of small businesses.[27] Two of my own studies, published in 1979 and 1982, respectively, examined the relationship between small business growth and regional development in southern Alaska and in central Ohio.[28] My works suggested that necessary to the successful development of small businesses were many factors, some internal to the firms, others having to do with their external environments. More recently, Steven Fraser, Amos Loveday, and Michael Santos have paid special attention to the interactions among technological changes, managerial strategies, and labor relations in small firms in the men's clothing, nail-making, and iron-making industries.[29]

Particularly noteworthy, however, have been Philip Scranton's examination of small firms in Philadelphia's textile industry and John M. Ingham's study of independent businesses in Pittsburgh's iron and steel industry. In findings strikingly similar to those of Soltow some 20 years earlier, Scranton and Ingham have shown that by developing market niches, using flexible production techniques, and depending on a highly skilled labor force, small businesses could compete successfully with the much-larger firms across the nation. These studies also illuminate, however, the limits to small business success in manufacturing. Scranton's work in particular highlights the inability of the small Philadelphia textile makers to deal with the growing demands of ever-larger purchasers of their goods in the twentieth century, a failing that led to the demise of many of these textile firms in the 1920s, 1930s, and 1940s.[30]

Still other historians have explored connections between large and small companies in imaginative ways. Thomas Dicke has examined the history of franchising in the United States, looking at the relationships between large companies—Singer Sewing Machine, the McCormick Company, Ford Motors, Sun Oil, and Domino's—and their small franchise outlets. Dicke shows that over time, a general tightening of the controls franchisers exert over their franchisees has taken place. His work also illustrates that since World War II a fundamental change has occurred in franchising: the franchise outlets have become as much a product for sale as the goods sold through the outlets.[31]

Social scientists, as well as historians, have contributed to our growing understanding of the development of small business in America. Especially in the post–World War II years, political scientists and sociologists have probed—often in the hope of influencing government policies—the contributions of small business to the evolution of American culture. In 1947 the sociologist Kurt Mayer, in a study of small businesses as social institutions, lamented small businesses' loss of independence to larger concerns and called for a new public policy to address "the burning question of human dignity, of status and function in our industrial culture as a whole."[32] Seven years later, the political scientist Joseph Palamountain,

Jr., found that the efforts of small business people in the distribution of groceries, drugs, and automobiles to shield their firms from the encroachments of their larger competitors through protective legislation had "accomplished little." Neither did he think protective policies should be allowed, for their results might be "to subsidize inefficiency and reduce the vigor and creativity of this section [distribution] of the economy."[33] In a 1958 study focusing on firms with four or fewer paid employees, Joseph Phillips concluded that the independence of small firms was "illusory" and that most of the federal government's efforts to aid small businesses had "little or no relevance" to the problems they faced. The government should, he concluded, reassess its small business policies.[34] Several years later, Harmon Zeigler and John Bunzel, both political scientists, observed the continuing significance of the symbolic value of small business in American politics, despite the declining importance of small firms to the American economy.[35] In a wide-ranging 1975 examination of the roles myths play in politics, Richard Hamilton reached much the same conclusion. Elaborating on Zeigler's work, Hamilton showed that many of the organizations purporting to represent small businesses in national politics were far from being broadly based grass-roots associations; they were instead "creations of the entrepreneurs," scams concerned only with their own profitability and growth.[36]

Until very recently, most economists pictured big businesses as benefiting from scale economies that made their development nearly inevitable. Conversely, they sometimes depicted the persistence of small firms as the survival of relics from the past. After studying the evolution of relations between large and small firms, Harold Vatter concluded that large and small businesses were fundamentally different, with large companies forming an "oligopolistic core" in American industry and with the "remainder of the industry dispersed in . . . the small enterprise sector."[37] Later economists refined Vatter's ideas. Robert Averitt, John Kenneth Galbraith, and Joseph Bowring analyzed the development of a "dual economy" in the United States, an economy in which big businesses and small businesses exist in different fields and play different roles.[38] According to these accounts, big businesses tended to be capital-intensive firms that benefited from economies of scale and technological innovations. Found primarily in manufacturing, these companies were labeled "center firms" because they were seen as being at the heart of the American economy. Small businesses, which came to be designated "peripheral firms," were just the opposite: labor-intensive companies enjoying no economies of scale, benefiting from few technological innovations, and located mainly in the service and sales sectors of the economy.

The most current economic studies have, however, significantly altered the picture of the roles small firms have played in America's development and the relationship between large and small firms in the United States.

The economist and economic historian Jeremy Atack has stressed the importance of relatively small firms in the industrialization of the nation well into the nineteenth century.[39] By the same token, some economists examining the problems facing American manufacturers today have argued that the solution to America's economic crisis lies in moving out of the standardized mass production of homogeneous products and into a system of flexible production by smaller companies linked together in industrial communities. Michael J. Piore, an economist, and Charles F. Sabel, a political scientist, suggest in their best-selling *The Second Industrial Divide: Possibilities for Prosperity* that only in this manner can an industrial future be ensured for the United States. They see in flexible production "a strategy of permanent innovation: accommodation to ceaseless change, rather than an effort to control it." Such a strategy, they argue, needs to be based on "flexible—multi-use—equipment; skilled workers; and the creation, through politics, of an industrial community that restricts the forms of competition to those favoring innovation."[40] Similarly, Michael Storper and Susan Christopherson have recently offered a convincing picture of the emergence of small, flexible firms in the American motion picture industry in the 1970s and 1980s, as have Zoltan J. Acs in an examination of minimills in the steel industry and Bo Carlsson in a study of firms in metalworking industries.[41]

The findings of the historians Scranton and Ingham, mentioned earlier, should, however, give pause to any too-hasty acceptance of such prescriptions. As Scranton has observed, "Enthusiasm for recreating flexible industry in the absence of its history of efficacy and breakdown risks substituting a romanticized simplification for a creative alternative." Scranton himself is currently preparing a history of small nineteenth-century manufacturing firms. Tentatively entitled "Endless Novelty: The Other Side of Industrialization," the work will investigate "flexibility and batch manufacturing in various American industries ca. 1860–1950."[42]

Faculty members at colleges of business administration, as well as business writers in general, constitute the most recent group of scholars to deal with small business.[43] As David Gumpert, the editor of the *Harvard Business Review*, noted in 1984, "The literature on starting and managing small businesses has exploded in quality and quantity during the last few years" and the "number of colleges and universities offering courses on starting and operating small businesses has grown to several hundred from only a handful in 1970."[44] In the writings of these scholars small business people are often pictured as entrepreneurs.[45] For example, many of the papers presented at the annual conference on entrepreneurship sponsored since 1980 by the Center for Entrepreneurial Studies at Babson College have focused on small businesses.[46]

While recognizing that only a minority of small businesses survive their infancy to grow to maturity, these types of works have stressed the contributions those firms have made to the economic advance of the United

States in recent years. In several controversial studies, David Birch has expressed well the feelings of this school of thought.[47] Birch and scholars like him have attributed nearly all the jobs and technological innovations generated in modern America to small businesses. Not all scholars accept Birch's findings, however, and the precise role of small firms in creating jobs and making innovations remains unclear.

Owing to the work of historians, social scientists, and faculty in business administration, much more is known now about small businesses than was the case just two decades ago. Historians have studied the evolution of individual small businesses in a growing number of fields, and in recent works have underscored the importance of small flexible companies to America's advance while also recognizing their limitations. Sociologists and political scientists have been particularly concerned with the role America's small business ideology has played in the development of government-business relations in the United States and with the impact of public policies on small businesses. Economists have depicted the growth of a dual economy in America; though until the past decade or so such works have generally relegated small businesses to the periphery, recent economic studies have, by contrast, emphasized a more positive role for small flexible companies in America's development, especially in manufacturing. And like economists, business faculty members have in the 1980s and 1990s viewed small firms as the most dynamic segment of the American economy.

1

The Traditional Business System: Small Firms before 1880

WRITING IN 1849, JOHN BEAUCHAMP Jones, a small-scale Missouri storekeeper, captured well the importance of merchants in American life during the middle nineteenth century. "Wherever the surges of 'manifest destiny' scatter the seeds of civilization—whether it be in the solemn shade and solitude of the dark forests bordering the 'Mad Missouri,' or on the interminable prairies beyond the woods—the merchant or trader," Jones observed, "is always found in their midst."[1] Whether operating from offices called countinghouses in major cities, running small country stores, or roaming the backwoods as peddlers, it was merchants who held the business systems of colonial America and the early United States together. Thousands of small, personally owned and operated firms—such as Jones's country store—composed America's business system.

This chapter examines the myriad forms taken by small business development in merchandising, farming, nascent manufacturing, and service industries during the colonial and early national periods of American history. Before 1880, small businesses were the norm in most fields of endeavor, with single-unit, nonbureaucratic firms dotting the American landscape. Only in the 1880s would the dominance of small businesses be challenged by the rise of big business in America. Small businesses were important to Americans in noneconomic as well as economic senses, and this chapter probes the origins of a business ideology in America. From the first, America was a land dominated by

1

business people and business values. Setting off in the early 1830s for Arrow Rock, Missouri, then a frontier region, Jones expressed sentiments common in America. "I now determined to be a merchant, a millionaire, and nothing else," he exclaimed; "I resolved to make my way in the world, and to obtain wealth."[2] Getting ahead in America meant succeeding in the world of business, and at a time when few large firms existed, business success meant success as a small business person. Not surprisingly, a national ideology favorable to business, especially small business, developed from the time of the founding of the first colonies.

☐ Economic Growth and Limitations on Business Development

Rapid economic growth not only characterized the development of the American colonies and the new nation of the United States but also opened opportunities for the small business people who came to compose America's expanding commercial network. Technological, market, and financial limitations precluded the development of big businesses, except in a few fields, prior to 1880. Until these restrictions began to be lifted in the middle and late nineteenth century, small firms made up America's business system.[3]

Economic growth came from several sources in colonial America. The production of goods for foreign markets was a prime engine of growth. Throughout the colonial period the Atlantic Ocean served as a bridge connecting the colonies to overseas markets. By the 1760s and 1770s, the colonists were sending abroad a substantial share of all the crops they raised and the handicraft items they made—to the extent that perhaps 20% of the colonists' income derived from these exports. Domestic developments, as well as foreign trade, drove the colonial economies. As time progressed, trading networks based on major cities like Boston, Philadelphia, New York, and Charleston penetrated inland, and local and regional commerce came to rival overseas trade as a stimulus for economic growth.[4]

Domestic commerce became still more important as the United States developed as an independent nation. As people moved across the Appalachian Mountains, the focus of economic activity moved inland, and internal development replaced foreign trade as the most powerful force driving the American economy. An agricultural revolution greatly increased America's output of staple crops, especially cotton and wheat, and the beginnings of the Industrial Revolution in America spurred the production of manufactured items. Meanwhile, the construction of turnpikes, canals, and railroads encouraged local, regional, and interregional trade. The emergence of America as the world's largest domestic free-trade region provided the single most powerful stimulant to the business development of the United States throughout the nineteenth century and well into the twentieth.[5]

As the United States developed an increasingly unified business system, the individual firms making up that system became more and more specialized. For most of the colonial period, the largest merchants and other business people were generalists; markets were too small and fragmented and financial facilities too poorly developed to permit them to specialize very much. But from the 1750s on, the growth of commerce, industry, and agriculture, together with improvements in transportation, allowed business people to begin specializing. Merchants who had previously dealt in a wide variety of goods and markets now found it possible to specialize as brokers handling a specific product, such as cotton, wheat, or iron; others became involved in financing and insuring America's growing commerce; and still others entered the world of industry. Nonetheless, this transformation was far from complete at the time of the Civil War. Especially on frontiers, business people operating as generalists continued to run country stores and to work as peddlers.[6]

Nearly all colonial Americans were eager participants in the development of a commercial economy. Merchants were, as already suggested, one of the key groups—probably *the* key group—in the business system of colonial America. But so were artisans (skilled workers), many of whom possessed their own tools and shops and who may well be regarded as the owners of small businesses. Farmers, too, were part of the commercial development of colonial America. Only a relatively small proportion were subsistence growers. Perhaps three-quarters produced for the market and, like merchants and artisans, acted as small business people in their economic transactions.[7] With the development of a vibrant business system, colonial Americans experienced a rising standard of living that reinforced their commercial outlook. By the time of the American Revolution, the colonists (except for black slaves) possessed a standard of living higher in many respects than that of most Europeans. The involvement of Americans in the development of their nation's commercial economy increased in the early and middle 1800s, and most Americans continued to share in a rapidly rising standard of living. Despite economic downturns in 1837, 1857, and 1873, America's real per capita GNP rose by a third in the 20 years after 1839 and continued to rise in later years.

For all this economic activity, however, individual businesses remained small. Limitations in both the distribution and the production of goods prevented the rise of big businesses on a major scale until after the Civil War. What the historian Alfred D. Chandler, Jr., has called the "throughput" of business—the amount of goods and services passing through a nation's business system in a given period—remained so small in the antebellum years, compared with what would come later, that small businesses, linked together in America's commercial web, could easily handle it. Only after 1880 did large companies arise in substantial numbers to coordinate the greatly increased flow of goods resulting from accelerating industrialization.[8]

Limitations in distribution were those of speed and expense in transportation and communications. Wind and animal power long remained the energy sources in transportation. Ships in the transatlantic trade required months to reach their destinations, while those sailing to China required more than a year. In domestic commerce, roads were so poorly constructed as to be virtually impassable much of the time. Although an improvement, especially in the carriage of heavy, bulky goods like wheat and coal, canals were slow and unreliable. Only from the 1830s on did railroads begin hastening the speed of transporting goods over long distances. Similarly, in the 1840s and 1850s the telegraph began coming into use by business people in scheduling orders and keeping track of affairs, thereby quickening commercial life. Constraints in technology also limited the production of manufactured items. As long as power from animals, water, and wind ran mills and factories, their outputs remained relatively low. Breakthroughs along the East Coast started when anthracite coal from Pennsylvania began to come into use as a fuel for steam engines and as a source of heat in processes for the making of sugar, beer, chemicals, and the like during the 1830s. A bit later, the Midwest used bituminous coal mined west of the Alleghenies. Still, the changes in industrialization required decades to complete, and as late as 1880 most industrial firms were small businesses.[9]

☐ Enterprise in Trade and Commerce

Foreign and domestic commerce held together the economies of the American colonies and the new United States, and handling this trade were merchants of various types. Composing 2 to 5% of the work force in colonial times and probably a larger percentage in the early and middle 1800s, the merchants were all small business people. Even the largest and most important conducted their business affairs in single-unit enterprises lacking managerial hierarchies. They could do so because the pace of business was slow and its volume low. Thomas

Hancock, the leading Boston merchant of the middle eighteenth century, sent out, for instance, an average of only 62 letters per year.

Nonetheless, while all the merchants can be considered small business people, gradations appeared within their ranks. Relatively large sedentary merchants operated from offices in seaport cities, importing and exporting goods and selling at wholesale and retail. Smaller storekeepers located in inland towns supplied the countryside with goods and credit. Purchasing their products from the eastern merchants and selling them to farmers in return for their agricultural produce, the country storekeepers were, arguably, the most important small business people of their day. On their work pivoted the economies of colonial and early national America. Finally, peddlers owning only the goods on the backs of their horses or in their wagons reached beyond the country store—served areas to the farthest frontiers.

By the time of his death, in 1782, Aaron Lopez of Newport, Rhode Island, was one of the largest and wealthiest of the sedentary merchants of colonial America.[10] Lopez had come to America in the 1750s to escape the persecution of Jews in his homeland of Portugal. Beginning in a small way with funds borrowed from other Jewish families in Newport, Lopez sold soap and candles to merchants in Philadelphia and New York. Like many of the larger colonial merchants, he soon became involved in a variety of business affairs. In the 1760s and 1770s, Lopez extended his trade to include imports and exports of rum, textiles, naval supplies, pewter, indigo, tea, and sugar. He sold at wholesale and retail, came to own shares in some 30 ships, entered into the distilling of rum and the making of candles, and employed women to sew shoes and clothing in one of his shops.

Although one of the most important merchants of colonial times, Lopez was able to run his business affairs in a personal manner. When more and more of his commerce began going to Great Britain, he came to rely on Henry Cruger of Bristol as his foreign agent. Why? Because Lopez's father had known Cruger, and Lopez trusted Cruger's honesty and business judgment. Similarly, when Lopez extended his reach to Jamaica, he did so by sending his son-in-law there as his agent in 1767, only to find his trust abused (the son-in-law had to be recalled just two years later).

Personal trust, as in Lopez's choices in his overseas agents, lay at the heart of colonial American overseas business. At a time when communications were slow and the risks in business were traditional ones, such as shipwrecks, merchants found themselves having to rely on friends and relatives. Elaborate managerial hierarchies, whether staffed by relatives or not, offered no advantages and were not used. Colonial

American trading companies lacked the monopoly powers often granted European trading companies and consequently were much smaller.[11] A colonial American merchant ran his business from his countinghouse with the aid of only one or two—or at most a half-dozen—clerks, each of whom he knew personally. The merchant often spent afternoons away from the countinghouse in nearby coffeehouses and inns, discussing affairs with other traders. Neither did new business methods come into use, for they provided no advantages over traditional ones. The types of risks apt to be encountered in trading were well known and unlikely to vary much from year to year. New ways of doing things could not appreciably lessen such risks as storms at sea. Instead, techniques handed down with little change from medieval Europe remained in vogue: the use of single- and (occasionally) double-entry bookkeeping, promissory notes, bills of exchange, and samples.[12]

When the regional economies of the colonies and later of the new United States became better developed through transportation and financial improvements, mercantile specialization occurred. Here merchants engaged in just one type of trade: importing or exporting, trading with just one rather than many parts of the world, selling at wholesale or retail but not both. By the late 1850s, for instance, Boston possessed 218 wholesale establishments engaged in importing and selling shoes and another 70 houses doing business solely in hardware. As Americans moved inland, Cincinnati, St. Louis, and Chicago developed as wholesale centers. By 1859, Cincinnati boasted 50 wholesalers specializing in dry goods and another 50 in clothing, leading one writer to observe that "within the last eight or ten years Cincinnati has been gaining a position as a great centre of supply, by wholesale, to the country merchants of Ohio, Indiana, Illinois, and Kentucky, of their dry goods, groceries, hardware, boots and shoes, hats, drugs, and fancy goods."[13]

While relatively large merchants controlled the wholesale trade of the nation, smaller retailers brought the goods to customers throughout America. By 1839, there were 57,565 retail outlets in the United States, with the average amount of capital invested in each store amounting to $4,350.[14] The most common form of retailer was the country storekeeper. Operating in small towns, the storekeepers generally found their markets too restricted to allow specialization. Most of the retail outlets carried a broad assortment of goods, everything from groceries and drugs to hardware and dry goods. A traveler in Pennsylvania remarked on this feature of the country stores in 1806:

> These storekeepers are obliged to keep every article which it is possible that the farmer and manufacturer [artisan] may want.

> Each of their shops exhibits a complete medley; a magazine where are to be had both a needle and a anchor, a tin pot and a large copper boiler, a child's whistle and a pianoforte, ring dial and a clock, a skein of thread and trimmings of lace, a check frock and a muslin gown, a frieze coat and a superfine cloth, a glass of whiskey and barrel of brandy, a gill of vinegar and a hogshead of Maderia wine, &c.[15]

For all the variety in their goods, the country stores were, however, limited in both their physical size and their capital investments. The stores were the archetypical small businesses of their day. The cost of erecting a store came to only about $300. Log cabins some 20 feet per side were the norm into the 1820s and 1830s. The stores contained display counters, open barrels, and shelves for the goods, together with a small office where the storekeeper kept his ledgers and accounts. By the mid-1800s, these rude structures were giving way in the more settled areas to brick and clapboard stores with bay windows and other amenities. It was a rare store that stocked more than $10,000 worth of goods at a time (many carried only $1,500 to $3,000 in goods), most of these purchased on credit from wholesalers.[16]

The main economic function of the stores was to facilitate the exchange of goods. Once or twice each year the storekeeper made a trip to purchase goods from wholesalers in New York, Philadelphia, and Baltimore, or from those in emerging regional centers, such as Chicago and St. Louis. The storekeepers usually bought their supplies with a bill of exchange payable in 12 months (no interest was charged for the first 6 months, but 6 to 10% was charged for the second 6 months). For western storekeepers these buying trips were often arduous, sometimes requiring six weeks or longer to complete. As John Allen Trimble, a storekeeper in Hillsboro, Ohio, wrote of his early nineteenth-century experiences, poor transportation facilities made travel difficult: "Turnpikes, rail roads & steam boats were not then in existence; and the roads over the mountains were the most indifferent wagon ways conceivable; without grading, ruts & gutters, mudholes and other obsticles [*sic*], never mended, and being hilly, broken & uncommon mountainous country made it toilsome in the extreme."[17]

The storekeeper sold his items to nearby farmers, accepting goods of all types in payment. Cash might be in short supply, especially on frontiers, and most storekeepers conducted a portion of their trade on a barter basis. Storekeepers allowed liberal credit terms to their customers, often as long as 12 months, for the farmers could settle their accounts only in the fall and winter after they had harvested their crops.

Storekeepers accumulated corn, pork, cotton, and wheat—as well as more esoteric products, such as ginseng, beeswax, feathers, and beaver pelts—in their trade. These they either sent east directly to pay off their debts to the wholesalers or processed locally, as in the grinding of wheat into flour, before shipping them east.

Country stores played especially significant economic roles in the predominantly rural South. Small farms were at least as important as large plantations in southern development, and country stores grew up at crossroads throughout the antebellum South to serve them. While larger merchants—called factors—operated directly from such southern cities as Charleston and New Orleans to handle the purchasing, marketing, and credit requirements of the planters, country storekeepers took care of the smaller farmers. On average, each storekeeper supplied 300 to 400 farm families with goods, allowing, as in other regions of the United States, up to 12 months' credit on the purchases. Storekeepers also acted as marketing agents for the cotton, tobacco, corn, and other crops taken in trade—selling them in large lots to urban-based factors and commission houses, selling them in other regions or even abroad through partners residing in cities, or sending them out in peddling wagons for sale to whoever would buy them.[18]

Even more than the merchant, the storekeeper found that traditional forms of business organization sufficed. Most storekeepers operated as single-owner proprietors. Almost none of the storekeepers organized their businesses as corporations. Their capital needs were scanty, and working capital could be provided by credit from their wholesalers. Although less common than single-owner proprietorships, partnerships did exist. In the most prevalent form of partnership both partners gave full-time service to one store and contributed to its capital stock. Less commonly, a partnership might control two or more stores, with different partners running the individual stores and acting as agents in eastern cities. Occasionally, family-based partnerships grew up to control chains of country stores. In 1803 Andrew Jackson operated three stores in different parts of Tennessee, and in the same year James and Archibald Kane ran four stores in villages around Albany, New York. The Andrews family entered merchandising with a store in Huntsville, Alabama, in 1826; opened a second store in Tuscaloosa three years later; and soon had family members in New York and Philadelphia employed as buying and selling agents for the stores.

In running their businesses, the storekeepers depended on their own efforts, with perhaps the help of unpaid family members. Multi-level managerial hierarchies did not exist. At most, a storekeeper might employ a young man as a clerk. In fact, by the 1840s clerking had become the most commonly followed road to store ownership, at least in the West, where some 70% of the storekeepers had started as clerks in other people's stores. (Of the others, 15% had entered merchandising directly from agriculture, and 5% had first been schoolteachers; few day laborers or skilled artisans became storekeepers.) Most stores opened early and closed late. Nonetheless, stock turnover was slow, sometimes painfully so. When John Jones and his brother opened their first store in Missouri in the early 1830s, they sold $150 worth of goods on their first day of business, but receipts soon fell to less than that per week. As Jones glumly noted, "We had dull days there as well as elsewhere."[19] The stores' average weekly sales, which varied considerably with the seasons, came to roughly $200 to $300.

In this situation of slow business, traditional bookkeeping methods saw little change. A few storekeepers simply marked their walls with chalked tallies of their accounts; others ran columns of figures on shingles, the forerunner of the visible file. One storekeeper kept his cash account by hanging up a pair of boots, one on each side of a fireplace: into one boot went the money received during the day; into the other went pieces of paper covering the money paid out; and to arrive at a balance, the storekeeper simply emptied the boots! Most storekeepers found it necessary, however, to maintain more complete accounts based on single-entry bookkeeping. They used two books—(a) a waste book or daybook containing a running record of all their transactions and (b) a ledger in which accounts were arranged by customer, with a debtor page on the left showing what was owed and a creditor page on the right showing what had been paid. The accounts were usually settled only once a year, generally in December or January.[20]

The daybook of Abraham Simpson, a storekeeper in the small town of Lafayette, Ohio, shows the variety of goods in which merchants dealt. The page from his book for 11 May 1838 covers transactions in butter, cloth (calico and muslin), thread, tobacco, sugar, gunpowder, and other goods. The entries illustrate the generally small scale of the business, for total sales for the day came to under $10, all but 87½¢ of which were made on credit. The daybook reveals too that, while most people purchased goods for themselves, they also bought them for relatives and friends who lacked the time to go into town. Travel was still difficult, and whoever was in town might buy goods to take home to neighbors on nearby farms.

Joseph Hath for son
butter   35 [¢]

Madison McGray self
  calico $87\frac{1}{2}$
  by cash
Daniel Wright self   1.00
  muslin   .15
  bleached muslin $18\frac{3}{4}$
  calico $1.46\frac{1}{4}$
  thread
Benjamin Blair self
  tobacco $18\frac{3}{4}$
William Minster
  sugar $66\frac{1}{2}$
Crawford
  powder $12\frac{1}{2}$
John Minster for W. Welch
  1 Fine Combe $18\frac{3}{4}$
  1 Side ? $12\frac{1}{2}$
Mathias Furrow self
  1 tobacco $18\frac{3}{4}$
  1 sugar $16\frac{2}{5}$
Thomas Kirkpatrick
  sugar $33\frac{1}{3}$[21]

In retailing as in wholesaling, specialization began in the antebellum years in areas where markets were large enough and concentrated enough to support it. While country stores selling a broad range of goods remained important in some rural areas well into the twentieth century, in cities they soon gave way to more specialized outlets. Retail drugstores, bookstores, and jewelry stores made their appearance in the antebellum years. Shoe and furniture stores were less common but not unknown. Although fully developed department stores came into existence only after the Civil War, forerunners were on the scene in the 1840s. By 1847, one Philadelphia dry-goods store had systematized and departmentalized its operations. According to a contemporary account,

> Each department of the store is alphabetically designated. The shelves and rows of goods in each department are numbered, and upon the tag attached to the goods is marked the letter of the department. . . . The proprietor's desk stands at the farther end of the store, raised on a platform facing the front, from which he can

see all the operations in each section of the retail department. From this desk run tubes, connecting with each department of the store, from the garret to the cellar, so that if a person in any department, either porter, retail or wholesale clerk, wishes to communicate with the employer, he can do so without leaving his station.[22]

Peddlers formed the third type of sellers of goods, after wholesalers and retail storekeepers. Serving regions in which the population was too sparse and dispersed to justify the operations of a country store, peddlers usually offered a wide range of goods for sale from wagons or from packs on the backs of horses. Peddlers were numerous in the antebellum years: 10,699 in 1850, 16,594 a decade later. Wagon peddlers started each season with goods valued at $300 to $2,000 (about the same as the value of the goods in a small country store) and turned their stock in about three months. While most handled a variety of goods, some in more densely settled regions specialized in one type of product, such as tinware, clocks, spices, patent medicines, or hats. In the antebellum years an increasing proportion became manufacturers' representatives, working directly for early industrial companies. In 1828, for example, the Scovil Company of Waterbury, Connecticut, sent representatives into Ohio to peddle its brass buttons and other products. By the early twentieth century few independent peddlers remained in the United States, as most were tied in one way or another to manufacturers.[23]

☐ The Business of Farming

The United States was still mainly an agricultural nation in 1880, and most of the products entering into the nation's internal commerce and foreign trade—cotton, tobacco, wheat, and corn—came from the farm. Despite the beginnings of industry in the late colonial and antebellum years, agriculture remained more important than manufacturing to America's economic advance until very late in the nineteenth century. In 1860 the value of the nation's corn, wheat, and hay crops surpassed the value added by manufacturing for all industries combined, and in the same year the value of the nation's farmlands and buildings was six times as great as the capital invested in all industries. On the eve of the Civil War, agriculture employed nearly three times as many people as manufacturing nationwide, and even in the industrializing Northeast farmers outnumbered industrial workers. Only in the 1880s did the value added to goods by manufacturing exceed the value of agricultural products in the United States.[24]

For the most part, colonial and antebellum farming was commercial, not subsistence, agriculture. Even in the 1600s and 1700s most farmers were market-minded, and this orientation heightened in the early and mid-1800s. Only those lacking good transportation to markets lived by subsistence farming. Most agriculturalists ran their farms as small businesses. In only a few areas did large agricultural establishments exist; even in the cotton belt of the antebellum South small farms, not large plantations, were the most common units of production.

Roughly 85% of colonial Americans were farmers, and the owner-occupied family farm was the typical unit of production (tenancy rates were much lower in colonial America than in other agricultural societies of the time). Often some 100 acres in size, the farms had only about 15 to 35 acres of planted crops, the remainder being composed of forest, pasture, or fallow land. Most colonial farmers engaged in diversified agriculture, raising enough food for their own personal needs but usually also producing for markets at home, in the Caribbean sugar islands, and in Europe. In the southern colonies the market production of such staples as rice, tobacco, and indigo was particularly pronounced, and there large plantations based on slave labor did develop. Even in the southern colonies small farms were common, however, and they too shipped to foreign markets. Farmers in the middle colonies produced surpluses of foodstuffs for export. From New England to North Carolina some colonists gathered forest products for the shipping industry.[25]

The majority of colonial farmers had an entrepreneurial outlook.[26] Still, most farmers sought economic gain less for themselves as individuals than for their families.[27] Most put the subsistence needs of their families and the long-run security of their farms ahead of short-run income maximization, but most also aimed, wherever possible, for a steady increase in their property. They sought more than a comfortable status quo by clearing new lands, constructing barns and fences, building up livestock herds for later sale, and hiring workers to plant and harvest crops for the market.[28] Massachusetts farmers, for instance, carefully considered the best markets in which to sell their produce, often traveling as far as 150 miles to make the most advantageous sales.[29] Even many tenant farmers were entrepreneurially motivated. For many, tenancy was simply a passing stage in their lives before they bought their own farms, and they invested a considerable share of their earnings in productive assets, such as slaves and livestock, before coming into possession of their own lands.

Changes occurring abroad and within the United States reinforced the profit orientation of American farmers in the antebellum years. A growing European demand for American corn and wheat stimulated the expansion of northern agriculture and pulled an increasing proportion of farmers into market production.[30] Similarly, the expansion of urban markets inside the United States, increasingly linked to the newly opened farming areas by canals and railroads, further spurred the production of commercial grain. There can be little doubt that most antebellum agriculturalists sought profits from their farming. A strong positive correlation existed between the price of wheat and the sale of public land. When the price of wheat rose, more land was sold, as farmers strove to take advantage of profitable opportunities. By the late 1850s, farmers were raising a considerable crop surplus for sale in American cities and overseas. In 1859 the average midwestern farm grew enough food to support two other families, and northeastern farms raised enough for one other family. That same year, northern farms earned a 12% return on their capital investments (more than the 10% return then being earned in cotton production but less than the 25% return being made in manufacturing). In addition to these operating profits were returns that could be earned from the sale of farmlands that appreciated in value.[31] Alexis de Tocqueville, the French social thinker, observed the growing commercialization of farming, including the involvement of farmers in land speculation, in the early 1830s: "Almost all farmers combine some trade with agriculture; most of them make agriculture itself a trade. It seldom happens that an American farmer settles for good upon the land which he occupies; especially in the districts of the Far West, he brings the land into tillage in order to sell it again, and not to farm it."[32]

At the center of antebellum agriculture in the United States lay the family farm. The expansion of farming, like the growth in trade, was based on family enterprises. The family farm and family retail store marched across America in tandem. Agriculture based on grain in particular boosted the growth of small family farms. Farm families owning about 75 to 100 acres and in some places even less could produce successfully for the market. Plantation production was not advantageous, for there were few economies of scale. The improvements needed to increase grain and livestock output—such as putting more land into cultivation, laying out new pastures, and spreading manure—could be done adequately by farmers and their families in their off-seasons.[33] Even in the South, as in colonial times, family farms remained important, as farms produced cash crops and foodstuffs for local consumption and long-distance trade. A dwindling proportion of antebellum farms were self-sufficient producers in remote areas. The per capita value of goods manufactured on the farm in America fell from $1.70 in 1840 to only 78¢ two decades later. Instead of making items for their own use, farmers resorted to purchasing them from country stores. Writing in the early 1850s, the president of the New York Agricultural Society commented on this trend,

> He [the farmer] now sells for money, and it is in his interest to buy for money, every article that he cannot produce cheaper than he can buy. He cannot afford to make at home his clothing, the furniture or his farming utensiles; he buys many articles for consumption for his table. He produces what he can raise and sell to the best advantage, and he is in a situation to buy all that he can purchase, cheaper than he can produce. Time and labor have become cash articles, and he neither lends nor barters them. His farm does not merely afford him a subsistence; it produces capital, and therefore demands the expenditure of capital for its improvement.[34]

As farming became increasingly market-oriented, farmers became more and more rational in managing their farms as small businesses. While many continued to trust tradition, using almanacs and Benjamin Franklin's maxims to determine how they ran their farms, some began to think in terms of new methods. Farmers experimented with crop specialization, used horses rather than the slower oxen to work their lands, and in general made conscious choices about how to farm. A farm manual published in 1839 captured the growing emphasis being placed on the necessity of running a farm along rational principles. "The business or management of a farm," the manual observed, "is a practice that demands constant care and attention, as well as much activity and judgment, to conduct it in a proper and advantageous manner." Good management, the manual concluded, "requires an intimate and practical knowledge of every kind of live-stock; and still further, a perfect acquaintance with the various modes of buying and selling."[35]

Yet while profits became the primary goals of American farmers, they were not the only objectives. Farming, especially on family farms, was a way of life providing psychic as well as monetary rewards. Americans remained on the farm when they could have earned greater returns on their capital in other fields of endeavor, such as small-scale manufacturing. Freedom and independence for themselves and their families, as embodied in the security of owning their own land and controlling their own supplies of food, motivated many northern farmers in particular. These values combined with ties to their families and communities to provide farmers with nonentrepreneurial reasons for leading their lives the way they did. Tradition, as well as rationality, lay behind the actions of many colonial and antebellum farmers.[36]

A page from the daybook of Daniel Kaufman, a farmer in Richmond County, Ohio, illustrates how even commercially minded farmers blended business and noncommercial affairs. Covering the last week or so in December 1864, the page shows that Kaufman kept careful track of how he used his time, perhaps in the interests of business rationality. Daybook entries show that Kaufman was buying and selling goods at the nearby market town of Mansfield; that he hired workers for special tasks, such as butchering and woodcutting, and paid them in cash; and that he, like most farmers, settled his accounts at the end of the calendar year. Yet personal comments, such as those about the weather, the "soft rain," also intersperse his business accounts. Notable, too, is that Kaufman abstained from all work on Sunday.

1864

Dec.	23	Sold in Mansfield 6 turkeys		
VERY COLD		at 10 cts lb		6.00
		Bought 6 plates 125 spoons 125 per set	2.50	
		Groceries and etc.	3.75	
	24	Cut wood & cleaned stables		
	25	White Christmas tho rather soft rain in the evening a little		
	26	Fixt to Butcher		
	27	Killed 3 hogs and one beef		
		Pd. Dale Cr. for 1 days butchering	1.50	
		Wm. Mackly Ditto	1.25	
		E. Charles Dr. to 90 lbs. beef hindquarter at 8 cts per lb.		7.20
	28	Settled with Mrs. Williams paid her	3.90	
	29	Wm Mackly cr. by 1 days cutting wood	1.25	
	30	Dito $\frac{3}{4}$ Dito [sic]	1.00	
		Wm. Mackly to cash also cash	2.00	
	31	Cleaned stables		

1865

Jan.   1 Sabbeth[37]

□ Artisans and Manufacturing

Although the United States was still primarily an agricultural nation at the time of the Civil War and for several decades thereafter, industrialization was beginning to reshape the economic and social contours of the land. Some industry existed in colonial times, but it developed more rapidly after independence was achieved from Great Britain. Small businesses were as important as large enterprises in bringing industrialization to America. In the colonial period skilled artisans operated as small business people, producing and selling a vast array of wood, metal, and leather goods. In the antebellum years artisan production continued. In addition, many artisans made the transition to industrial production, setting up firms using new sources of power and new methods of production. Although some large industrial businesses began to develop in antebellum America, the most typical sort of manufacturing company remained, as late as 1870 or 1880, the small firm. Like farms and stores, most of these manufacturing ventures continued to be run as family businesses.

Artisans plying their trades in shops they owned supplied colonists with myriad handicraft goods. Composing about 10% of all the white workers in colonial times, artisans included coopers (barrel makers), tailors, shoemakers, carpenters, tinsmiths, and silversmiths. Many artisans owned their tools and shops, maintained inventories of raw materials and goods-in-process, and handled their own accounts. In short, they operated as small business people. The most successful often owned a few acres of farmland as well, and many possessed a few head of livestock. Like country storekeepers, most ran their businesses as single-owner proprietorships, though some operated them with others in partnership arrangements.[38]

The situation of artisans in prerevolutionary Charleston was probably typical of that in most colonial cities. In Charleston were two groups of artisans. First were carpenters, bricklayers, carvers, joiners, and tinsmiths, who operated as workers but usually did not possess their own shops. Second were saddlers, cabinetmakers, shoemakers, and others who operated as small business people, fashioning their own wares for sale in their own shops. This second group of artisans often ran their businesses by themselves but sometimes took in partners to secure needed capital or skills. While all these businesses were small enterprises (all were single-unit businesses without managerial hierarchies), some became large by colonial standards. In fact, as the businesses became larger and more complex, newspapers carried advertisements offering to bring up to date the account books of artisans as well as those of merchants.[39]

As in farming and shopkeeping, more was involved in the work and lives of artisans than a quest for profits: a concern for family and community matters was also present. The family nature of colonial artisanship was clearest in the practice of apprenticeship. Carried over from the Old World to the New, apprenticeship was widespread until the 1840s. Young boys and girls left their families to live with another family, usually at around age 12. In their new family the head of the household taught a young man farming or a craft and instructed a young woman in cooking and household management. Artisans were expected to initiate their apprentices into all aspects of the "mysteries" of their crafts. In return, apprentices worked for their masters for five to seven years with no pay (the master usually provided his apprentices with new clothes each year, and many apprentices took their meals with the families of their masters). The apprentice system was more than an economic system, for it had social ramifications as well. Masters had a great deal of authority over their apprentices and were expected to ensure that they received a basic education and moral and religious training.[40]

While artisans produced a diversity of articles for sale in the colonies, industrial production truly began only in the nineteenth century.[41] The term *industrialization* is usually taken to mean the substitution of water and steam power for human and animal power, the increased use of machinery in making products, and the gathering of work forces in central locations called factories. These changes did not necessarily occur simultaneously, however. Nonmechanized factories, for instance, replaced workshops in some fields well before new sources of power were tapped. Moving from scattered beginnings, industrialization grew in importance in the middle nineteenth century. Between 1810 and 1860, the value of manufactured goods produced in the United States rose tenfold, from $200 million to $2 billion. In the same period the amount of capital invested in manufacturing facilities increased still more rapidly, from $50 million to $1 billion—signaling that industrialization would spread even further after the Civil War.[42]

Merchants and storekeepers were instrumental in bringing industrial enterprise to America. Using surplus funds earned in trade, the large sedentary merchants of the eastern seaboard financed early industrial projects and were also key in importing the necessary new technologies into the United States. The Rhode Island merchant Moses Brown worked with the British artisan Samuel Slater to establish, in the 1790s, the first successful cotton textile mill in America. The Boston merchant Francis Cabot Lowell and his friends, calling themselves the Boston Associates, built the nation's first fully integrated cotton textile mills at Waltham, Massachusetts, just after the War of 1812.[43] Operating on a smaller scale, country storekeepers played significant roles in their communities. As small capitalists, they often invested in gristmills, iron forges, fulling mills, distilleries, and so forth.[44]

Just as important as merchants and storekeepers in the industrialization of the United States were artisans. While some craft-oriented artisans found themselves unable to compete with businesses using new production methods and went out of existence, others made the transition to industrial production. Both individual artisans in specific fields of endeavor, such as Jonas Chickering in piano making, and a broad range of craftsmen in particular locales, such as those in Newark, New Jersey, illustrated how artisans successfully entered the new industrial world.

Jonas Chickering's career was typical of those artisans who became early-day industrialists.[45] Chickering began as an artisan in Boston. After working in the establishments of several piano makers, he broke away to form his own firm in 1826. Like many artisans moving into industry, Chickering initially depended on the capital and marketing skills of a merchant to help him get started, but within a decade he bought out the merchant's interest to run his business as a sole proprietorship, doing so until his death, in 1853. An aggressive entrepreneur, Chickering used advertising and business agents to expand his sales beyond Boston to much of America. Chickering transformed piano making from a craft to an industrial operation by building a manufacturing plant that in 1850 employed 100 men to turn out 1,000 pianos worth $200,000. Within this factory, work was divided into different tasks. Chickering's establishment had 20 different departments, each devoted to a different step in the manufacturing process. Moreover, outside the factory Chickering employed an additional 100 men in preparing the wood and the cast-iron frames going into the pianos. In contrast to skilled artisans, no workers in Chickering's establishment were knowledgeable in all the steps in making the pianos.

Although Chickering set up the first modern production works in the American piano industry, he remained something of a craftsman at heart. Older ways of thinking and acting died hard. Chickering personally approved the quality of each piano before it was sold and continued to spend much of his time on the shop floor rather than in his office. Chickering knew his workers by name. Worth $300,000 on his death, Chickering was deeply respected by his workers, who turned out in large numbers for his funeral.

In some communities entire groups of artisans came to specialize in one form of manufacturing, a situation that developed in the Connecticut Valley. There many craftsmen went into the industrial production of cutlery.[46] The inventiveness of its artisans in acquiring capital, making technical innovations in the production process, and opening transportation links to markets was a key factor in the development of the industry. From a handicraft operation in the 1820s and 1830s cutlery making became, over the following three decades, an industry relying on steam-powered machinery to turn out an ever-more-specialized assortment of knives. No single company emerged to dominate the industry, which continued to be controlled by a group of small businesses into the middle twentieth century.

By remaining flexible in their production techniques and by adjusting their products to take advantage of market niches, the cutlery companies in the Connecticut Valley continued as industry leaders in the United States until World War II. Even as something approaching mass production began, however, a concern for craftsmanship lingered well into the late nineteenth century. Most of the firms, though now organized as corporations, remained closely held family businesses. Like Chickering, their owner-managers continued to be more interested in producing high-quality goods than in increasing profits. They also remained closely identified with their communities, in which they were commonly recognized as social and political leaders.

In still other localities large numbers of artisans in a broad range of crafts made the transition to industrialization. One such place was Newark, New Jersey, America's leading industrial city in 1860. There artisans making shoes, saddles, jewelry, trunks, leather goods, and hats transformed their lines of work from craft to industrial production in the middle nineteenth century.[47] Well-educated by the standards of their day and innovative and flexible in their outlook toward business, these artisans—like their counterparts in the Connecticut Valley—sought and obtained the capital needed to change their shops into small factories and opened new markets for their products. Possessing a high sense of self-worth and joined together by cooperative institutions—such as the Newark Mechanics Association for Mutual Improvement in the Arts and Sciences, formed in 1828 by 114 craftsmen, and the Mechanics Bank of Newark, many of whose directors were craftsmen—the artisans looked to the future, not the past, for inspiration. Far from opposing mechanization, Newark's artisans embraced and controlled it. For instance, in 1840 no factory in Newark used steam power; just six years later more than 100 did.

It was artisans who brought industrialization and the beginnings of big business to Newark. By 1860, some 22 firms in the six fields mentioned earlier possessed capital of at least $50,000 and employed 100 or more persons, making them large businesses by the standards of the time; three-fifths of these firms had started as artisans' workshops. Despite the growth in the size of their enterprises, most of Newark's artisans-turned-industrialists remained faithful to many of their older values. Like family farmers, they continued to honor hard work, thrift, and independence, and they continued to value their work because they saw it as being useful to society.

Since many of the industrial businesses of the United States had their origins in the workshops of artisans, it is not surprising to find that as late as 1870 small businesses dominated the industrial landscape of the nation. While average plant output rose dramatically in a few industries in the antebellum years, production figures rose more slowly in most manufacturing fields. In cotton textile production median plant output jumped from $5,000 in 1820 to nearly $100,000 a half-century later, and in iron making it soared from just $2,000 to more than $200,000. In most other leading American industries increases in plant size occurred more gradually, however. The median output of flour mills rose from $4,500 in 1820 to $6,300 in 1870, and the figures for lumber mills were $590 and $2,200. The median output of boot-making establishments actually fell from $3,100 in 1820 to only $2,300 a half-century later.[48] The number of workers per plant showed much the same tendency. There was a considerable increase in the number of employees per plant, but as late as 1850 the average number of employees remained relatively low, by later standards.

Average plant size remained small, because in most industrial fields the establishment of many small plants offset the growth of a few large ones. In the antebellum years and for a few years right after the Civil War, small plants generally held their own with large ones in manufacturing. In most industrial fields in these years, large plant size was not generally needed to obtain full economies of scale. Only after 1880, as we shall see in chapter 2, did production breakthroughs and other events occur to spur decisively the growth of big businesses in manufacturing, and even then small firms continued to perform well in certain fields.[49]

☐ Service Businesses

Service businesses developed concurrently with the growth of farming, trading, and manufacturing enterprises. Banks, insurance companies, and credit-rating businesses were not latecomers to the business scene; their evolution was an essential part of growth of the business systems of colonial America and the antebellum United States. In fact, service businesses have been important worldwide in stimulating and facilitating production for the market, helping developing nations make the transition from subsistence to commercial economies.[50] As can be seen in Figure 1, service business became increasingly important to the

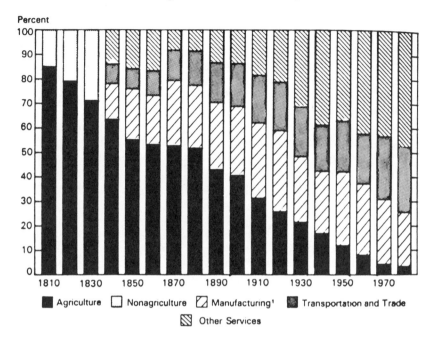

Figure 1. Labor Force Shares by Industry. *Economic Report of the President, 1988* (Washington, D.C.: U.S. Government Printing Office, 1988), 190.

American economy from the 1840s onward, and, as in other forms of American business endeavor before the Civil War, the service industries were a home of small firms.

Banking had existed in an informal manner in the colonial period, as merchants and storekeepers loaned funds to each other and to other members of their communities. Robert Morris, a merchant in charge of the finances for the newly formed federal government, set up the first bank in America when, in 1781, he established the Bank of North America in Philadelphia to provide credit services for the government and for merchants. More banks soon followed, often established by merchants seeking profitable forms of business specialization. In addition to commercial banks, the first savings banks and investment banking houses grew up. Savings bank deposits totaled $1 million by 1820 but amounted to 10 times as much just 15 years later. Investment bankers began dealing in railroad securities in the 1850s, branching out to the stocks and bonds of industrial enterprises at a later date.[51]

As in banking, merchants were active in developing the field of insurance. Colonial merchants shared risks by operating through partnerships that owned ships and their cargoes on ocean voyages. The merchant Thomas Willing formed the first insurance company in North America in 1757, and by 1807 some 40 companies had been set up to insure ships and their cargoes. Fire and life insurance enterprises also grew up in the antebellum period, until, by 1860, 81 general insurance companies, many of which wrote fire insurance, and 43 life insurance companies were doing business.[52] Merchants were also instrumental in forming the first credit-rating agencies—a step necessitated by the economy's geographic expansion, which made it impossible for business people to know who were good and poor credit risks on the farms and in the towns springing up across the nation. By 1858, one agency had branches in 17 cities.[53]

While a handful of credit-rating agencies developed into multiunit enterprises in the antebellum years, most service businesses did not. Nearly all operated in just one locale, and the vast majority—like most stores, farms, and industrial ventures—were run as family enterprises. Nowhere was this clearer than in banking.

Most antebellum banks, at least in New England, functioned not so much as modern commercial banks as they did as the financial arms of extended kinship groups. Family-controlled banks raised funds through deposits and the sale of stock in their banks to the public (the families, however, retained a controlling share of bank ownership for themselves). The banks then loaned the bulk of their resources to family insiders who in turn invested them in their industrial or trading ventures. Whether the banks were privately held or incorporated, the longevity of family control was often great. The Brown, Ives, and Goddard families controlled the Providence Bank from 1791 to 1926, and the Richmond, Chapin, and Taft families dominated the Merchants Bank of Providence from 1818 to 1926. Like their modern counterparts, these family-controlled banks channeled surplus funds in their communities into profitable investment opportunities. In doing so, they successfully adapted traditional ways of conducting business—the reliance on family ties—to new needs.[54]

The only commercial banks to develop any real hierarchical management were the two nationally chartered institutions, the First (1792–1812) and Second (1816–36) Banks of the United States. Headquartered in Philadelphia, the Banks of the United States had branches in major cities across the nation—8 in the case of the First and 25 in the case of the Second. But the fate of these large banks was sealed when President Andrew Jackson vetoed the rechartering of the Second Bank in 1836. Unlike the case in most other nations, where banking normally became oligopolistic, in America banking remained atomized. By 1840, there were 901 banks in the United States; by 1860, 1,562; and by 1880, 3,355.[55] With few economies of scale adhering to larger banks, banking was conducted as small business everywhere, except in the largest cities, such as New York.

☐   Toward a Business Ideology

The United States has developed as a nation with a business culture, and business people have generally been admired and looked up to as leaders in society. As we have seen, many colonists were eager participants in the expanding commercial economy of the British Empire, and the economic growth of the nineteenth century brought still more Americans into the commercial arena. Country storekeepers, farmers, artisan-industrialists, and bankers all sought material gain.[56] De Tocqueville was struck by this orientation of most Americans during his travels in the early 1830s. "Fortunes, opinions, and laws are in ceaseless variation," he found. The only constant in the new United States was the quest for wealth. "The love of wealth," de Tocqueville concluded, "is therefore to be traced, either as a principal or accessory motive, at the bottom of all that Americans do: this gives to all their passions a sort of family likeness."[57]

The embrace of business by Americans contrasts with the attitudes of people in many other nations. In Great Britain, the first nation to industrialize, business people, especially manufacturers, never achieved the level of acceptance won by their counterparts in the United States. Something of an antibusiness bias lingered from feudal times even as Great Britain industrialized, and may have been reinvigorated in the late nineteenth century. As late as 1927, Samuel Courtauld, whose company was a leading producer of textiles, denounced the profit motive he associated with the American way of life. "I view the so-called 'Americanization of Europe' with the utmost dislike," he observed; "I doubt whether American ideals of living—purely materialistic as they are—will finally lead to a contented working nation anywhere when the excitement of constant expansion has come to an end." In Japan, the first Asian nation to modernize its economy, business people were long held in low repute because they were seen as seeking profits, not service to society, as their goal. As the head of the Mitsui Trading Company noted with dismay in 1900, "Men of commerce and industry . . . are not the equal of other classes in social prestige."[58]

Relatively little such antibusiness feeling has existed in America. In the colonial period the large sedentary merchants played important social and political roles, sitting on boards of selectmen (city councils), serving as members of colonial legislatures, and acting as advisers to governors. As respected members of their communities, country storekeepers played much the same roles in the antebellum years. Usually older than the farmers of the surrounding countryside, the storekeepers were accepted as leaders in their communities. Many were deeply involved in politics, often rising from a humble office like that of hogreve, the official who kept hogs from running loose, to become a member of the state legislature. About a quarter of the storekeepers in the antebellum Midwest held some type of political office at one time or another.[59] Storekeepers were also often leaders in church, school, militia, and lodge affairs. John Jones, the Missouri trader, summarized well the importance of storekeepers to their communities: "He [the storekeeper] is the general *locum tenens*, the agent of everybody, and familiar with every transaction in his neighborhood. He is a counselor without license, and yet is invariably consulted, not only in matters of business, but in domestic affairs. Parents ask his opinion before giving their assent to their daughters' marriages; and he is always invited to the weddings. . . . Candidates for the state legislature, for Congress, for Governor, bestow upon them their most gracious smiles; for they are supposed, and very truly, to possess considerable influence over the minds of their customers."[60]

There was more, however, to the acceptance of business by Americans than simply a desire to get ahead economically. While most Americans were by choice actively engaged in business activities for commercial purposes, nonmonetary motivations also prompted them. They thought they saw in their businesses a way to achieve or maintain personal independence, security for their families, and strong social ties to their local communities. Throughout the antebellum years and later, a desire for individual advancement through entrepreneurial activities coexisted in an uneasy alliance with a search for personal and family security.[61]

As we have seen, most colonial and antebellum businesses operated as family enterprises. Not surprisingly, the short-term goal of maximizing profits often took second place to the long-term goal of ensuring family survival and advancement. Neither is it surprising to find that, especially through the colonial period but even into the antebellum years, business people normally got ahead less as individuals and more as members of families. Thus, Thomas Hancock, the Boston merchant, ran his trading firm as the House of Hancock. In these family businesses management succession was often limited to children or other close relatives. And although some aspects of the family nature of business began eroding in the antebellum years—the spread of mechanization in manufacturing destroyed the apprentice system, for example, by devaluing skilled labor—the family nature of many small businesses would nonetheless persist into the late twentieth century.

For women and blacks, as for white males, business was largely a family affair. Those women who succeeded in business as merchants, storekeepers, and artisans did so not as individuals on their own but as "deputy husbands." That is, they took the places of their husbands in business when the husbands were out of town, were disabled, or died.[62] Thus, Rebecca Lukens took over the management of her husband's iron mill on his death in 1825, expanding its operations and laying the foundations for Lukens Steel.[63] Only rarely did women operate on their own outside family bonds. For a relative handful of blacks, businesses— especially very small enterprises such as one-man cartage companies and barbershops—offered some hope for advancement. Free blacks made up about 10% of the nation's black population of 4.5 million in 1860, and in that year there were about 2,300 black-owned businesses in America. Like their white counterparts, black entrepreneurs often used inherited wealth, connections, and apprenticeships in family enterprises to get ahead.[64]

Even as farmers, artisans, and other business people sought upward mobility and family security through business success, they hoped to gain other rewards as well. Beyond economic matters, many Americans adhered to the notion that only on a base of widespread property holdings could a framework of political freedom and morality stand.[65] And in fact there was more economic equality in the United States before the rise of big business than would exist in later times, at least in the North.[66] Although writing specifically about farmers in his *Notes on the State of Virginia* in the 1780s, Thomas Jefferson provided a classic statement on the value of free enterprise for the inculcation of morality, a notion that small business people would return to time and again in the nineteenth and twentieth centuries, despite vastly changed economic circumstances: "Those who labor in the earth are the chosen people of God, if ever he had a chosen people, whose breasts he has made his peculiar deposit for substantial and genuine virtue. . . . Corruption of morals in the mass of cultivators is a phaenomenon [*sic*] of which no age nor nation has furnished an example. It is the mark set on those, who not looking up to heaven, to their own soil and industry, as does the husbandman, for their subsistence, depend for it on the casualties and caprice of customers. Dependance [*sic*] begets subservience and venality, suffocates the germ of virtue, and prepares fit tools for the designs of ambition."[67]

□ Conclusion

The idea that morality and freedom were somehow associated with the flourishing of many independent business enterprises—in Jefferson's case, family farms—would animate much of American life and thought over the next 200 years. Over time, notions of independence would become identified in the minds of many Americans with the ownership of small business units. This situation developed as economic realities changed. The business systems of colonial America and the antebellum United States evolved as congeries of small businesses. A tremendous amount of economic growth took place between the time of the founding of the first permanent British colony in North America at Jamestown in 1607 and the beginning of the American Civil War in 1861, but, with just a handful of exceptions, few big businesses arose during these years. With the conflict of the Civil War behind them and with technological and market restrictions lifting, Americans would develop a large number of big businesses in the late nineteenth and early twentieth centuries, as we shall see in chapter 2. Nonetheless, it was in this period that the general business ideology of earlier years was transformed into an ideology specifically glorifying the small firm and small business person.

2

Small Business in the Age of Giant Enterprise, 1880–1920

In *THE VALLEY OF DECISION,* MARCIA DAVenport's novel about life in Pittsburgh in the late nineteenth and early twentieth centuries, the owner of a small steel mill explains how he competed successfully with the much-larger Carnegie Steel Company: " 'I could not compete with the steel rail production proposed for this Edgar Thomson Works [one of the Carnegie plants],' he said slowly. But he added, 'they cannot compete with me if I concentrate on special alloys for tools and farm machinery, that kind of thing. Nobody,' he said slowly, 'is opening up that kind of field much.' "[1] Davenport's fiction described reality. By turning out specialty products and by creating market niches for themselves, small manufacturers persisted as viable concerns into the age of giant industrial enterprise.

From the 1880s onward, big businesses arose in America, especially in certain forms of manufacturing, and small businesses, although continuing to increase in absolute numbers, declined in their relative importance to the American economy. One indication of this shift is that, while the number of Americans who were self-employed rose from 1.2 million in 1880 to 2.6 million in 1920, their representation in the nation's work force fell from 8 to only 6.5% over the same 40 years.[2] This chapter explores the relationships between large and small companies that evolved in America during the late nineteenth and early twentieth centuries, paying special attention to the strategies small businesses adopted in the growing competition with their larger counterparts.

Since businesses never exist in a vacuum but are instead always a part of their fluid social, political, and legal environments, this chapter examines as well shifting public attitudes toward small business and governmental policies for business development.

☐ Industrialization and the Rise of Big Business

As we have seen in chapter 1, industrialization began in the United States well before the Civil War, but only after the conflict did the process reach maturity. Between 1869 and 1919, the value added to products by manufacturing rose from $1.4 billion to $24 billion. Economic growth accompanied the speedup in industrialization. Between 1869 and 1921, the GNP of the United States increased from $9 billion to $72 billion, and GNP per capita tripled, from $223 to $683.[3]

Though this acceleration in industrialization originated in numerous sources, of key importance were market developments and technological breakthroughs. The unification of the national market by the completion of America's railroad and telegraph networks—railroad trackage rose from about 30,000 miles in 1860 to nearly 170,000 miles by 1890—allowed manufacturers to locate their factories in one or two cities and sell throughout the United States.[4] Moreover, the market was there. America's population more than tripled between 1860 and 1920, growing from 31 million to 106 million persons, most of them eager to purchase industrial goods. At the same time, technological breakthroughs in prime industries—the distilling and refining of liquids and semiliquids like oil, the processing of agricultural goods, and the making and working of metals—greatly sped up and increased the output of America's industrial plants.[5] The adoption of the Bessemer and open-hearth processes, for example, made the United States the world's leading steel-producing nation by 1900—with an output of 10.2 million tons, up from only 500,000 tons in 1876.

With improvements in transportation and communications and with the breakthroughs in manufacturing technologies came the rise of big businesses in America. In the 1850s, aside from a few railroads, cotton textile mills were the largest businesses in the United States. Only a handful, however, were capitalized at more than $1 million or employed more than 500 workers. By contrast, when the United States Steel Corporation was formed in 1901, it was capitalized at $1.4 billion, thus becoming the first "billion-dollar company" in American history, and employed more than 100,000 workers (by 1929, 440,000). As late as

1860, no single American company was capitalized at as much as $10 million, but by 1904 more than 300 were.[6]

Big businesses developed especially when companies combined mass production with mass distribution to become vertically integrated enterprises controlling all or most of the stages in the production and sales of their products. Vertical integration became a hallmark of significant segments of America's industrial system well into the twentieth century. To a lesser degree, big businesses also grew through horizontal integration—a process by which a company sought to control all of one stage of making or selling its products. Central to vertical and horizontal integration—and some companies engaged in both at the same time—was a quest for control over company operations, a search that took various forms.

As the throughput of their businesses rapidly increased, executives in some manufacturing fields found it hazardous to rely on established market mechanisms to ensure the movement of raw materials to their plants, the flow of the work-in-process through their factories, and the distribution of their finished products throughout the United States. Many manufacturers, such as Andrew Carnegie in the steel industry, purchased their own supplies of raw materials—in Carnegie's case, iron ore, coking coal, and limestone. Others, experiencing particular difficulties with the nation's established marketing and distribution network, set up their own national sales systems. In some cases, the issue was the speed of distribution, for makers of perishables required timely sales; Pabst Brewing, for example, established its own distribution systems lest its unpasteurized beer spoil en route to market. In other cases, the growing complexity and rising costs of industrial products made it difficult for independent merchants to demonstrate, finance, and service them adequately. And in still other cases, the tremendous increase in output simply overwhelmed established marketers, again bringing manufacturers into the picture. In all these cases businesses were, through vertical integration, internalizing transactions formerly occurring in the marketplace.

At the same time that America's business leaders sought to gain control over the internal operations of their firms, they tried to dampen competition in their markets. The development of a national market was a mixed blessing for industrialists: on the one hand, as the largest free-trade area in the world at the time, it offered tremendous scope for their entrepreneurial energies; on the other hand, it brought them into increasing competition with one another across the country. The United States experienced its first big merger movement between

1895 and 1904 as several thousand companies disappeared into consolidations. A desire for market control lay behind many of the mergers; in half of them, the consolidations accounted for more than 40% of the manufacturing capacity of their industries, and in a third of them, more than 70%.[7]

The giant firms that resulted clustered in just a few fields. Nearly all were in industry. Of the 278 American companies with assets of $20 million or more in 1917, 236 were manufacturing companies. By contrast, only 5 were agricultural firms (1 each in ranching, the growing of sugar cane, and the harvesting of crude rubber, and 2 diversified multinationals, the United Fruit Company and its competitor, the Atlantic Fruit and Sugar Company). Of the manufacturing businesses, 171 firms, or nearly three-quarters, were in just six groups: 39 in primary metals, 34 in food processing, 29 in transportation equipment, 24 in machinery making, 24 in oil refining, and 21 in chemicals. These companies shared certain characteristics. They were capital-intensive enterprises, producing large quantities of homogeneous products for mass markets. Some 85% had integrated production with distribution by the time of World War I. Nearly all were multiunit enterprises with operations spread across the United States.[8]

In their management systems, these industrial companies differed in important ways from the small artisan workshops of the antebellum years. Informal arrangements based on family and personal ties no longer sufficed, for companies had become too large and too complex for any one person to manage. Bureaucratic organization replaced personal management in big businesses. Functionally departmentalized corporate offices—offices composed of managers grouped together in committees set up to handle the different functions of a company's operations, such as production or sales—emerged to set corporate strategies and coordinate operations. By 1917, four-fifths of America's largest 236 manufacturing ventures had adopted management systems based on departmentalized corporate offices. At the same time, middle management developed to handle the daily work of the companies. The number of managerial employees in American firms, mainly middle managers in big businesses, increased from 161,000 to 1 million and from 1.1 to 2.6% of the work force between 1880 and 1920.[9] In short, managerial hierarchies began emerging.

Providing the sinew binding the disparate parts of the companies was greatly improved financial reporting that went far beyond the simple double-entry bookkeeping that had earlier been adequate. Railroad executives and industrialists developed increasingly sophisticated methods of financial accounting, including the use of operating ratios, capital accounting with its provisions for depreciation, and cost accounting to keep track of past and current operations and help plan for the future.[10]

☐ Public Attitudes and Government Policies

Americans' attitudes toward the rise of big business were complex and ambiguous. From the 1880s well into the twentieth century, Americans' relationship with big business was a love-hate affair. Most Americans associated big business with material abundance, efficiency in production methods, and a rising standard of living. Nonetheless, many Americans, especially in the late nineteenth and early twentieth centuries, also feared big business. Perhaps as a result of this uneasiness, the public continued to have a sentimental attraction to small business, to the "little guy." The development of big business was so sudden and so disruptive of traditional ways of work and life that most Americans looked on it with anxiety.[11]

The attitudes of middle-class Americans toward big business passed through three stages between 1879 and 1914.[12] The first generation to come into contact with big business maintained an uneasy acceptance of it into the early 1890s. There was relatively little public hostility to big business during these years among professionals, who viewed economic efficiency as resulting from the spread of large firms. Farmers, hurt by falling prices and angered by what they saw as the economic depredations of railroads and other "trusts," expressed more hostility, especially in the late 1880s and early 1890s. So did skilled workers concerned about the power large companies could exert over wages, hours of work, and working conditions. Nonetheless, even many farm and labor groups found praise for big businesses as stabilizing and progressive forces in the nation's economy. A major depression that devastated the United States in the mid-1890s signaled the start of a second stage: one of heightened hostility of all groups toward big businesses, a hostility that ran deepest among labor bodies. The return of prosperity in the late 1890s and in the opening two decades of the twentieth century brought forth a third stage: one marked by a more favorable attitude toward large firms. By 1902, most Americans, even most workers, were resigned to the continued presence of big business in their lives, and many welcomed large firms for the outpouring of goods they brought. This second generation of Americans to live with big businesses increasingly accepted large firms as a part of the socioeconomic landscape.

In fact, during the Progressive Era (roughly the first two decades of the twentieth century), a growing number of Americans viewed small firms as anachronistic, obsolete, and inefficient.[13] Small businesses came to be seen as outdated, vanishing forms of enterprise, and their replacement by larger firms was viewed as a natural evolutionary movement. Even so, Americans expressed concern about the fate of the small business person (as distinct from the small business) and the effects that his or her decline would have on American society. What would become of economic independence, of economic freedom, as large businesses squeezed out small companies? Something of the ambivalent attitudes that most Americans had held toward large firms in the 1890s continued into the twentieth century.

These mixed attitudes found expression in governmental actions. Americans expended considerable effort in seeking to control, and sometimes to break up, big businesses through lawsuits—brought under common law before 1890 but under the terms of the Sherman Act thereafter. Rather than try to destroy or atomize big businesses through antitrust actions, however, the main thrust of government policies was to regulate big businesses by newly formed independent regulatory commissions at both the state and the federal levels.

Control through legal actions was the initial response of Americans to the rise of big business.[14] The common law tradition of the United States encompassed well the ambivalent attitudes most Americans harbored toward big business: while placing restrictions on how big companies could act, it fell far short of outlawing large combinations. Conversely, the common law tradition protected small firms from some, but not all, of the depredations of their larger competitors. A new level of action began with the passage of the Sherman Act by Congress in 1890. Its supporters intended that the act encompass the common law tradition. Although the Sherman Act outlawed restraints of trade, the law's sponsors intended that "reasonable" restraints— those not injurious to the public and not preventing new firms from entering business fields—be allowed to continue. It remained for the courts to decide matters. In a series of cases in the mid-1890s federal courts did permit reasonable restraints, but in another series of cases decided between 1898 and 1911 the justices took a narrower view and forbade nearly all types of restraints that came before them. Reversing themselves once again, the justices returned to the common law tradition in cases involving the American Tobacco Company and the Standard Oil Company—both decided in 1911—to declare that reasonable restraints were permissible.

Although Standard Oil and American Tobacco were broken up as constituting unreasonable restraints of trade, few other big businesses suffered similar fates. In fact, of the 127 actions taken under the terms of the Sherman Act between 1905 and 1915, 72 were filed against loose combinations of smaller firms (such as cartels), 32 against tight combinations (such as trusts), 12 each against labor unions and agricultural produce dealers, and 10 against miscellaneous others.[15] Thus were law, public attitudes, and economics reconciled. As interpreted by the U.S. Supreme Court from 1911 onward, the Sherman Act has generally permitted large firms to exist, as long as they have grown big through reasonable means.

Final pre–World War I antitrust actions were worked out in 1914, when Congress passed both the Federal Trade Commission Act, setting up the Federal Trade Commission (FTC), and the Clayton Act. Like many pieces of business legislation passed during the Progressive Era, these acts resulted from compromises between various groups of business people—no single, monolithic business community existed—and politicians. For more than a decade, business groups had debated the wisdom of having a governmental body to oversee competitive conditions, and by 1914 most agreed that such an agency was needed. Small business people, such as retailers and grain dealers, wanted the creation of an agency that could look into the monopolistic practices of big businesses that they thought were threatening them with financial ruin. Larger firms, interested in bringing predictability to their relations with the federal government, sought the establishment of an agency that would clearly delineate what businesses could and could not do in their competition with one another. Officers of large firms especially wanted the establishment of a government agency that could offer businesses advance legal advice on their proposed actions, such as mergers. The FTC Act partly satisfied each camp. The legislation stated that "unfair methods of competition are hereby declared unlawful," created the FTC with the powers to decide just which methods were unlawful, and empowered the FTC to order offenders to "cease and desist" from engaging in unfair methods. The Clayton Act, a companion piece of legislation, sought to define more clearly than the vague Sherman Act what constituted restraint of trade. In addition to condemning any forms of price discrimination that limited competition, the Clayton Act forbade (a) certain types of interlocking directorates and (b) "tying contracts," mechanisms by which large firms prevented their suppliers and customers from doing business with competitors. While protecting small businesses to some degree, these laws also created a more stable political and legal environment for large firms.[16]

Similar compromises characterized much of the business legislation passed during the Progressive Era. Unwilling to forgo the fruits of big businesses, most Americans turned to politics to regulate but not destroy them. Much of the regulation was undertaken by the federal government through the creation of a new device, independent regulatory commissions (the FTC was one). Once established, these bodies operated with a fair degree of independence from both the legislative and the executive branches of government. The Interstate Commerce Act of 1887 set up the Interstate Commerce Commission to regulate first railroads and later trucks and buses, and the Elkins Act (1903), the Hepburn Act (1906), and the Mann-Elkins Act (1910) greatly increased the agency's powers. The Meat Inspection Act and the Pure Food and Drug Act, both passed in 1906, gave the federal government responsibility for the regulation of America's food and drug industries, and the Food and Drug Administration was established that same year.

The Federal Reserve Act of 1913 established the Federal Reserve System to regulate banking practices and the money supply in the United States. Spurred by financial panics in 1903 and 1907, bankers joined politicians in seeking federal legislation to bring stability to their industry. The resulting legislation was a compromise between the desires of big-city bankers, especially those in New York, who wanted a centralized banking system, and the desires of bankers in regional centers and small towns, who wanted a more decentralized one. The Federal Reserve Act established a Federal Reserve Board composed of five members, each from a different region, appointed by the president. Rather than set up a single central bank, as many New York financiers wanted, the act created 12 Federal Reserve district banks, each owned by the banks in its region. Each Federal Reserve district bank had a nine-member board composed of three members from the national Federal Reserve Board, three from district banks, and three nonbankers. The board for the Washington district sought to coordinate overall banking policies—control of interest rates and the money supply—for the 12 districts, with, however, only partial success. The Federal Reserve System was thus a compromise between centralized and decentralized banking.[17]

While Congress passed much of the most important legislation regulating businesses, state legislatures took significant steps as well. During the Progressive Era, they initiated or extended state regulation of railroads, public utilities, insurance companies, oil producers, banks, lumber companies, and some types of farm operations. As was occurring at the national level, much of the business legislation passed at the state level embodied compromises between politicians and competing business groups, often groups of large and small business people. In California, for instance, rifts often separated big-city bankers in San Francisco and Los Angeles from their counterparts in small towns scattered throughout agricultural regions. Only when these two groups of bankers could reconcile their differences, as they did following the Panic of 1907, was the state government able to pass significant regulatory legislation—the Bank Act of 1909, which for the first time clearly separated commercial, savings, and trust banking in California.[18]

Reflecting public attitudes, the impact of court decisions and political actions on small business was ambivalent. Some protection was afforded from the most blatant abuses of large firms, as the federal courts and Congress sought to prevent vaguely defined forms of unfair competition. For the most part, however, few impediments were placed in the way of the development of big business. As long as they developed by reasonable means and as long as they submitted to federal and state regulation, big businesses were permitted to grow and prosper. Small businesses persisted, and in some fields thrived, after 1880 less as a result of protective political actions than because of the important contributions they continued to make to America's evolving business system.

☐ Small Business in Manufacturing

Together, America's large and small industrial firms transformed the nation. From a country based on farms and small towns in the antebellum years America became a nation of factories and large cities in the late nineteenth and early twentieth centuries. It was in the 1880s that, for the first time, more people worked in nonfarm than in agricultural jobs, and it was in the 1920s that more people first came to live in towns and cities than in villages and on farms. Table 1 illustrates the changes that occurred in America's work force as the nation industrialized. Particularly noticeable is the decline in the proportion of Americans who earned their living as farmers and the rise in the proportion who were in clerical and sales positions.

With the development of industry, the dominance of the merchant yielded, after the Civil War, to that of the manufacturer. Small businesses found themselves in an ambiguous position. The opportunities of the nation's expanding industrial economy beckoned to small business owners, and they continued to increase in numbers throughout the late nineteenth and early twentieth centuries. Nonetheless, the proportion of America's industrial output coming from small businesses dropped as large manufacturing ventures rose to prominence. Corporations—the legal form assumed by most big businesses but by relatively few small businesses (most small firms remained single-owner proprietorships or partnerships)—accounted for three-quarters of America's industrial pro-

Table 1. The Occupational Distribution of the American Work Force, 1880–1920

Occupational Group	1880	1890	1900	1910	1920
In Thousands of Workers					
All gainful workers	15,265	21,546	26,707	34,856	39,764
All employees	9,628	14,273	18,489	25,675	30,408
Wage earners	8,048	11,714	15,088	19,896	21,874
Clerical and sales employees	995	1,618	2,136	3,882	5,845
Professional employees	424	680	913	1,284	1,681
Managerial employees	161	261	352	613	1,008
All enterprisers	5,637	7,273	8,218	9,181	9,356
Farmers	4,243	5,304	5,705	6,132	6,387
Business enterprisers	1,218	1,719	2,198	2,682	2,573
Professional enterprisers	176	250	315	367	396
As a Percentage of All Gainful Workers					
All gainful workers	100.0	100.0	100.0	100.0	100.0
All employees	63.1	66.2	69.2	73.7	76.5
Wage earners	52.7	54.4	56.5	57.1	55.0
Clerical and sales employees	6.5	7.5	8.0	11.1	14.7
Professional employees	2.8	3.1	3.4	3.7	4.2
Managerial employees	1.1	1.2	1.3	1.8	2.6
All self-employed enterprisers	36.9	33.8	30.8	26.3	23.5
Farmers	27.8	24.6	21.4	17.6	16.0
Non-farm business enterprisers	8.0	8.0	8.2	7.7	6.5
Professional practitioners	1.1	1.2	1.2	1.0	1.0

Spurgeon Bell, *Productivity, Wages, and National Income* (Washington, D.C.: The Brookings Institution, 1940), 10.

duction by 1904. By that year, too, a third of the income generated from manufacturing came from industries in which the four biggest companies accounted for more than half the sales. Small businesses also became less important as employers. By 1914, nearly a third of all industrial workers found employment in plants with 500 or more in their labor forces, and another third in those with 100 to 499. As large, vertically integrated companies arose in manufacturing, a growing share of industrial workers found employment in companies operating more than one plant; at least a third of the nation's workers had done so by 1923.[19]

Small businesses did not, however, disappear from the industrial scene in the United States. The same set of census statistics just alluded to show that in 1914 a third of America's industrial work force found employment in firms with 100 or fewer laborers. If small businesses are defined as those with 250 or fewer workers, 54% of those employed by manufacturing concerns worked for small firms. Moreover, some 54,000 little businesses, those with 6 to 20 workers, were still in operation on the eve of World War I.[20] Those small businesses which survived and prospered in manufacturing did so by following several strategies. In some fields—such as leather working, furniture making, and lumber milling—few economies of scale existed and big businesses did not develop. In these areas small manufacturers continued to turn out their goods much as they had in the antebellum years.

In those realms in which big businesses did emerge, small industrialists had to adapt to the presence of their larger counterparts. Some small businesses were able to operate on the fringes of an industry dominated by big businesses, making up an oligopolistic core, either as suppliers of intermediate parts for the larger firms or as independent producers.[21] The evolution of the flour-milling and the men's clothing industries illustrates this approach.

In flour milling the adoption of new technologies—mechanical rollers and purifiers—in the late nineteenth century made the industry more capital-intensive than in earlier times and began a trend toward concentration. Large companies located in Minneapolis came to dominate the industry by taking advantage of scale economies in production and by setting up their own nationwide marketing networks. Many small mills went out of existence, and the flour-milling industry came to be dominated by a few giants. By 1921, the five largest companies were milling 23% of America's flour, and by 1939, some 38%, of which General Mills accounted for about a fourth. While declining in their overall importance in the flour-milling industry, small businesses remained significant in several respects: as millers turning out special blends of flour; as millers in interior towns away from the big cities; and as national producers during times of peak demand.[22]

The men's clothing industry experienced similar changes. Between 1880 and 1920, the industry came to consist of two segments: (a) a handful of large firms that operated year-round, were organizationally and technologically sophisticated, and manufactured high-quality garments and (b) thousands of small firms that came and went with great frequency, were technically more primitive, and produced mainly lower-quality and lower-priced clothing. Since the demand for clothing was seasonal and generally unstable, the small firms in the secondary sector, with their low capital investments, were well suited to handle the variable component of demand. By 1927, only 14 of the nation's 4,118 men's clothing firms employed more than 1,000 workers, and only 110 employed more than 300. Yet half of the industry's work force found employment in just the largest 6% of the companies.[23]

Most small businesses that succeeded in manufacturing chose a different route from those in flour milling or in the making of men's clothing, however. They succeeded by differentiating their products from those of their larger counterparts. Doing so often meant producing a wide range of goods for rapidly changing regional and seasonal markets. Part of the ability to accomplish this task lay in the possession of intelligent, innovative work forces; another part lay in the flexible use of the most advanced (not primitive) technologies. In short, by carving out market niches, and by developing new production methods, small businesses could remain as independent enterprises in successful coexistence with larger firms.[24] Among the fields in which small firms prospered well into the twentieth century were textiles and metal making.

As the nineteenth century progressed, the textile industry divided into two segments.[25] In Waltham and Lowell in New England, large factories employed unskilled workers to turn out standardized goods for the mass market. The mills quickly became fully integrated in the production of textiles, with all the steps—preparation, spinning, weaving, and dyeing—carried out on different factory floors linked by elevators. These milling companies were among the largest businesses of the antebellum period. As early as 1832, eight of them were capitalized at at least $600,000 apiece. They each employed hundreds of workers, and their physical plants were large. In 1849 one company possessed five mills, each of which was five stories tall, with each story taken up by one room measuring 40 by 151 feet. By the 1830s and 1840s, all the companies had adopted the corporate form of organization, and most were run through rudimentary managerial hierarchies. Few small textile firms developed in Waltham or Lowell, for the large businesses controlled the available plant sites and sources of waterpower, denying access to others. By 1850, 12 corporations employed 12,000 textile workers in Lowell. Not even the cotton shortage of the 1860s and the nationwide depression of the mid-1870s changed things much. When pressed by rising expenses for their raw materials and falling demand for their finished goods, the companies contracted their operations, laying off workers and reducing wages in the process, but did not alter their approach to business.

The textile business developed differently in Philadelphia. In 1850, 326 firms employed 12,400 textile workers. Two-thirds possessed 25 or fewer workers, and 28 of the largest 32 employed only between 102 and 225 workers. Though employing as many workers in the aggregate as their counterparts in Waltham and Lowell, the Philadelphia firms were capitalized at much less—$4.7 million, about a third of the amount invested in the Lowell and Waltham companies. Most of the Philadelphia companies were organized as single-owner proprietorships. Only about 17% were partnerships, and even fewer—a scant 3%—were corporations.

The Philadelphia firms competed successfully throughout the nineteenth century with the much-larger mills of New England by stressing specialization and flexibility in production and marketing. Few Philadelphia firms tried to master all aspects of textile production; most specialized in one or two steps, which they then did very well indeed, using the most up-to-date machinery and employing skilled workers, often men, at high wages. Their productivity levels were high. In their labor practices as in their management methods, the Philadelphia mills differed from the larger mills in Lowell and Waltham. The Lowell and Waltham mills employed young, unskilled farm women as workers and treated them very paternalistically, housing them in company dormitories and strictly supervising their morals. Turnover rates were probably higher in Lowell and Waltham than in Philadelphia, thus probably making productivity lower in the northern mills. With skilled work forces and modern machinery, the Philadelphia mills could also more rapidly switch to various types of cotton, wool, and other fabrics as needed.

For the most part, the owners of the Philadelphia textile establishments did not become members of their city's social elite—in sharp contrast to the situation in New England, where mill owners became influential figures in cities like Boston. Instead, the Philadelphia mill owners remained close to their work, and a commercial elite of merchants long dominated Philadelphia's affairs. This circumstance paid an unexpected dividend. Although Philadelphia was not immune to labor unrest, disturbances were mitigated by bonds uniting managers and workers. Workers and managers knew each other personally through work on the plant floor and through membership in the same churches and social organizations. Moreover, many mill owners had started as skilled artisans, often renting space for their nascent ventures and only later expanding their enterprises. Workers and owners "talked the same language" and respected each other, even when they disagreed.

The flexibility of the Philadelphia firms served them well during the crises of the 1860s and 1870s. Most adjusted better than their counterparts in Lowell and Waltham to the cotton shortage and the wartime demands of the Civil War by shifting to the production of woolen goods and other items. Similarly, their flexibility allowed the Philadelphia mills to prosper and expand even during the hard times of the mid-1870s, a period in which many New England mills encountered severe difficulties. By the early 1880s, Philadelphia possessed 849 textile establishments employing 55,000 workers, the largest such concentration of firms and workers in the nation. These were mostly profitable firms. The return on capital in Philadelphia's cotton textile companies averaged 23% in 1890, compared with 6% in the Lowell and Waltham companies and 8% in cotton textile firms nationwide. Most of the Philadelphia companies remained what they had been in the antebellum years—small, family firms in which the owner-manager personally supervised every aspect of his firm's operations. As a spokesman noted with pride, Philadelphia's textile community was "composed almost exclusively of individuals and individual firms . . . no corporations."[26]

Small size and versatility continued to be hallmarks of the Philadelphia textile firms into the twentieth century. Not even the depression of the 1890s, which ushered in merger movements in many industries, led to concentration in Philadelphia's textile industry. Economic factors militated against mergers—the flexible, batch system of production; the ease of entry into the industry; and the near-absence of scale economies—but more important was the character of the men owning the mills. They identified personally with their businesses, which they often viewed as extensions of their families. Philadelphia remained the domain of small firms. In 1905, 728 textile companies capitalized at a total of $100 million employed 60,000 workers within the city of Philadelphia (there were additional firms in the suburbs and nearby areas). As before, these were flexible, specialized companies attuned to making rapid production changes as markets altered (in 1910, for example, a carpet maker celebrated its twenty-fifth anniversary by bringing out its 25,000th pattern).[27]

If the experiences of the Philadelphia textile makers illustrate continuing opportunities for small business people in manufacturing during the age of giant enterprise, they also reveal limitations. Most unsettling was the growth in the power of the intermediate purchasers of the textiles. In the late nineteenth and twentieth centuries, chain stores and department stores emerged as big businesses in America. Using their buying power and emphasizing the rapid turnover of their stock, they demanded lower prices and more frequent deliveries from their Philadelphia textile suppliers. Wedded to traditional family business methods (few mill owners understood or adopted new accounting methods, for instance), Philadelphia's textile producers failed to mount an adequate defense. They failed, for instance, to form any sort of trade association to combat the demands of the larger companies buying their goods. Their continuing desire to maintain independent family firms prevented any combined defense of their businesses. The new demands of mass retailers put strains on these small manufacturing units that eventually overwhelmed their owner-managers. Flexibility gave way to rigidity, and the industry went into long-term decline.

When national economic problems joined the particular problems of the Philadelphia mills during the Great Depression of the 1930s, the destruction of the textile businesses was assured. Between 1925 and 1933, Philadelphia suffered a net loss of nearly 300 textile firms. Rather than merge with their competitors, most mill owners used up their capital and went out of existence. A corresponding decline occurred in the number of workers in the city's textile industry. Employment peaked in 1925 with 72,000 workers. From that point on, the course was downhill: 60,000 in 1929 and 42,000 in 1932. Some recovery occurred in the late 1930s and during World War II, only to be followed by further decline in the postwar years, until a scant 22,000 textile workers remained in Philadelphia in 1960.

A similar story developed in America's iron and steel industries. In these fields large companies, such as Carnegie Steel and later the United States Steel Corporation, did come to dominate important segments of their industries. By using new, large-batch production methods, they turned out vast quantities of homogeneous steel products, mainly rails and structural steel, for America's expanding national market. Nonetheless, smaller iron and steel mills continued to thrive alongside the giants, even in Pittsburgh, the heart of the nation's iron and steel industry, well into the twentieth century.

Pittsburgh's iron and steel industries took form as collections of relatively small businesses.[28] As late as 1870, the typical firm was capitalized at just $210,000, produced 3,000 tons of iron and steel annually, and employed only 119 workers. Like their counterparts elsewhere in America, Pittsburgh's iron and steel mills were unintegrated enterprises. They engaged in only one or two, not all, of the steps involved in turning out iron and steel products. The companies were for the most part family businesses, with about 40 families dominating the industries. The owners lived in Pittsburgh or nearby areas and ran their businesses themselves, eschewing the use of managerial hierarchies.

The switch from iron to steel, and with this change the use of the capital-intensive Bessemer and open-hearth methods, altered the situation in Pittsburgh, but only somewhat. Despite the expansion of new methods of steel making, iron production continued to grow as well, and older methods of steel making, such as the crucible process, continued to enjoy popularity. Many mills did become larger, but few approached the enormous size of the Carnegie operations. By the late 1880s, the average Pittsburgh iron and steel firm was capitalized at $805,000, produced 14,000 tons of iron and steel, and had a work force of 332. Many of these firms continued to be run by well-established Pittsburgh families (Carnegie was considered an outsider). The rise of a few giant firms, such as Carnegie Steel, should not obscure the continuing importance of the many smaller companies, for there remained 58 independent iron and steel mills in Pittsburgh in 1894.

The independent Pittsburgh mills (those not part of the expanding Carnegie empire) survived and indeed prospered by specializing. Rather than compete with Carnegie Steel in the large-batch production of rails and structural steel, most coexisted side by side with the Carnegie enterprises by producing specialized goods for niche markets. In pursuing this strategy Pittsburgh's independent iron and steel producers closely resembled the approach to business taken by Philadelphia's textile makers in their competition with the larger companies of New England. Oliver and Phillips, the Sable Rolling Mill, Vesuvius Iron, Juniata Iron, Crescent Steel, Hussey Wells and Company, and LaBelle Steel were some of the firms that successfully specialized. Oliver and Phillips, for instance, went into the making of nuts and bolts, wagon hardware, and barbed wire, while Vesuvius engaged in the production of bar and sheet iron, rods, hoops, and nails.

The coexistence of many smaller iron and steel companies with a few giant ones continued well into the twentieth century. Not even the formation of United States Steel in 1901 radically altered the situation. Only a few of the old-line independents became part of United States Steel, and between 1898 and 1901 16 new iron and steel firms were set up in Pittsburgh. In 1901, the 40 independent producers in Pittsburgh had a production capacity of 3.8 million tons of iron and steel, compared with the 2.6-million-ton capacity of United States Steel. In 1920 fully 78% of the independents in existence two decades earlier were still doing business, and even after America's second large merger movement, which occurred in the 1920s, about 50% were active. The Great Depression ended the existence of more, but on the eve of World War II, 28% of the independents remained. By 1938 the independents had not only survived but increased their combined production capacity to 7.9 million tons.

Throughout the nineteenth century and into the twentieth, the independent mill owners composed much of the social elite of Pittsburgh, in marked contrast to the lesser social role played by the textile makers in Philadelphia. From the 1840s through the 1890s, 141 families owned and operated iron or steel mills in Pittsburgh. About half of these families were considered to be among the city's upper class. This situation continued into the middle twentieth century, as many iron and steel families entered banking. It was this social elite—based on iron, steel, and finance—that largely controlled Pittsburgh's political and cultural life for many years, losing its hegemony only after World War II.

Their positions as leaders in their community influenced how the independent iron and steel mill owners dealt with their labor forces. Perhaps both because they were close to their workers in relatively small plants and because they cared deeply for the welfare of Pittsburgh, most tended toward a grudging acceptance of unions and a pragmatic willingness to try to work with them. More so than the operators of the much-larger Carnegie mills, the owner-operators of the small independent facilities sought to achieve a harmonious relationship with their workers, especially in the 1870s and 1880s. In the 1890s and later, following the lead of the larger firms, the independent mill owners became less tolerant of labor. As they adopted more capital-intensive equipment and were influenced by the examples of violence against labor at Carnegie Steel, they turned more of their attention to breaking unions.

The success of small firms in the iron and steel industries was not limited to the Pittsburgh region. The growth of the Buckeye Steel Castings Company of Columbus, Ohio, suggests the continuing significance of small businesses in manufacturing across the nation.[29] Formed as a partnership in 1881, Buckeye Steel was initially simply one of some 20 companies producing a variety of cast-iron goods for the local market in central Ohio. Buckeye lacked a specialty product or any other advantage over its competitors and came very close to failing during the hard times of the mid-1880s. Through personal ties, however, the company's founders were able to attract new investors, most important a man named Wilbur Goodspeed. Hailing from Cleveland, Goodspeed moved to Columbus in 1886, assumed the presidency of Buckeye Steel, and reorganized the company as a corporation.

Goodspeed saved Buckeye Steel, and how he did so illustrates some of the ways by which small firms were able to coexist with their larger counterparts in the late nineteenth and early twentieth centuries. Like many of the independent Pittsburgh steel companies, Buckeye Steel developed a specialty product for a niche market, an automatic railroad-car coupler. Made out of cast iron in the 1890s but out of stronger cast steel in the twentieth century, this technologically sophisticated coupler gave Buckeye an edge over its competitors and allowed the company to break into the national market. In entering this market, Buckeye Steel's executives relied heavily on their personal connections with other business people. While in business in Cleveland, Goodspeed had come to know high-ranking executives at the Standard Oil Company, which was headquartered in that city. Soon after he took over at Buckeye Steel, Goodspeed negotiated an arrangement favorable to both parties. In return for receiving a large block of common stock in Buckeye Steel for free, the Standard Oil executives agreed to use their influence to persuade all the railroads that shipped Standard's petroleum products to market (few long-distance pipelines existed then) to purchase their couplers solely from Buckeye Steel.

Railroad orders soared, and Buckeye Steel emerged as a highly successful business, becoming a medium-size firm by national standards at the time of World War I. Personal connections continued to play a substantial role in Buckeye Steel's growth. Almost every officer in the company had connections to railroads and used them to help sell Buckeye Steel's couplers. Beyond this fortunate circumstance, other factors contributed to Buckeye's rise. The firm's owner-managers reinvested the company's earnings in their corporation, building what became in the first decade of the twentieth century the most up-to-date steel mill of its type in the United States. Deeply interested, like the independent iron and steel mill owners in Pittsburgh, in the progress of their community, Buckeye Steel's officers were closely involved in community affairs. This concern, combined with a desire to lessen the turnover rate of labor in their steel foundry, led Buckeye's officers to institute a broad range of corporate welfare activities for their workers. Largely successful in achieving a sense of harmony with their work force, Buckeye's owner-managers kept their plant free of labor strife.[30]

In brass making—the final example offered here on small business success in manufacturing—the competitive situation differed from conditions in the production of textiles, iron, and steel. Because of the small size of the total market for brass products, no truly large companies emerged. Rather, a host of small firms composed the brass-making industry.

The development of the Smith and Griggs Company of Waterbury, Connecticut, was probably typical of that of the many small firms in the brass industry.[31] Founded as a partnership in 1865, the company was incorporated a few years later but nonetheless continued into the twentieth century to be run as a family business. Smith and Griggs moved ahead by devising technical innovations in the manufacturing of specialty products for a distinct market niche—mainly buckles and buttons—and by maintaining close personal ties between its owner-managers and the wholesalers purchasing its goods. In 1900 the company earned $47,000 on sales of $220,000; 85% of these sales were made to just 10 customers, underlining the necessity of keeping good relations with the wholesalers.

Successful in its nineteenth-century operations, Smith and Griggs went into decline in the twentieth century. A new president, a person still related to the founding families of the company, assumed power in 1908. He failed to meet several pressing challenges. In particular, many former customers were integrating backward to set up their own production facilities, as the availability of new types of machinery made this step feasible. At the same time, a deterioration in its service cost Smith and Griggs orders from many of its largest and oldest wholesalers. Strapped for funds, the company engaged in less research and development than previously and failed to develop a new market niche to compensate for the one it was rapidly losing. As was occurring in many of Philadelphia's textile companies at about the same time, flexibility was replaced by inflexibility at Smith and Griggs. Faced with mounting losses during the Great Depression, the firm went out of existence in 1936. A possible lesson to be drawn from the experiences of Smith and Griggs is that small firms survive only if new technology does not preempt their "niche" status.

Common themes run through the successes of those small companies which proved capable of coexisting with big businesses in manufacturing. Consciously or unconsciously, the small manufacturers adopted a growth strategy that would remain one of the keys to success in small business into the late twentieth century: they developed specialty products that they then sold in niche markets, thereby often avoiding direct competition with their larger counterparts. To make this growth strategy work, the firms usually adopted (or developed themselves) the most advanced production technologies available. These small companies were not backward workshops using obsolete equipment but were instead among the most advanced industrial establishments of their day.

Running the companies were managers deeply committed to their success. Most of the companies, even those organized as corporations, continued to be operated as family enterprises. The businesses remained single-unit enterprises devoid for the most part of managerial hierarchies (though some of the independent Pittsburgh mills did develop simple hierarchies in the late nineteenth century). More than a quest for profits animated their owners. A sense of personal satisfaction, almost a sense of craftsmanship, remained a primary motivating factor for their executives and workers. Writing his wife about business affairs in 1908, the president of Buckeye Steel captured this feeling when he observed, "We have had hard times to bear, but surely we should not care to have our lives easy, for there would be no accomplishment, no development."[32] Not surprisingly, personal connections and informal ways of conducting business continued to be important in the daily operations of the firms.

Nevertheless, new management techniques crept into the world of small business manufacturing. As small manufacturing companies became more capital-intensive, some emulated their larger counterparts in instituting new accounting practices. The adoption of innovations, especially in cost and capital accounting, helped them compete with larger companies. For instance, some firms in the cut nail industry of the Ohio Valley, small businesses all, developed new cost accounting methods as early as the 1850s and 1860s. In the decades after the Civil war the nail companies improved their systems of inventory control, and by the 1870s and 1880s the most successful of the firms were using cost accounting as a diagnostic tool in their planning processes, one of the first group of American companies to do so.[33]

At Buckeye Steel, as well, both cost and capital accounting were well advanced as early as 1903, when the company was still small. In his approach to cost accounting, Buckeye's plant superintendent was among the most advanced managers of his day, pioneering in the inclusion of indirect and overhead expenses as part of his costs of production, at a time when many manufacturers, large and small, simply ignored them. In capital accounting, the superintendent carefully figured monthly charges for furnace, building, and machinery repairs, together with depreciation charges—again at a time when many industrialists failed to account for such expenses. A page from the superintendent's notebook reveals his concern for capital expenses:

> For instance, we produced 18,500 tons of castings from the beginning of operations to Dec. 31, 1903. Total cost furnace repairs $12,129 = $0.70 ton.
>
> Repairs of buildings about $3,600 = $0.20 per ton.
>
> Repairs of machinery about $6,000 = $0.35 per ton.
>
> Depreciation of buildings figures at 3% per year.
>
> Buildings are worth $200,000. Depreciation is $5,000 or $0.35 per ton.
>
> Depreciation on machinery is figued at 10% per year. Machinery is worth $250,000. So depreciation comes to $25,000 or $1.40 per ton.[34]

Perhaps because of their continuing personal involvement in their businesses, small-scale industrialists were often more concerned about the welfare of their labor forces than their larger counterparts were. Many of the smaller, more profitable manufacturers were both more receptive to unions and more willing to engage in welfare capitalism. This situation was most apparent in the iron and steel industries, at least into the 1890s, but existed as well in textiles.[35] Particularly in textiles, the small Philadelphia industrialists relied heavily on highly skilled workers who—like the managers of the companies—were flexible in their approaches to their tasks. Despite its reputation of being antilabor, small business was, as these cases show, often receptive to the needs of workers.

Not all small business owners adopted a benevolent attitude, however. The picture of small business response to labor was complex. In 1895 owners of small- and medium-size firms formed the National Association of Manufacturers, which soon grew to become a national trade association and which in the twentieth century became virulently antiunion.

External factors also prepared the way to success for small businesses. In some instances government aid helped. Such was the case with Buckeye Steel. In 1893 Congress passed legislation requiring that all railroad cars be equipped with automatic couplers within five years. (This act was a piece of safety legislation designed to protect trainsmen, who were often injured while using the old-style manual couplers to join cars together.) This law helped create a national market for Buckeye Steel's main product. In other cases, a favorable local environment proved valuable. In Philadelphia the textile companies benefited from various sorts of local government aid and were also able to unite to support for many years a trade school to ensure the availability of a steady supply of skilled workers.

☐ Agriculture: The Continuing Family Farm

Although the United States was fast becoming an urban industrial nation in the late nineteenth and early twentieth centuries, agriculture remained a vital part of the American economy. At the heart of the agricultural picture lay the family farm, which, despite the growing mechanization and commercialization of agriculture, changed little from the antebellum years. Farming was still, in 1900 or even 1920, dominated by family farms operating as small businesses.

Yet there were also suggestions of the beginnings of agribusiness complexes that would largely supplant family farmers in later years. The term *agribusiness* is usually taken to mean a cluster of related farming practices and beliefs. Foremost is the notion of farming for profit, to the exclusion of other motives. Closely related is the idea of making farming scientific and efficient. Doing so may in turn mean moving away from the family farm as the primary unit of production. Instead, corporations may own and operate farms much larger than those run by most individual families. Specialized farming almost completely replaces general farming, and, as "factories in the field," agribusiness enterprises may be operated by managers employing gangs of hired farm workers. Moreover, the farms themselves often become simply parts of vertically integrated companies that raise, process, and market agricultural produce—with most of the profits being earned in processing and marketing.[36]

While growing in absolute importance, agriculture declined steadily in terms of its relative significance to the American economy. The number of farms rose from 1.5 million in 1850 to 6.5 million in 1920, and during the same years the land in farms increased from about 300 million to just under 1 billion acres. Despite these impressive increases, the still-more-rapid rise of industry ensured that agriculture's overall contribution to the economy of the United States would fall. In 1880 self-employed farmers composed 28% of the total work force of the United States; by 1920, a scant 16%.[37] If farmers and farm laborers are considered together, the trend is the same. In 1860 about 60% of the nation's workers were on the farm; 40 years later, only 37%. In 1860 farm income was 30% of the national income; by 1900, a smaller 20% (the per capita income of farm workers, however, rose from $70 in 1859 to $112 in 1900, in constant dollars).[38]

It was not that farming regressed; rather, agricultural incomes failed to keep pace with the tremendous advances being made in industry and the service sector. Agriculture, though successful in terms of its overall efficiency, primarily benefited consumers more than it did farmers. The markets for farm products remained highly competitive, forcing the less efficient farmers to shift to the manufacturing or service sectors. As one farmer observed in 1909, "To the man who regards the mere accumulation of great wealth as the sole or even the chief criterion of success the occupation of farming will present few attractions."[39]

Just as the place of agriculture in the American economy changed, so too did farming methods. The mechanization and technological improvements begun in the antebellum years continued after the Civil War. Technological innovations—haying machines, wheat harvesters, combines, mechanical seed drills, and new types of plows—were particularly important for the spread of agriculture in the Midwest and on the Great Plains. The impact of the innovations was sometimes dramatic.

The number of man-hours needed to produce 100 bushels of wheat fell from 233 in 1840 to only 87 in 1920, and the corresponding number of man-hours required for corn dropped from 276 to 113. The use of new types of farm equipment was less widespread in the South and on the Pacific Coast, for the cultivation and harvesting of tobacco, cotton, fruits, and vegetables remained labor-intensive.[40]

The mechanization of farming was part of a larger trend, the commercialization of American agriculture. Even more so than in the colonial period or the antebellum years, American farmers became deeply involved in the national and international trade in agricultural commodities. Communications and transportation improvements—the telegraph, transatlantic cables, the railroad, and steamships—furthered this trend. Individual family farmers across the nation found themselves increasingly at the mercy of market forces they neither understood nor controlled. A rise in the demand for their wheat by British consumers might boost the prices paid Great Plains farmers for their harvests in some years, while bumper crops in the Ukraine or Argentina might lower prices in others. The foreign market remained, as it had been earlier, an important outlet for American farm products. Between 1869 and 1900, nearly a fifth of the nation's farm goods found overseas markets, and in the same period, despite the expansion of industry, farm goods composed about three-fourths of all American exports.[41]

The family farms, which, as in times past, continued to lie at the center of America's agricultural system, remained much as they had been a century before. In 1900 the average family farm encompassed 146 acres, of which about 72 were improved—a considerable increase, to be sure, from the 100 acres, of which perhaps 35 might have been cultivated, in late colonial times, but nevertheless not an astronomical rise. Despite the mechanization that had occurred in some fields of agriculture, the average farm still possessed only $131 worth of machinery at the turn of the century. Most farms were diversified to some degree; few specialized entirely in just one crop. Despite the spread of a commercial economy across America, general farming remained the norm, as farmers raised livestock, fruit, and vegetables for their own consumption, as well as such staple crops as wheat and corn for the market.[42]

The tension already apparent in colonial and early national times between a desire for family self-sufficiency and a need to participate in a market economy grew more pronounced in the late nineteenth century. While profit-motivated, farmers also valued agriculture for nonpecuniary reasons: for what they viewed as their independence, for close personal relationships with their family and local communities, for nearness to the soil and nature in general.[43] Speaking before the U.S. Industrial Commission in 1916, a tenant farmer from Texas summarized the nonmonetary aspects of agriculture so important to many family farmers. After telling the commission a story of hard work, poor health, and poverty, he testified that farming nonetheless offered a contented life— "a legitimate life, a happy life, a useful life, useful to humanity, useful to all developments of every nature."[44]

The career of Lewis D. McMillen illustrates well the sometimes-contradictory aspects of farm life. Raised in an Ohio farm family, McMillen acquired his own farm of 125 acres in northern Ohio in 1891 at age 33. Here he and his growing family made a living for the next 35 years. After surviving the depression of the mid-1890s, McMillen prospered as a general farmer, raising wheat, corn, livestock, and some fruit.[45]

McMillen took part in the commercial market for farm products in the United States. Like many American farmers, he bought his farm on credit, paying off his mortgage some years later. He made most of his profits by purchasing sheep and cattle in the Chicago market, fattening them on his corn, and then selling them throughout the nation. A progressive farmer, he practiced crop rotation (wheat or oats, clover, and corn in yearly succession) and was always interested in new types of machinery, farming techniques, and crops, including sugar beets. His son recalled that McMillen paid "particular attention to market reports in the daily paper he received from the Pittsburgh stockyards."[46]

For McMillen, farming was, however, much more than a commercial enterprise. He valued his farm for the independence it provided him and his family. As his son remembered, "He had always wanted to be a free American, living on and within his own resources, unobligated to anyone for favors or support. . . . One reason he liked the farm was that it was a business he could run without becoming obligated to others."[47] In fact, the McMillen family raised most of the chickens, eggs, milk, vegetables, fruit, and meat that they consumed, and even in the twentieth century made their own soap. Although he was astute in his trading (he was able to save about $1,000 a year, a large sum then, most of which he reinvested in his farm), a quest for luxury did not dominate McMillen's life. His son recalled, "We did know that people somewhere were richer than we, and perhaps did not have to work so much or so hard, and we heard that many more were poorer than we were. We did not expect to strike it rich and did not know how we could relieve distant poverty. In our neighborhood the range from richest to poorest was not wide."[48]

Not all family farmers were as progressive as McMillen; for many farmers, traditional techniques and beliefs remained chief arbiters in the conduct of agricultural affairs. For example, "moon farming" continued to be widely practiced across the United States. As one adherent explained, "We plant, we sow, we reap and mow; we fell trees, we make shingles, we roof our houses, secure bacon, make fences, spread manure, when the moon is auspicious." Almanacs showing the phases of the moon were in great demand.[49] Not surprisingly, many farmers resisted the "country life movement," which aimed at improving farming in the early twentieth century, because they viewed the campaign as an effort by urbanites to force city ways of life and thought on them (indeed, much of the movement was concerned with introducing urban education practices to rural areas).[50]

Nonetheless, farm practices did change, and in some of the alterations may be glimpsed the faint beginnings of agribusiness and the corresponding origins of the decline of family farming. Although not fully developed until after World War II, agribusiness can be traced to the late nineteenth and early twentieth centuries.

"Bonanza farms" growing wheat in California and on parts of the northern Great Plains in the 1870s and 1880s provide an early example of agribusiness. By 1880, there were 29,000 farms of more than 1,000 acres apiece in the United States, many of them in the West. While some of these operated as large family farms, many were organized as corporations designed to earn quick returns for their stockholders. Typical were the efforts of the Dalrymple interests, which controlled 100,000 acres in North Dakota. In 1880 the company raised wheat on 25,000 acres (most of the rest was still uncultivated), divided into farms of about 6,000 acres of plowed land. Each farm was under the control of a superintendent and was subdivided into three segments, averaging 2,000 acres apiece. According to a federal government census report, "Each subdivision [had] its own farm buildings, boarding-houses, stables, blacksmith-shop, and so on, this size being considered the most convenient, and as large enough for systematic management."[51] Most of the labor came from harvesting crews that each year traveled across the Great Plains as migrant workers.

Most of the nation's bonanza farms disappeared during the depression of the 1890s (many smaller family farms also failed); however, the trend toward larger farms reappeared with the return of agricultural prosperity in the early 1900s. These changing relationships in farm sizes—as seen in Table 2—suggest the rising importance of large-scale farming during the first two decades of the twentieth century. Farms larger than 260 acres experienced a rapid growth rate. The increase in the numbers of farms of less than 50 acres, many of which were proba-

Table 2. U.S. Farms by Size, 1900–1920 (thousands of farms)

	1–49 acres	50–259 acres	260–499 acres	500–999 acres	1,000+ acres
1900	1,931	3,278	378	103	47
1910	2,254	3,489	444	125	50
1920	2,300	3,455	476	150	67

U.S. Bureau of the Census, *Historical Statistics of the United States, Colonial Times to 1957* (Washington, D.C.: U.S. Government Printing Office 1960), 279.

bly run by part-time farmers, continued, though at a slower rate. The numbers of medium-size family farms (those of between 50 and 260 acres) increased at a still-slower rate during the first decade and then declined over the next 10 years.[52] While far from conclusive, these figures suggest the emergence of a skewed pattern of farm landholding that would become more pronounced after World War II: a growth in the proportion of farms that were either small or large, coupled with a decline in the proportion of medium-size units.

Even medium-size family farmers discovered that they needed to devise new methods to market their crops. As they became increasingly drawn into the commercial economy, they formed selling organizations to deal with the complexity of their commercial affairs. Beginning in the 1870s and 1880s, farmers set up cooperatives to market their produce. Through pooling their marketing efforts, agriculturalists hoped to limit competition among themselves, thus raising the prices they received for their crops. They also sought through combined actions lower railroad rates and faster service to get their crops to markets before they spoiled. Finally, they joined forces to open sales agencies in eastern cities and abroad, something they could not afford to do as individuals. Even McMillen, much as he valued his independence, marketed through a cooperative. Some cooperatives went beyond selling by branching into the purchasing of an assortment of products, ranging from gasoline to insurance, for farmers. By 1907 more than 1,000 farm cooperatives were operating in America, mainly in wheat, milk, fruits, and vegetables, and their numbers would increase in later years.[53]

Cooperatives proved most useful for those farmers, family and corporate, who turned away from general farming to specialize in just one or two crops. This trend was most pronounced in California, where more and more farmers came to specialize in raising fruits and vegetables that they then shipped via fast trains to eastern and midwestern markets. By the time of World War I, California's farmers had set up cooperatives to market oranges, grapefruit, lemons, apples, pears, walnuts, berries, rice, almonds, tomatoes, string beans, lima beans, and cantaloupes. Altogether, cooperatives handled more than half the Golden State's produce and helped farmers survive as small- to medium-scale economic units.[54]

☐ Small Business in Distribution and Services

The rise of big business led to significant changes in the distribution and sales of both agricultural and industrial products. Nonetheless, small-scale merchants continued to thrive, and the distribution of goods, particularly at the retail level, long remained the domain of small business. The number of people working in wholesale establishments rose from 170,000 in 1869 to 1.2 million a half-century later, and in the same period the number employed in retail outlets jumped from 720,000 to 4 million—rates of increase much greater than the threefold population rise in the United States during those years. While a growing proportion of America's selling establishments were large, many remained small stores. As late as 1929, 168,000 wholesalers employed 1.6 million persons, for an average employment per establishment of just under 10 persons. Retailing remained even more the province of small businesses. In 1929, 1.5 million retail establishments employed 5.7 million persons, for an average employment of just over three persons per store.[55]

The growth of big businesses in marketing assumed several forms. Large commodity dealers used the telegraph and the railroad to operate nationwide buying and selling networks for agricultural goods. By 1921, for example, just 21 firms marketed three-fifths of America's cotton. Full-line and full-service wholesalers and jobbers established nationwide organizations to move consumer products—dry goods, hardware, drugs, and groceries—from manufacturers to retailers. As early as 1870, Alexander T. Stewart, America's leading distributor of dry goods, boasted sales of $50 million and employed 2,000 workers. And as we have seen, many manufacturers set up their own sales outlets to reach customers across the United States. Soon, however, mass retailers challenged these marketers. Department stores—Macy's, Bloomingdale's, Lazarus, and a host of others—grew up in cities, and catalog stores—Montgomery Ward and Sears, Roebuck—served rural and small-town America.

Chain stores also got their start. The Great Atlantic and Pacific Tea Company (A & P) began operations in 1859 and by 1900 had about 200 stores selling tea, coffee, and selected groceries. Beginning in 1879, F.

W. Woolworth set up five-and-ten stores that by 1905 had a sales volume of more than $15 million.[56] Most sales—especially at the retail level—continued, however, to be made by small neighborhood stores in cities or by small general stores in the countryside as late as World War I. In 1890 just 10 chains (each composed of at least two stores) existed in America, and even in 1915 there were only 515.[57]

If most of America's consumer goods still moved through long-established wholesale and retail channels at the time of World War I, changes were occurring in those channels. The merchandising methods of the mass retailers had an impact on the independents. Mass marketers stressed high volumes of sales through quick stock turnovers and low unit costs as the paths to profits. Independents responded in several ways. Even more so than in the antebellum years, urban retailers streamlined their operations by specializing in the goods they handled. Moreover, they often embraced new technologies as eagerly as their larger competitors. Cash registers made by the National Cash Register Company were, for example, cheap enough for even small retailers to purchase and came into common use throughout the nation by around 1900.[58]

General country stores were less successful than independent urban retailers in their adaptations to the social and economic changes taking place in the United States. Owners of general stores did, though, make some alterations in their business methods. The coming of the railroad allowed them to order stock directly from manufacturers' and wholesalers' representatives, known as "traveling men," rather than make tiresome, month-long trips to eastern cities to purchase their supplies. The more progressive shopkeepers installed attractive showcases in which they grouped their goods by category or department and, like their urban brethren, began carrying more and more brand-name packaged goods, such as Ivory Soap, Uneeda Biscuit, and Quaker Oats. These moves were not enough. As they extended their reach, commodity dealers usurped the roles country stores had played in the purchasing and selling of farm goods. Even more damaging was farmers' adoption of the automobile, which allowed farmers to shop in nearby towns and cities. By the 1920s and 1930s, country stores were fast disappearing from the American scene, except in those few remaining isolated rural areas. As one commentator observed, "So it was with the passing of the general store. It just slowly dried up, like a farm pond in the August heat, scarcely changing from one day to the next, until it was gone."[59]

The development of an urbanized and industrialized society in America spurred the demand for the services of credit-rating agencies, insurance companies, and banks. Like firms in wholesaling and retailing, companies in the service industries felt the impact of the rise of big business. A few big businesses grew up in these fields. Two companies dominated credit rating: by 1880, R. G. Dun had 69 branch offices and employed 10,000 credit investigators, while its main rival, the Bradstreet Agency, also operated across the nation; Dun and Bradstreet was later formed from a merger of these two companies. But while a few big businesses grew up in the service industries, it was mainly small firms that dominated them, just as in the antebellum years. Not even the Dun and Bradstreet agencies could avoid competition. With few barriers to entry, the credit-rating business was open to all, leading one Dun employee to comment in the late 1870s that other credit-reporting agencies were "getting as thick as blackberries."[60]

The late nineteenth and early twentieth centuries witnessed a rapid expansion in the number of insurance companies in the United States. The growing impersonality of life in big cities led to a tremendous growth in the life insurance business, as families came to rely on these companies to provide benefits they had once given their members. In 1880, 59 companies had $1.5 billion worth of life insurance policies in force; by 1920, 335 companies had $41 billion in force.[61] The "Big Three" life insurance companies—New York Life, Equitable of New York, and Mutual Life of New York—dominated their industry for many years. These companies wrote, for instance, half the policies in force in California in 1885. Their dominance was broken, however, in the opening decades of the twentieth century, as government investigators revealed fraud in some of their practices and as new companies grew up to challenge them. Fire insurance also became necessary, as a growing proportion of people and businesses existed in crowded circumstances susceptible to conflagration (the fire following the 1906 earthquake in San Francisco laid waste five square miles of the city's downtown district). There were 81 general insurance companies, most of which wrote fire insurance, in the United States in 1860, but nearly 500 just 40 years later.[62]

Even more than the insurance industry, commercial banking remained a home for small businesses in the United States.[63] Unlike many industrialized or industrializing nations, the United States possessed no central bank, following the dissolution of the Second Bank of the United States in the late 1830s and the 1840s. Nothing resembling the Bank of England or the Bank of Japan lent coherence to commercial banking in the United States. Instead, Americans depended on a mixture of thousands of national- or state-chartered banks to meet their commercial needs. In 1896 there were about 11,500 commercial banks with assets of roughly $6.2 billion in the United States; by 1920, some 30,300 possessing assets of $47.5 billion.[64] Because of changes in federal banking laws in the mid-1860s, many commercial banks previously chartered by states chose to become nationally chartered institutions. Nonetheless, these institutions remained small and independently owned. As the members of the Indianapolis Monetary Commission, a body set up to examine the nation's banking system, observed in 1898, "Nowhere save in the United States is there such a multitude of small and unconnected institutions. There is perhaps no more striking characteristic of the banking system of the United States than the immense number of banks of low capitalization, and the absence of institutions of large capital with branches."[65]

This financial system possessed both strengths and weaknesses. On the positive side, most commercial banks were owned, as in earlier times, by individuals or small groups that provided the original funding. Bankers served their local areas, giving loans to merchants, farmers, and manufacturers about whom they had personal knowledge. Living in their communities, the bankers were in close touch with the business needs of their neighborhoods, towns, and surrounding areas. On the negative side, each bank operated to a considerable degree in isolation, having few outside resources on which to rely during hard times. Some correspondent banking—an arrangement in which small country banks deposited reserve funds in larger city banks—existed, yet this system was unable to prevent bank runs and panics in 1873, 1884, 1893, 1903, and 1907. And though branch banking might have provided some stability, state and federal laws, inspired by fears about the development of financial monopolies, placed so many restrictions on branch banking that only 21 commercial branch bank systems existed as late as 1920.[66] As we have seen, only with the establishment of the Federal Reserve System in 1913 did America begin moving toward the creation of a centralized banking system, and even then the steps were halting.

Small firms thrived in other types of banking as well. The 149 savings banks in existence in 1860 ballooned to almost 2,500 40 years later. Spurred especially by the voracious capital needs of America's railroads, investment banking houses developed out of mercantile establishments. While often large in terms of the funds in which they dealt, most of the houses operated as if they were small businesses. Many investment bankers continued to think of themselves as merchants, and personal relations and trust pervaded the industry. While some investment banking houses became multiunit enterprises with branches in different cities, none were organized as corporations or established elaborate managerial hierarchies.[67]

J. P. Morgan's House of Morgan—by the early 1900s the nation's and arguably the world's most important investment banking house—offers a good example of how investment banking houses continued to operate along personal lines. Morgan worked through four interlocking partnership arrangements—one each for New York (his headquarters), Philadelphia, London, and Paris. He and his 10 or 11 partners handled most of the work of the firms by themselves, meeting as needs dictated rather than according to any set schedule. Morgan himself made the final decisions on all important pieces of business. The supporting staff was minimal: in 1903 the New York office had fewer than 150 employees, of whom only a half-dozen were salaried associates; in the decade before World War I the Paris house had about 20 employees, the London office fewer than 50, and the Philadelphia office perhaps 75. Personal relationships, rather than organized hierarchies, lay behind the work of the Morgan firms.[68]

☐ America's Businesses in a Dual Economy

The rise of big businesses combined with the persistence of small firms to begin creating a dual economy in the United States in the late nineteenth and early twentieth centuries. That is, America's economy began separating into two parts, with large and small businesses often found in different segments.

As we have seen, the nation's largest companies developed primarily in manufacturing as vertically integrated enterprises. Benefiting from scale economies, they tended to be capital-intensive firms that used large-batch or continuous-process manufacturing techniques. Sometimes called center or core companies by economists and historians, these large firms often came to exist in oligopolistic industries.[69] By 1904, just a handful of companies controlled at least half the output in 78 different industries in the United States. In these industries management substantially determined the prices and outputs of the companies, as the "visible hand" of management replaced the "invisible hand" of the market.[70]

Small companies generally clustered in different segments of the economy: in labor-intensive manufacturing, in farming, and in sales and services. Here economies of scale were fewer. In manufacturing, for example, smaller firms were able to coexist with their larger counterparts in fields in which the flexible output of specialized items using relatively short production runs counted for more than the mass production of homogeneous goods in long production runs. As we have seen, this situation existed in the textile industry and in some types of steel production. Sometimes called peripheral companies by scholars, the smaller firms did not control their markets but were instead at the mercy of them.[71]

The small business segment of the economy was much more vola-
tile than the big business sector. Small businesses came and went with
much greater frequency than was the case for big businesses. Of the 278
largest industrial companies in the United States in 1917, all but 14 were
still in operation 50 years later.[72] Small firms, even in the fields in
which they successfully competed or coexisted with big businesses,
formed and dissolved more often than that. The situation in Poughkeepsie, New York, may have been typical for businesses in the United States
as a whole. Small firms did not last long there. Of some 1,530 businesses, most of them small companies, evaluated for credit there by R.
G. Dun and Company and its predecessor agency between 1845 and
1880, about 32% lasted three years or less, and only 14% remained 20
years after their founding.[73]

Large and small firms also differed in the types of people they
attracted as owners and managers. Almost without exception, big businesses were run by well-educated men who came from middle- or
upper-class backgrounds and were native born. No women or minorities
and few immigrants rose to the top of large firms in the nation's emerging industrial economy.[74] To the extent that they succeeded at all in
business management and ownership, women and minorities moved
ahead in small firms. Women secured white-collar positions as buyers
for department stores, as clerical workers, and as saleswomen in large
companies. The handful who were able to strike out on their own as
managers and owners did so in small companies.[75] For minorities, too,
small firms offered opportunities not found in larger enterprises, although minorities' participation in small business varied considerably
by group and by type of business.

Hindered by both racism and law from pursuing careers in manufacturing and farming, many Chinese and Japanese ended up in domestic
service. Those who went into business on their own did so by running
retail outlets, especially grocery stores, and service businesses, such as
restaurants and laundries. In effect, the Chinese and Japanese succeeded
by creating market niches for their small firms. Few white business
people either wanted to go into their lines of work, as in laundries, or
had the necessary knowledge to do so, as in the operation of stores and
restaurants specializing in Asian food. As in the case of many white
small businesses, these minority small businesses were predominantly
family operations, ones in which the proprietor often employed unpaid
family members. Some Chinese and Japanese also formed various sorts
of insurance companies and banks to serve their compatriots. Here they
were less successful. Hampered by hostile state legislation, none of the
10 banks started by Japanese in California survived the 1920s.[76]

Black involvement in small business differed from that of the Chinese and Japanese. A study of black business ownership in eight leading American cities in the 1920s showed that most black businesses were in the service and retail trades. At the local level, blacks started grocery, dry cleaning, and personal service businesses.[77] Nonetheless, faced by competition from knowledgeable white business owners eager to sell to them, blacks proved less successful than Asian-Americans in the operation of these businesses. At the regional and national levels, blacks, like Asian-Americans, formed insurance companies and banks to serve their communities, and here they proved relatively more successful, though the overall success rates were still very low. Between 1880 and 1910, for example, blacks formed a host of fraternal insurance organizations. By 1927, the 32 largest black insurance companies, which accounted for 85% of all of the black-held insurance written by black-owned companies, had $316 million worth of policies in force. Nevertheless, these companies were relatively small firms. That same year a single white-owned company had $900 million worth of insurance in force on blacks, and in 1940 one large white-owned company had a greater value of policies in force on blacks than the top 40 black companies combined.[78]

Although there were major differences between small and large firms and while the two types of companies often existed in separate realms of business, there was as well a considerable degree of interaction between them. To describe America's emerging modern business system simply in terms of center and peripheral firms misses some of the complexity of the situation. In fact, large and small firms grew up symbiotically, at least in some fields. While many large industrial businesses became vertically integrated to a certain extent, few were totally integrated. Small firms frequently acted as subcontractors for their larger brethren. Buckeye Steel, for example, supplied the automatic couplers that large railroad-car manufacturers used in their production efforts. Both Buckeye Steel (and other coupler manufacturers) and the car makers benefited from this arrangement. A similar example of mutually beneficial arrangements lay in sales. As they expanded their output to meet the voracious demands of America's growing national market, some manufacturers, as we have seen, set up their own sales outlets. Others, however, came to rely on franchised agents. Rather than own their sales outlets—a costly proposition—manufacturers depended on agents closely tied to, but still legally independent from, their firms to make the sales. The I. M. Singer (Sewing Machine) Company and the McCormick Harvester Company employed primitive franchise sales systems in the nineteenth century—a practice that would be refined and become widespread in the twentieth century (and that is discussed in more detail in chapter 4).[79]

☐ Small Business Thought

Small business owners—men and women, minority and nonminority alike—continued, as in the colonial and antebellum years, to value their small firms for nonpecuniary as well as monetary reasons. The psychic and social independence they derived from their businesses remained important for them. As we have seen, many of the owners of small metal-making and metalworking companies continued both to take pride in the quality of the products their shops turned out and to approach their work as craftsmen. Farmers like Lewis McMillen of Ohio identified with their land and their localities, even as they produced for America's expanding national market.

Actual socioeconomic independence was, however, becoming elusive by the turn of the century, as the United States was transformed from a land of isolated small farms, shops, and towns into a country in which more and more people lived in large cities and worked in the plants and offices of big businesses. In this situation, Americans formed organizations to mediate between themselves and the socioeconomic forces changing their country. Through organizational life they sought to achieve a new sense of order in the United States.[80] Industrial workers formed nationwide labor unions, professionals founded societies like the American Medical Association and the American Bar Association, farmers formed buying and selling cooperatives, and large business owners established trade associations and chambers of commerce. Small business owners were sometimes caught up in this organizational thrust of American society.[81] Yet their continuing desire for independence meant they would participate less fully than most other Americans in the organizational life of the United States, even when such participation would have been in their best economic interest.

Of the small business organizations that did develop, most common were those which grew up at the local and state levels. Perhaps typical of local business organizations was the Manufacturer's Association of Montgomery County, Pennsylvania.[82] Formed in 1908 by small industrialists worried about labor legislation then under consideration in their state, the body soon became more than a reactive organization. By the time of World War I, the association was offering a variety of services to its members, and the scope of these services expanded still more in later years. By 1927 the organization had 212 members, and by 1958 nearly

300—all served by a salaried staff in association headquarters. At the state level, the experience in California provides examples of how business people running enterprises of all sizes established organizations during the Progressive Era to advance their economic causes. There family farmers set up cooperatives, one of which became Sunkist; bankers joined the California Bankers' Association, whose officers worked through both voluntary methods and state legislation to upgrade banking practices; investment bankers formed their own associations for much the same reasons; and insurance agents established bodies to try to improve business practices and influence state legislation.[83]

At the national level, small business organizations were less common, but two typify the varied approaches small business owners took to the problems they faced. As we have seen, in 1895 small- and medium-size industrialists, mainly in the Midwest, formed the National Association of Manufacturers (NAM) to press for federal government policies that would further the development of exports. Beginning in 1902 and under the leadership of David M. Parry, the NAM became an antiunion organization that rose to national prominence, with 3,500 member firms by 1914. Differing from this broad-based association was the industry-specific National Association of Retail Druggists (NARD). Established in 1898, the NARD was, just eight years later, powerful enough to enforce a "Tripartite Agreement" among drug manufacturers, wholesalers, and retailers. This agreement set uniform prices through manufacturers' sales contracts binding distributors to charge only agreed-on resale prices. Declared to be in violation of the Sherman Act, this agreement was broken up in the Progressive Era—whereupon the NARD became a leading advocate of resale price maintenance legislation in the 1920s.[84]

☐ Conclusion

The rise of big business dramatically changed the world of small business in the late nineteenth and early twentieth centuries. In the colonial period and in the antebellum years, nearly all American businesses had been small firms, single-unit enterprises without managerial hierarchies. With the acceleration in industrialization that occurred after the Civil War, this situation changed. Especially in the field of manufacturing, large companies benefiting from economies of scale supplanted smaller ones in some lines of work. While continuing to grow in absolute numbers, small firms became proportionally less important to the American economy.

Nonetheless, small business remained a vital part of that economy. Beginning a trend that would continue into the post–World War II period, small businesses using flexible production methods and creating market niches for their products successfully coexisted with their larger counterparts in manufacturing. In agriculture the family farm remained the norm, though the beginnings of agribusiness enterprises became visible. In the sales and service industries, too, small businesses continued as the dominant form of business organization; however, in these realms as well they faced increasing competition from big businesses.

3

Government Policies for Small Business, 1921–1971

IN 1938, AT THE SUGGESTION OF HIS SECRE-
tary of commerce, President Franklin D. Roosevelt invited 1,000 small
business people from around the nation to a conference in Washington,
D.C. Roosevelt hoped to show that small business people, unlike their
big business counterparts, supported the New Deal. Convened on 3
February, the Small Business Conference achieved no such consensus.
From beginning to end, the meeting was in almost constant turmoil, as
the delegates divided by region, type of industry, and size of business
(some small businesses were larger than others). At the start of the first
afternoon session, a typical disagreement surfaced. Seventeen New York
business people seized the front of the Department of Commerce audito-
rium, demanding to be heard on behalf of the millions they said they
represented, whereupon non–New Yorkers broke into the raucous chant
of "New York sit down! New York sit down!" Lasting for several more
days, the conference accomplished little except to show a lack of unity
among small business people. No more than in the past did small businesses compose a monolithic group.[1]

Throughout the middle twentieth century, at times it seemed, as in
1938, that there were as many types of small businesses—each with its
own agenda—as there were small business firms. Yet all operated in a
similar environment. The 50 years following 1921 witnessed a decline
in the importance of small firms relative to larger companies, a decline
that became particularly pronounced in the postwar years. During the

middle twentieth century American business people, building on the accomplishments of their predecessors, brought their nation's economy to a new level of maturity through the completion of a national market for their goods. Only after World War II, and then especially in the 1970s and 1980s, did world trade come to rival domestic commerce as an engine driving America's business system. As America's national economy matured, small businesses in many fields found their roles shrinking relative to big businesses.

As we saw in chapter 2, public attitudes and governmental actions have helped shape the external environment of business in the United States, thus partly determining what firms can and cannot do. Government policies became increasingly important in influencing business decisions in the middle twentieth century. This chapter surveys public attitudes and governmental actions in the context of the erosion in small firms' economic significance in the United States. Chapter 4 provides a more complete account of the fortunes of small business by sector of the economy—manufacturing, sales and services, and agriculture.

☐　American Attitudes toward Small Business

The mixed emotions Americans had long held toward big business continued into the 1970s. As in earlier years, Americans harbored fears about the threats big businesses might pose to economic opportunities and, though to a much lesser degree, to political democracy in their land. As the second, third, and fourth generations of Americans exposed to big business, however, citizens after 1920 showed greater acceptance of it. Criticism became muted. Not even the Great Depression shook the faith of most middle-class Americans in their nation's business system. Yet at the same time—especially from the 1930s on—a growing number viewed small firms and their owners in a more positive light. Small businesses came to be seen as institutions that by their very nature could make valuable contributions to the development of America's business system.

Many of the attitudes established by the turn of the century continued to hold sway into the 1920s and 1930s. During the twenties, most professionals, landowning farmers, and skilled workers admired big businesses for the prosperity, job security, and material goods they seemed to provide. Rising incomes, the fact that many were themselves now members of large organized groups—cooperatives, labor unions, and professional associations—and the fact that big business had been part of the American scene for 40 years led most Americans to accept its permanence. The depression decade sorely tried the faith of Americans in big businesses, as many blamed them for the coming of hard times. Still, this break with big business was remarkably brief. By the close of the 1930s, as some prosperity returned, most Americans had reaffirmed their acceptance of the large corporation.[2]

The boom times of World War II sealed the pact, and there existed little active opposition to big business in the first quarter-century after the war. (There was some. Members of the beat generation of the 1950s and the more numerous members of the counterculture of the 1960s felt themselves alienated from big business and large organizations in general.) For the most part, these were years of rapid economic growth, from which the middle class especially benefited, and most of its members viewed large firms favorably. Surveying the nation's graduating college class of 1949, the editors of *Fortune* found that the typical graduate "wants to work for somebody else—preferably somebody big." "No longer," they concluded, "is small business the promised land."[3] By the same token, an extensive public opinion poll taken by the Institute of Social Research of the University of Michigan in 1951 revealed that old suspicions of big business were fading fast. Asked to assess the general social effects of big business, most Americans responded in a favorable vein:

The good things outweigh the bad things: 76 percent

The bad things outweigh the good things: 10 percent

They seem about equal: 2 percent

Confused: 12 percent[4]

These were years in which most middle-class men aspired to be "organization men" (at this time almost no women were in the top or even the middle ranges of management in big business). Far from being innovative risk takers, organization men were primarily interested in security, which they sought in the embrace of the large corporation. Writing in 1956, the sociologist William H. Whyte, Jr., described the aspirations of men just leaving college to enter business: "They have an implicit faith that The Organization will be as interested in making use of their best qualities as they are themselves, and thus, with equanimity, they can entrust the resolution of their destiny to The Organization. . . . Somewhat inconsistently, trainees hope to rise high and hope just as much not to suffer the personal load of doing so. Frequently they talk of finding a sort of plateau—a position well enough up to be interesting, but not so far up as to have one's neck outstretched for others to chop at."[5]

Their acceptance of big business did not, however, preclude Americans' liking the small business person and small business. To the contrary, many continued to admire small business owners and, as time passed, to see a growing role for small business in the American economy.[6] As in earlier times, some Americans who worked for large corporations hoped, on retiring, to start their own independent small businesses. Reflecting public attitudes, such popular magazines as the *Saturday Evening Post*, *Harper's Monthly*, and *Colliers*, while sometimes glorifying the small business person as a staunch individualist, portrayed small businesses in the 1920s as part of a vanishing breed: as retail concerns in small towns, enterprises without much of a future in the face of growing competition from chain stores. Writers for such business journals as *Printer's Ink*, *Industrial Management*, and *Nation's Business* adopted a more positive viewpoint. They perceived small businesses as serving useful roles in an economy dominated by big businesses. Small businesses could fill market niches ignored by larger concerns and, by using flexible management and manufacturing methods, might even compete with large industrial enterprises. Marking a reversal from their earlier stances, popular magazines in the 1930s picked up this trend and began picturing small businesses as vibrant parts of the nation's economic system. By the close of the decade, articles in popular magazines were promulgating the notion that small and large firms could coexist and that small firms were not necessarily doomed by the rise of big business.

Even as most Americans embraced big business after World War II, they deepened their admiration of the small business person. A perceptive political scientist writing in 1962 observed that most citizens viewed small business owners favorably "as a kind of modern-day American underdog." It was, he found, "very much in keeping with our own traditions to react with sympathy or outrage, as the case may be, when it is felt the 'little guy' is being pushed around." Even more significant, he concluded, was "the fact that the small businessman has always been identified with all of the homely virtues of Main Street America and thus is in something of a charmed if not sacred category along with Motherhood and the American Flag." In the cold war atmosphere of the 1950s and 1960s, small business also came to be seen as "a cornerstone of American democracy" and as part of the American way of doing things.[7]

American attitudes toward small business were clearly complex. As in the late nineteenth century, Americans continued to favor big businesses for the rising standard of living they were perceived as creating. Yet small business as a way of life still tugged at the heartstrings of Americans, who longed for independence from concentrated economic power. As in earlier times, these attitudes helped shape public policies toward business, policies every bit as tangled as the attitudes themselves. From the 1920s into the 1970s, the policies of the federal government toward business in general and small business in particular followed a labyrinth of twists and turns. Astute politicians and governmental officials sought to balance an appreciation for the economic benefits of big business with a sensitivity to the ideological needs of Americans. A penetrating editorial published in *Colliers* in 1938 observed the ambivalent feelings of Americans toward small business and the varied policies taken by the government with regard to them: "The record is that for a hundred years and longer we have been building our business big and at the same time cheering patriots who advocated laws commanding our business to stay small. We built business big because we craved the fruits of large-scale production. . . . Surely the time is ripe for common sense and plain speech on this vital issue. Business is going to be big and small, too, for that matter, and it should not be beyond the wisdom of statesmen to contrive policies and laws which will preserve the obvious advantages of the industrial system which is so distinctly American."[8]

☐ Government Policies during the Interwar Years

During World War I, business leaders benefited from increased outputs, higher profits, and a growth in industrial efficiency in their cooperation with the federal government. To coordinate the output of war goods, President Woodrow Wilson established in 1917 the War Industries Board (WIB) as a federal agency empowered to set uniform prices that all government organizations, including the army and navy, would pay for war materials produced by private industry. The WIB also established production quotas for different industries and set priorities for the distribution of scarce raw materials among different industries and individual companies within industries. Directed by Bernard Baruch, a former Wall Street whiz, the WIB operated through committees, one for each major industry. The committees were composed of government officials and representatives from private industry, usually big business leaders who headed industry-specific trade associations.[9]

The WIB set the prices paid by the government considerably above prevailing market prices to encourage maximum production of war materials. An unexpected result was that larger, more efficient firms made greater profits than most small companies. For instance, in the steel industry the four largest and most highly integrated producers earned an average 31% return on their capital, while smaller firms earned an average of 16%. Small businesses sometimes fell behind in other ways. When raw materials were in short supply, they usually went to big businesses, not small companies. The federal government found, not for the last time, that working with a relative handful of big businesses to boost output quickly was far easier than trying to coordinate the work of thousands of smaller enterprises. Nonetheless, some small firms benefited as subcontractors for larger companies, and still others won prime defense contracts. The Buckeye Steel Castings Company of Columbus, Ohio, earned rich profits turning out gun casings and other products for the army and navy.[10]

Many business leaders wanted collaboration with the federal government to continue after World War I. Business and government leaders had worked together in a diversity of industries, including the railroads, shipbuilding, and food production, as well as those producing materials needed directly for fighting on the front lines.[11] After the war, some big business executives hoped to work with federal government officials in smoothing out the ups and downs of the business cycle to achieve steady economic growth. In Herbert Hoover, secretary of commerce under Presidents Warren Harding and Calvin Coolidge, they found a ready ally: Hoover wanted government and business to work together voluntarily to bolster the economic strength of the nation. While largely unable to moderate swings in the business cycle, as the economic collapse in the early 1930s graphically demonstrated, such government-business cooperation—which scholars have labeled associationalism—reached a new high point in the middle and late 1920s.[12]

The impact of associationalism on small business was mixed. Hoover and other federal government officials worked most closely with trade association officers, who were usually the heads of big businesses, and many of the resulting policies favored large businesses more than small ones. At the same time, U.S. Supreme Court decisions, based on the "rule of reason," first enunciated in 1911, continued to favor the development of big businesses. The Supreme Court also permitted trade associations to engage in many cooperative activities previously forbidden.[13] Not surprisingly, given these favorable political policies, concentration proceeded in the American business system. The United States experienced its second large merger movement between 1925 and 1931, as 5,846 mergers occurred.

Yet Hoover's policies also strengthened small businesses in some fields. Over the course of the 1920s, the proportion of gainfully employed Americans who were self-employed, nonfarm business people remained steady, rising slightly from 6.5 to 6.6%.[14] In the lumber, movie, and aviation industries conferences for business people—many of them small business owners—sponsored by the Department of Commerce led to the adoption of more efficient production methods and more cooperation among firms. For instance, conferences in 1922, 1923, and 1925 led the owners of lumber companies to adopt standard sizes and grades for their boards and, in general, to reduce waste in their mills.[15]

Much of the cooperation between government and business begun during World War I and the 1920s continued into the early years of President Roosevelt's New Deal. Yet the situation had changed: by the time Roosevelt took office, in 1933, the economic growth of the 1920s had vanished, replaced by the hard times of the Great Depression. By 1932, industrial production had fallen to half of its level just four years earlier, and at least a fourth of the nation's work force was unemployed. In the four years following the stock market crash of 1929, some 110,000 businesses failed.[16]

Initially, Roosevelt's main weapon to pull the economy out of the Great Depression was the National Recovery Administration (NRA), a federal government agency modeled partly on the WIB.[17] Established by the passage of the National Industrial Recovery Act in the summer of 1933, the NRA was intended to mobilize the economy for recovery. As had the WIB, the NRA set up committees organized by industry and staffed by government officials and business executives, usually big business leaders who were officers in trade associations.[18] The goal of the NRA was to raise business profits and thereby, its proponents hoped, bring about a return of prosperity. To do so, the industry committees of the NRA adopted "codes of fair business practices." Under these codes, businesses limited competition with one another by cutting back production and raising their prices (the nation's antitrust laws were suspended to allow these actions). As had happened in the operations of the WIB, big business generally benefited more than small business from the work of the NRA, for once again big business officers called the shots in the operations of the agency. Declared unconstitutional by the Supreme Court, the NRA went out of existence in 1935.[19]

Roosevelt also sought to bring about recovery by having the government make loans directly to businesses, and here too large firms generally benefited more than small ones. Established in 1932 under President Herbert Hoover, the Reconstruction Finance Corporation (RFC), a federal agency, was empowered in 1934 to make loans to industrial and commercial businesses. By the end of 1946, the agency had made 35,000 loans, totaling $3.3 billion. Most of the money went to big businesses. Just 298 transactions of more than $1 million apiece accounted for 55% of the agency's loans by value; by contrast, 11,000 loans of $5,000 or less composed 1% of those loans by value. In 1934 legislation also empowered the Federal Reserve System to grant direct loans to private businesses under certain conditions. Again, big businesses received most of the loans. During the first three years of this program, for example, only 564 of the 2,406 loans approved were for $5,000 or less—about 1% of the total value of all loans. After analyzing the capital needs of small businesses, a federal government investigatory body concluded in 1941 that the RFC and the Federal Reserve banks "[had] contributed only slightly to the alleviation of this difficulty" and "[could not] be considered important factors in this area."[20]

Even as part of the New Deal sought economic recovery through aid to big business, other programs tried to help small firms. Far from being a carefully thought-out blueprint for redesigning the American economy, the New Deal constituted a series of ad hoc measures hastily thrown together to stimulate recovery from the worst economic crisis in America's history. As such, the New Deal contained many anomalies and inconsistencies.

At the same time that Roosevelt and Congress worked with big business leaders through the NRA, politicians sought to protect small businesses from competition with some of those same large firms. In the 1920s chain store operations developed to challenge smaller mom-and-pop stores in the grocery and drug trades. Some state legislatures passed protective laws, and Congress followed suit. Between 1933 and 1942, Congress considered 390 bills designed to protect small businesses and enacted 26, most of which pertained to retailing. Dismayed by this mass of small business legislation, officials in one governmental commission wryly observed in 1941, "We have now entered the era of quantity production of statutes."[21] Two pieces of legislation were of most importance: (a) the Robinson-Patman Act of 1936, which outlawed volume discounts often given by manufacturers and wholesalers to their largest retail customers, and (b) the Miller-Tydings Act, passed a year later, which sought in a variety of ways to protect small retailers from the competition of the chains. (Chain stores and the legislative measures aimed at them are discussed in more detail in chapter 4.)

As time passed, Roosevelt soured in his views on big business leaders. Failing to win their support for many of his New Deal measures, Roosevelt increasingly turned to other groups, especially labor, for backing.[22] Coming to believe that the nation's economic recovery was being retarded by the monopoly power of big businesses, Roosevelt in 1938 asked Congress to fund an examination of competitive conditions in American business. Congress responded by establishing the

Temporary National Economic Committee (TNEC), which carried out a series of economic investigations. At the same time, Roosevelt appointed a new attorney general, Thurmond Arnold, and, reversing his earlier stance, instructed Arnold to enforce the nation's antitrust laws.[23] Bolstered by the findings of the TNEC, Arnold prosecuted a number of companies and won several convictions. His efforts did little, however, to change the economic structure of the United States and in any event were soon cut short by World War II. With the coming of war, the federal government shifted its emphasis to ensuring the production of war materials by private industry. A chagrined Arnold shelved his antitrust actions, as wartime demands once again took precedence over other concerns.

Just as the New Deal was ending, however, the federal government took several actions to help small businesses, steps that paved the way for additional aid in the postwar years. Congress set up committees to look after the needs of small businesses—the Senate Committee on Small Business in 1940 and the House Committee on Small Business a year later.[24] At about the same time, a Small Business Division was established within the Department of Commerce, charged with "reinforcing the position of small enterprise and retarding the trend toward concentration."[25]

What impact did these mixed and sometimes-contradictory actions have on small business? The depression decade witnessed a surge in the ranks of small business. The proportion of gainfully employed who were self-employed, nonfarm business people rose from 6.6 to 8% during the 1930s.[26] This rise in the share of Americans engaged in small business did not, however, indicate a revival in the health of small firms but instead resulted from a lack of other employment options. Laid off by large firms, some Americans tried to survive by setting up their own small businesses. An especially large increase, for instance, occurred in the number of small retail outlets formed between 1929 and 1933—grocery stores, restaurants, and gasoline stations—constituting what one scholar has called a "flight into independence."[27] The number of gasoline filling stations, for example, rose from 98,976 in 1929 to 156,538 just four years later—not because the American economy required such an expansion but because the jobless sought employment through opening such stations (the financing came from oil companies eager for their own reasons to expand their retail operations). To some extent, the same phenomenon developed in manufacturing. Unemployed cigar makers became "buckeyes," self-employed cigar makers with few or no employees, and in the Patterson broad silk industry unemployed workers became owners of petty "cockroach" shops. Despite the formation of these new small busi-

Table 3. U.S. Business Population, 1900–1938 (in thousands)

	Listed Concerns[1]	New Enterprises[2]	Discontinued[3]
1900	1,174	272	248
1901	1,219	286	248
1902	1,253	304	265
1903	1,281	305	272
1904	1,320	308	268
1905	1,357	329	287
1906	1,393	334	299
1907	1,418	339	302
1908	1,448	361	325
1909	1,486	360	331
1910	1,515	358	348
1911	1,525	365	326
1912	1,564	369	316
1913	1,617	387	348
1914	1,655	388	369
1915	1,675	380	347
1916	1,708	369	344
1917	1,733	361	385
1918	1,708	307	305
1919	1,711	308	197
1920	1,821	459	353
1921	1,927	483	427
1922	1,983	491	478
1923	1,996	469	417
1924	2,047	477	411
1925	2,113	496	451
1926	2,158	484	471
1927	2,172	483	456
1928	2,199	476	463
1929	2,213	453	483
1930	2,183	423	481
1931	2,125	355	404
1932	2,077	338	454

1933	1,961	345	332
1934	1,974	379	319
1935	1,983	392	385
1936	2,010	408	382
1937	2,057	400	351
1938	2,102	388	365

1. Listed concerns refers to the total of industrial and commercial names in the July issue of the Dun & Bradstreet Reference Book. In general it excludes financial institutions including banks, railroads, professional enterprises such as lawyers and doctors, farmers and others not ordinarily users of commercial credit in the accepted sense. In general, branches are listed, except in the case of chain distributors.

2. New enterprises refer to names added, but does not include cases arising from change in style or geographical location within the community. The figures refer to calendar years.

3. Discontinued enterprises include those which have discontinued operation as a result of any of the following types of action: Assignment, attachment, voluntary petition, involuntary petition, receivership, absconding, compromise, execution, foreclosure and other voluntary discontinued operations in which there is no official record of loss to creditors. The figures refer to calendar years.

U.S. Temporary National Economic Committee, "Problems of Small Business," monograph no. 17 (Washington, D.C.: U.S. Government Printing Office, 1941), 66.

nesses, more businesses discontinued operations between 1929 and 1932 than began them: the depression years were hard times indeed for small as well as large businesses. This fact reversed the past trend, for in every year since 1900, except 1917, more businesses had been formed than discontinued—as shown in Table 3.[28]

These new small enterprises led tenuous lives. A comprehensive survey of corporations engaged in manufacturing, mining, and trade between 1931 and 1936 revealed that a direct relationship existed between size and profitability: the smaller the firm, the lower the profit margins.[29] As we saw in chapter 2, only a few small businesses lasted very long between 1880 and 1920. During the Great Depression the situation probably worsened. Generalizing from dozens of separate business mortality studies, the TNEC officers concluded, "To the extent that local studies in scattered communities of the United States represent the general experience, approximately 30 percent of retail firms discontinue business within the first year. An additional 14 percent dissolve before reaching their second anniversary."[30] Manufacturers and wholesalers, the TNEC report showed, performed slightly better, but most went out of existence fairly quickly.[31] After surveying mortality studies for all types of firms, the head of the TNEC concluded that small businesses led perilous lives: "The material makes it very clear that business mortality is a problem of major proportions. In study after study, in industry after industry, in area after area, the record is the same. The chance of a newcomer becoming an established member of the business community is sadly slight. He carries on until his funds are exhausted, and then he disappears from the scene."[32]

☐ Small Business and Government during World War II

World War II brought a return of prosperity to the United States, but small businesses did not benefit as much from it as their larger counterparts. As during World War I, the federal government's main concern was to increase the output of war materials as rapidly as possible, and governmental officials paid scant attention to ensuring that defense contracts went to small firms. Army and navy procurement officers found it easier and faster to work with big businesses than to encourage the participation of small companies in production for the war effort. A Senate committee reported in February 1942 that just 56 of the nation's 184,000 manufacturing establishments had received 75% of the value of the army and navy contracts awarded to that time. Small companies often suffered as well when they tried to maintain their production of civilian goods, because scarce raw materials were often allocated to big businesses. With so much government spending going to large firms and so little to smaller concerns, it became a bittersweet joke that a small business was "any business that is unable to maintain a staff in Washington to represent its interest."[33]

Congress took actions to try to correct this situation with the passage of the Small Business Act in June 1942. This law sought to increase small business participation in the war effort by setting up a Smaller War Plants Division (SWPD) within the War Production Board, the federal agency coordinating the production of war materials. The SWPD was charged with seeing that a greater share of defense contracts went to small businesses. The act also established the Smaller War Plants Corporation (SWPC) to make loans to small firms that needed them to enter into defense businesses. Hindered by poor leadership, lacking strong support from small businesses—which remained, as at the 1938 meeting, quite divided—and inadequately funded by Congress, the SWPD and the SWPC were only partly successful in achieving their goals. Most of the contracts flowed to big businesses. Officers in the army and navy continued to argue that only large companies were "equipped with the plant and machinery, specially skilled workers, managerial know-how, financial stability, and established contracts with a wide variety of suppliers" needed to produce the vast quantity of goods on time.[34]

Big businesses received the lion's share of governmental wartime spending. Of the $175 billion worth of prime defense contracts awarded between June 1940 and September 1944, more than half went to just 33 companies. Altogether, the largest 6% of the contracting firms received 90% of the contracts, all the others combined only 10%. Neither was the picture for small businesses much brighter with regard to subcontracts. A survey completed by the SWPC in 1943 revealed that, while a group of 252 of the largest prime contracting companies did subcontract about a third of the value of their prime contracts, three-fourths of the subcontracts went to businesses having more than 500 employees, not to smaller firms.[35] A Senate committee concluded in 1945 that "in the period in which the greatest effort was presumably being made to speed contracts to small business, nothing was actually accomplished."[36]

Big businesses continued to win more from government actions than small firms did during the postwar reconversion to civilian production. Large firms were in a better financial position to purchase production facilities built by the government during the war than small firms were. And so they did. Two-thirds of the government plant and equipment sold at war's end went to only 87 big businesses.[37]

What was true for the war years was also true for the entire period 1921–46: small businesses fell behind larger firms in their participation in the nation's economic development. Beginning with the merger movement of the late 1920s, many fields of business became increasingly concentrated. This was particularly the case with manufacturing. Establishments having more than 250 workers employed 46% of the wage earners in American industry in 1914, that proportion rising to 56% in 1937. The movement toward bigness accelerated during World War II. Between 1939 and 1944, firms with 100 or fewer employees saw their share of industrial employment drop from 26 to just 19%. By contrast, firms with 10,000 or more employees increased their share from 13 to 30% during the same period.[38] Industrial concentration continued with postwar reconversion. Despite increasing their numbers from 206,000 to 255,000 between 1947 and 1954, single-plant firms saw their share of the nation's value added by manufacturing drop from 41 to 32%. Multiplant businesses, despite experiencing a decrease in numbers from 35,000 to 32,000, increased their share from 59 to 68%.[39]

A pessimistic verdict put forward by the TNEC in 1941 was perhaps applicable to the interwar and war years. The TNEC concluded that, unless the federal government intervened, the future of small business would be dim. "There can be no denying the fact that the long-run trend of the competitive battle in most lines has been against small business," a report of the agency observed; "the small businessman has been displaced from entire industries."[40]

☐ Postwar Government Policies and the Formation of the Small Business Administration

America experienced accelerating economic growth during the first 25 years following World War II. A postwar recession feared by some political and business leaders failed to materialize, as Americans rushed to spend income saved during the war years. Between 1945 and 1960 the nation's real GNP rose by 52%, with per capita GNP increasing 19%; in the 1960s real GNP climbed an additional 46%, with per capita GNP rising by 29%.[41] Federal government policies lay behind much of this growth. Through its support of the Bretton Woods Agreement in 1944 and the General Agreement on Tariffs and Trade three years later, the government spurred the opening of new global markets for American goods. In 1950 American firms sold 9% of their output abroad; 20 years later, 13% (foreign markets would become still more important for Americans in the 1970s and 1980s).[42] Some industries received direct help. The building of an interstate highway system, authorized by Congress in 1956, aided the trucking industry, and federal funding for airports helped commercial airlines. With the advent of the cold war, defense spending grew in importance, accounting for between 4 and 8% of the nation's GNP in the 1950s and 1960s.

While not specifically designed to spur the development of big business, many of the federal government's policies had that effect. Big businesses benefited more than smaller concerns from the opening of world markets to American goods. Not until the middle and late 1980s did small companies begin exporting their products in appreciable volume. Neither did small businesses benefit as much as their larger counterparts from defense spending. One report found that "from 1940 to 1964 the fifty largest corporations in the country always received somewhat more than half of all prime military contracts, while small businesses never received as much as 20 percent."[43] In 1964 just 10 big businesses accounted for $3 billion of the $5.1 billion the Department of Defense awarded in research and development funds.[44] Similarly, the construction of highways and airports helped large companies operating on a national scale more than it helped smaller local and regional firms.[45]

Even as many of their actions continued to aid big business development in America, however, federal government officials took steps to help small businesses. As in the interwar years, the federal government's business policies remained complex and often confused. Reflecting the existence of contradictory public attitudes, no single, unified government policy existed.

Antitrust matters were a case in point. As we have seen, public attitudes favored big business development after World War II, and no public clamor arose to revive antitrust actions in the postwar years. As one observer noted in the mid-1960s, "The antitrust movement is one of the faded passions of American reform."[46] Nonetheless, despite the decline in public interest the federal government did revive prosecutions. In 1950 Congress passed the Cellar-Kefauver Act, which allowed the Justice Department to use market share as proof of practices in restraint of trade. The administration of President Dwight D. Eisenhower established an Attorney General's National Committee to Study the Antitrust Laws in 1955, and this body reported favorably on keeping the nation's antitrust legislation intact. By 1962, the Antitrust Division of the Justice Department had a budget of $6.6 million, employed 300 lawyers, and was prosecuting 92 cases. Judicial decisions forced some large firms to divest themselves of parts of their operations, as in cases involving Alcoa and Du Pont, and, less frequently, punished price-fixing arrangements, as in a case decided against General Electric and other large firms in the electric manufacturing business.[47]

At about the same time that the federal government was mounting its antitrust actions, it established the Small Business Administration (SBA).[48] In part, the SBA grew out of federal agencies set up earlier to help small businesses—the RFC, SWPD, and SWPC. In addition, after World War II some of the RFC's programs for small business were delegated to the Commerce Department, which set up an Office of Small Business. Moreover, in 1951 Congress established the Small Defense Plants Administration (SDPA) to help small firms win defense contracts during the Korean War.[49] Throughout these years, the RFC continued to offer funding and other forms of assistance to some small firms. During the early 1950s, however, the officials in the RFC were indicted in a series of well-publicized scandals involving favoritism in granting loans, and it was out of these scandals that the SBA was born.[50]

Coming to power in 1953, President Eisenhower and many other Republicans wanted to abolish the RFC, which they viewed as a holdover from the Democratic New Deal and as a symbol of political corruption. At the same time, they realized that they needed to ensure the continuation of the aid given by the agency to small business. Even if the actual amount of aid was not great, its symbolic value was. From these concerns came new legislation ending the RFC and creating the SBA. The bills worked their ways through the House and Senate with relatively little debate. Support came from two small business groups that had been formed in the wake of the Small Business Conference in 1938, the National Federation of Independent Business and the American Association of Small Business. Small business people remained divided, however, and other small business organizations opposed the creation of the SBA, preferring that government get out of business affairs altogether. The National Small Business Men's Association and the Conference of American Small Business Organizations took this stance.[51] Opposition also came from certain big business groups, whose members argued that small firms needed no special aid. Most politicians agreed, however, with Secretary of Commerce George M. Humphrey, who asserted, "In theory there should be no difference between lending money to a large business or lending money to a small business . . . [but] in practice, in just good common sense, I think, there should be some additional body arranged to assist small business."[52] As signed into law by President Eisenhower, the legislation set up the SBA as a temporary agency in July 1953.

Made permanent five years later, the SBA was charged by Congress to "aid, counsel, assist, and protect, insofar as is possible, the interests of small-business concerns in order to preserve free competitive enterprise . . . to maintain and strengthen the overall economy of the nation." But what *were* small firms? This was the first question SBA officials had to answer. The enabling legislation establishing the SBA was intentionally vague on this matter: "For the purposes of this Act, a small-business concern shall be deemed to be one which is independently owned and operated and which is not dominant in its field of operations." SBA administrators soon found it necessary to devise size categories based on the type of industry in which a firm operated. Small businesses in manufacturing came to be defined as firms with no more than 500 employees, those in wholesaling as companies with no more than $5 million in annual sales or receipts, and those in retailing and services as businesses with no more than $1 million in annual sales or receipts. SBA officials granted exceptions to these rules, however. In 1966, for example, the American Motors Company, then one of the largest 200 businesses in the United States, was defined as "small" because it was not as large as any of the Big

Three automakers—leading observers at the time to raise the question, How big is small?[53]

Employing 3,800 persons within 13 years of its founding, the SBA sought to aid small businesses through four major programs. First and most important was its loan program: by 1966, the SBA had granted $3.1 billion in financial assistance to 70,000 small firms, mostly in the form of regular business loans offered either directly or with the participation of commercial banks. Second, SBA officers sought to work as well with other federal government agencies in procuring government contracts for small businesses. Management advice offered to small business people by regional offices—three-fourths of the SBA staff worked outside Washington, D.C.—constituted a third type of aid; seminars, conferences, and minicourses were all part of the SBA's offerings. Perhaps the most significant form of advice was the establishment in 1964 of the Service Corps of Retired Executives (SCORE), a nationwide group of retired business people recruited to counsel small business owners; by the end of 1965, 3,000 SCORE members in 135 chapters had advised 10,625 small business people. Fourth, SBA administrators sought in various ways to increase the supply of equity capital available to small firms.[54]

Questions quickly arose about the SBA's effectiveness. The loss ratio on the agency's loans was about the same as that of commercial banks, leading critics to suggest that there was "an unwillingness to take risks" on the part of the SBA (the agency was supposed to make riskier loans than those granted by commercial banks). This circumstance was particularly pronounced in the loan program for minorities; one respected analysis concluded, "The SBA has done something . . . but the effort has been unimaginative and too narrow in scope." Similarly, the efforts to help small firms raise equity capital came under fire, with critics finding that "no one really knows about this aspect of the effectiveness" of the SBA's program.[55] Nor did the procurement work as well as had been hoped. As noted earlier, big businesses benefited more than small firms from government spending, especially Defense Department spending.

Underfunded and lacking consistent leadership, the SBA proved a disappointment to many of its proponents. An administrative assistant to Rep. Wright Patman, a strong advocate of government aid for small business, expressed this feeling shortly after the enabling legislation for the SBA had won approval. "The 1953 act was more to get rid of the RFC than to set up the SBA," he observed. "It's no more than a sop," he concluded; "the administration wanted only to get rid of the RFC." For others, disillusionment came later, as it became apparent that the SBA would not fund all desired projects. In fact, after studying the record of the SBA, one scholar concluded, in 1961, "It seems reasonable to suggest that the culmination of eighteen years of activity to establish a separate small business agency actually resulted in a reduction of the government's program for small business."[56]

☐   The Postwar Impact of Government Policies

Neither antitrust actions nor the work of the SBA slowed the development of big business in the United States. For the most part, the Justice Department directed its antitrust suits against large vertically integrated or connected companies. Thus, Du Pont was forced to sell its shareholdings in General Motors because General Motors was a major customer for Du Pont products. The Justice Department took few actions against a new type of merger that developed in the 1960s—the conglomerate merger. Conglomerates were companies that had operations in many unrelated fields, and business executives often formed conglomerates by merging previously independent companies.

Throughout the 1950s and well into the 1960s, the Justice Department looked favorably on the formation of conglomerates as a means of bringing new competition into established fields of business. Asked in 1966 whether he was worried about possible antitrust actions against his firm, the president of Litton Industries, one of the nation's fastest-growing conglomerates, replied that he was not. "I think we've generally been on the side of the Justice Department because we've so often been the challenger in a field where someone else had a dominant position," he remarked.[57] The permissive attitude of the Justice Department set the stage for America's third big merger movement, which took place in the 1960s. This movement peaked in 1968; in that year 2,500 mergers of manufacturing and mining companies occurred, including 715 conglomerate-type mergers.[58]

The companies resulting from these mergers and the businesses that continued to develop through internal growth were large indeed. By 1962 the top 5 industrial companies in the United States controlled 12% of all the nation's manufacturing assets, the 50 largest accounted for a third, and the 500 largest accounted for more than two-thirds. By 1965, General Motors, Standard Oil of New Jersey (Exxon today), and Ford had a combined gross income greater than that of all the farms in the United States. And in 1963 General Motors possessed revenues more than eight times the size of those of the state of New York and almost a fifth the size of federal government revenues.[59]

In these circumstances, it is not surprising to find that the erosion of the position of small business relative to big business continued. Perceptions of the decline of small business, brought to the nation's consciousness by the TNEC investigations in the late 1930s, were renewed in the postwar years. As one scholar examining the social roles of small businesses in America observed in 1947, "The feeling that all is not well with small business has been growing."[60] The most thorough study of small business in the United States published up to that time noted in 1962 that "despite its numerical preponderance from the Bronx to Chula Vista, small business is not looking particularly healthy these days." Small business, the report concluded, "is weak, though not abysmally so; essentially it seems to be hanging on."[61] Statistics bore out the general validity of these gloomy assessments. The total number of nonfarm, self-employed business people in America declined steadily from 1950 to 1972, reversing the earlier upward trend. The total share of employment held by small firms (those with 500 or fewer workers) declined only slightly, from 41% in 1958 to 40% in 1977. More telling, however, is that between 1958 and 1979 the share of business receipts earned by those small companies plummeted from 52 to a scant 29% of the total for all American firms.[62]

□   Conclusion

The welter of federal government policies designed to protect small businesses from the competitive encroachments of larger firms and, in a more general sense, to promote the development of small businesses accomplished little. Government agencies set up in the 1930s, 1940s, and 1950s proved ineffective in either slowing the advance of big business in America or furthering the development of small firms. Perhaps the greatest disappointment was the SBA, already under criticism from some quarters by the late 1960s. The lack of effective actions in behalf of small business probably accurately reflected public attitudes. Most Americans favored the growth of big business, which they associated with an outpouring of consumer goods and a rising standard of living. Few favored the destruction of large firms through antitrust actions. At the same time, however, most Americans desired that the government take some steps, if only symbolic ones, to preserve small businesses. These symbolic actions were not enough to arrest the erosion of the place of small firms in America's business system; still, as we shall see in chapter 4, that erosion occurred at different rates and in different ways in the various sectors composing the American economy.

4

Small Business in a Maturing National Economy, 1921–1971

ASKED HOW HIS SMALL FIRM COMPETED
with larger companies in the late 1920s, the president of a New England metalworking concern specializing in the production of air valves captured the essence of the way in which many small businesses succeeded. "A small company must have a product with a limited market potential," he observed. "If the potential of a product developed by a small company is too big," he continued, "a large corporation will take it away."[1] As we saw in chapter 3, small businesses came under increasing pressure from larger enterprises during the middle twentieth century. In field after field, business became more concentrated and small firms found themselves squeezed by the growth in competition. Many failed to survive. Some did, however. Like the maker of air valves, a growing number specialized their products and services to exploit niche markets.

This chapter examines the positions of small businesses in manufacturing, sales and services, and agriculture from the 1920s to the early 1970s, a period when the completion of America's domestic market led to a maturing of the nation's economy. The chapter looks as well at the nature of the small business person at midcentury and, finally, draws conclusions about the changing relationships between small and large firms in the United States.

☐   Small Business in Manufacturing

Between 1880 and 1970, small businesses experienced a long-term decline in their relative importance in American manufacturing. As we saw in chapters 2 and 3, with the rise of large manufacturing companies the shares of small firms in both industrial employment and output dropped steadily. The decline was, however, especially pronounced during World War II, as companies employing 100 or fewer workers experienced a fall in their share of the nation's industrial employment, from 26 to only 19%.[2]

Interestingly, in light of the current debate over the significance of research and development in America's possible reindustrialization in the 1990s and the likely places of large and small firms in it, it was not a lack of involvement in industrial research that hurt small firms. In fact, smaller companies appear to have participated in industrial research nearly as much as the nation's industrial giants. Between 1921 and 1946, the rates of participation of the largest 200 manufacturers and smaller companies were about the same. Except in chemicals, in which large companies dominated research efforts, smaller firms held their own. Moreover, as time progressed, smaller firms increased their relative importance in the research being done.[3] The relative decline of small business in manufacturing stemmed more from the continued existence and exploitation of economies of scale in manufacturing by the larger firms, furthering a trend begun shortly after the Civil War.

This decline continued in the postwar period, especially in the 1950s and 1960s. Single-plant companies (a good proxy for smaller firms) decreased slightly in absolute numbers, from 255,000 in 1954 to 251,000 by 1972, while their share of America's industrial employment fell from 39 to just 25%. Continuing a trend from the nineteenth century, larger multiplant establishments rose in number from 32,000 to 70,000 and increased their share of industrial employment from 61 to 75%. These trends led one economist investigating the changing relationships between large and small industrial firms to conclude, "Relative crowding out of individual, small entrepreneurship from manufacturing was the apparent record of the U.S. economy in the quarter century after World War II."[4]

Not all small manufacturers suffered, however. As a perceptive essay appearing in the *Harvard Business Review* in 1957 showed, small companies continued to succeed even in the immediate postwar years. Foreshadowing many of the findings of economists and other scholars 20 to 30 years later, the author summarized well how some small firms (companies employing no more than 100 workers), admittedly a distinct minority of the nation's small businesses, prospered. Some served national markets whose total demand was too small to attract large firms. Others operated in areas that required "special knowledge and background, special methods and skills in manufacture, and contact with customers by men with particular backgrounds." Still others manufactured products for regional markets in which service and speed of delivery were of utmost importance. Finally, small businesses succeeded in fields in which flexibility, especially the capability to turn out rapidly small batches of goods in short production runs, was of most significance. Like the Philadelphia textile makers of the nineteenth century, these small firms got ahead by differentiating their products from those of larger manufacturers that relied on long runs in mass-production industries.[5] As the author explained, "As our economy becomes more mature, while still remaining dynamic, apparently the demand for nonconforming models is increasing. Short runs of special styles create management difficulties and increase costs for large companies in both production and marketing. . . . With sharper cost controls, many large organizations are finally coming to recognize that they are losing money on these short runs and special models. The small manufacturer, on the other hand, is often so organized in both sales and production that he can handle small lots and special types much more inexpensively and efficiently than can his bigger colleague."[6]

The metal-fabricating and machinery-making industry of New England provides an instructive example of the success of small business in American industry from 1890 to 1960. This industry was dominated by small companies. Of the 80 firms composing the industry, all but 18 employed fewer than 100 workers, only 15 possessed tangible assets exceeding $500,000, and only 10 had a net worth of more than $500,000. These companies shared common patterns of development, management, and success.[7]

Like those starting small manufacturing enterprises in earlier times, the Philadelphia textile makers and Pittsburgh's independent iron and steel makers, the entrepreneurs setting up the metal-fabricating and machinery-making shops usually had prior knowledge of the business. Often the necessary technical knowledge was gained through experience on the shop floor as skilled workers, although some of those entering the industry had engineering degrees from MIT and similar institutions. Most established their ventures because of a strong desire to control an independent business of their own, a desire that often extended back into their childhood. These entrepreneurs were far from the "organization men" so typical of American businesses in the 1950s and

1960s. One explained that he liked being "a lone operator," able "to make decisions instantly and to carry them out." Or, as another put it, "I can do what I want, and I don't have to take any bull from anyone."[8] A desire for freedom more than a quest for large profits provided their motivation. Still, a desire for self-preservation also played a role in the founding of the companies. More were started during the trough of the business cycle than during any other of its stages—suggesting again, as we saw in chapter 3, that many Americans go into small businesses when they find other employment options cut off.

Growth and success most frequently came through the development of specialty products for niche markets, a strategy that offered some hope of insulation from competition with other, often-larger firms. Some entrepreneurs, like the owner of the company making air valves, specialized in products having only a limited demand, thus avoiding competition with big businesses disdaining to enter such unappealing fields. Others engaged in just one process: metal stamping, heat treating, or electroplating. By performing custom work, they secured nonstandardized orders overlooked by larger, mass-production firms. Still others differentiated their products by providing extraordinary service and by building up reputations for dependability. For example, a manufacturer of screw-machine products won a competitive edge through its ability to make an item "in a hurry" for its customers "when it has to be right."[9]

Personal ties held these small businesses together. Most of the founders, like those in small businesses in other industries and in other times, began their enterprises as partnerships or single-owner proprietorships, though all except six eventually reorganized their businesses as corporations. Whatever legal forms they assumed, nearly all the businesses were directly run by their owner-founders. "One-man shows" characterized by hands-on, seat-of-the-pants administration were common. Except in the largest of the firms, little delegation of authority occurred and no managerial hierarchies came into being. Family enterprises in which fathers and sons or brothers jointly handled affairs frequently existed (sometimes wives participated, usually looking after the finances of the operations).

This personal approach to business carried over into financing and labor relations. Personal savings, supplemented by family funds, funds from local business acquaintances, and, to a much lesser extent, bank borrowing, provided most of the initial capital. Almost no use was made of borrowing from federal government agencies. Capital used to finance expansion came mainly from retained earnings and debt financing. Few of the entrepreneurs had access to equity markets. Even had they had such access, few would have made use of it, for they were unwilling to dilute their ownership and managerial control over their companies. More than half the companies began with five or fewer employees. As the firms developed, they were able to acquire and keep their growing number of employees through a combination of monetary and non-monetary incentives. Some offered more than the prevailing wage rate; others provided chances for rapid advancement and opportunities to learn new skills. And in all, the owner-managers continued to know their workers individually.

The history of one company, Burg Tool of Los Angeles, illustrates how small industrial firms could prosper in America after World War II.[10] Founded in 1946 by an inventive machinist, Fred Burg, the company enjoyed great success as a personal, family business producing high-tech products for niche markets. Only after its acquisition by a conglomerate and the subsequent introduction of new management goals and methods in the mid-1960s did Burg Tool falter.

Fred Burg had successfully operated a department store in Cicero, Illinois, but his first love had always been for things mechanical. Burg had been a skilled machinist before family concerns led him into the department store business, but in 1943, at age 47, he sold his store and moved to Los Angeles, ostensibly to retire. Once there, Burg found life more expensive than he had expected, however, and within four months was working as a tool-and-die maker for a defense contractor in the region's booming wartime economy. Always an innovator, Burg devised a new sort of machine tool that he was soon producing in his garage during his spare time. In 1945 Burg struck out on his own, leaving his salaried job and forming his own firm, Burg Tool.

Set up as a partnership in 1946, Burg Tool was family-owned and -operated. Fred Burg recruited his son Joe and his son-in-law Norm Ginsburg to join him in the business (incorporation came only in 1951). Using their own money and $5,000 borrowed from a sister, they entered the machine tool industry with the production of a turret drill they dubbed the Burgmaster. In the late 1940s and early 1950s, Burg Tool successfully broke into established markets with this product. Innovative in design, the Burgmaster was backed up by dependable, rapid service. Fred Burg himself traveled to factories using the tool in order to make any necessary repairs. If innovation, service, and the possession of a specialty product contributed to Burg Tool's initial success, so did the existence of a favorable external environment, for defense spending on the Korean War boosted Burg Tool's sales. In 1954 the company earned a net income of $35,000 on net sales of $574,000 and employed 62 persons.

Burg Tool's emergence as a machine tool builder of national repute during the Korean War marked the beginning of a decade of rapid growth. In 1964 the company's net sales reached $7.4 million and the firm employed 275 persons. Several factors lay behind this success. First, Fred Burg and the others running the company remained innovative. Trained in machine tool building themselves, they spent much time on the factory floor getting their hands dirty in devising new processes and new machines. Burg Tool was one of the first companies, for instance, to produce numerically controlled machine tools, tools that could be programmed by early-day computers (the advantage of such tools was that they could be quickly and cheaply reprogrammed for new tasks). Second, as a consequence of this approach, they worked closely with their employees in formulating new ways of doing things—encouraging and then using suggestions put forward by their machinists. The relationship between management and labor was paternal, complete with summer picnics, Thanksgiving turkeys, and Christmas dinners. Unionization did occur in the 1960s, but relations between the Burgs and their work force nonetheless remained cordial and mutually supportive. Third, Burg Tool provided its customers with state-of-the-art machines backed up by high-quality service. Finally, a continued favorable economic environment helped Burg Tool move ahead. Government spending on aerospace and defense and the expansion of the American automobile industry bolstered machine tool sales in the late 1950s and the early 1960s.

Burg Tool's rise attracted national attention, and the company found itself being wooed as a takeover target by a conglomerate, Houdaille. Running a company based on automobile parts, construction materials, industrial and engineering services, and machine tools, Houdaille's officers saw in Burg Tool a vehicle by which to continue a diversification drive begun several years earlier. The Burgs were willing to sell, for by this time Fred Burg was genuinely beginning to think of retirement, and even Joe Burg and Norm Ginsburg were aging. In the short run, the Burgs desperately needed funds to expand their factory to keep up with an exploding demand for their tools, funds Houdaille agreed to provide. Moreover, the Burgs thought they received verbal assurances that their ways of conducting business would be preserved. The result, after lengthy negotiations, was a friendly takeover in 1965.

That year marked a turning point in Burg Tool's fortunes: from 1965 the company's course was nearly all downhill. The most basic change was managerial, for over time the Burgs were forced out of management. The Houdaille executives who replaced them knew little about the machine tool industry. Taking a short-term approach to business, they insisted upon milking the company for profits at the expense of long-term investments in research and development. As a consequence, Burg Tool gradually lost its innovative edge and its reputation for high-quality production and service. Labor relations also soured. As the company, now a division within Houdaille, came to be run by executives trained in finance and marketing rather than production, a split developed between labor and management. Cooperation disappeared and strikes occurred. These developments in turn left Burg Tool ill prepared to meet the growing competition of machine tool imports from Japan. Unable to cope with competition from American and foreign firms, Burg Tool went out of existence in 1986.

The rise and fall of Burg Tool illustrates some of the factors needed for the successful operation of small businesses in modern American industry, and perhaps some of the reasons American manufacturers have recently lost their competitive edge. The Burg family succeeded in large part through constant innovation in their company's specialty products—innovation made possible, as in the cases of many of the New England metal fabricators and machinery makers, by their direct involvement in management. They got their hands dirty on the shop floor, with no managerial hierarchies separating them from their employees. After Burg Tool was acquired by Houdaille, this approach to business changed: immediate profits took precedence over other goals, managers untrained and unmindful of production methods took charge, and rifts increasingly separated labor from management. And whereas a favorable external environment, especially government purchases, aided the development of the machine tool industry in general and Burg Tool in particular in the 1950s and 1960s, this environment turned more hostile with the growth of foreign and especially Japanese competition in the 1970s and 1980s, competition that Burg Tool and many other American machine tool makers were poorly prepared to meet.[11]

□   Small Business in Sales and Services

As we saw in chapter 2, small businesses remained dominant in sales and services longer than they did in manufacturing. The 50 years following World War I, however, brought epochal changes in business organization to these fields, especially to sales. The rise of chain stores in the 1920s and the early 1930s, in particular, eroded independent retailers' importance in many trades, and the development of supermarkets from the 1930s onward further accelerated the decline of independents in the grocery field. Small service businesses also came under increasing pressure from large firms in some fields, though not to so great an extent as small retailers did. As in manufacturing, however, some small businesses continued to prosper in sales and services, often by adopting the strategy of specialization.

Writing in 1931, an expert on retailing correctly observed, "In the United States the major scene of the industrial revolution has definitely shifted from production to distribution."[12] The most notable change lay in the rapid increase in the significance of chain stores in retailing. The number of chains in the United States rose from 905 in 1921 to 1,718 just seven years later.[13] By 1929, the Great Atlantic and Pacific Tea Company (A & P) was operating 15,418 stores; Woolworth, 1,825; and J. C. Penney, 1,395.[14] In that year chains accounted for 10% of all retail stores in the United States and did 20% of the nation's retail business.[15] Although the expansion of chain stores slowed during the Great Depression and the immediate postwar years, chains remained a key part of the nation's retailing structure. By 1935, chains, while controlling 8% of the nation's retail outlets, had increased their share of sales to 23%, though this proportion dropped to 22% in 1939 and to 20% a decade later.[16]

The spread of chain stores was part of a more general trend in distribution, particularly in retailing: the growth in importance of large-scale stores. By 1949, in addition to the 20% of the nation's retail sales made by chain stores, department stores accounted for 8%; supermarkets, 7%; and mail-order houses, 1%. Independent retailers, which had handled nearly all the sales as late as 1890, accounted for only two-thirds of the sales by the time of the Korean War. Most of the nonindependent outlets were considerably larger than those of independent retailers. By 1939, for example, the average chain store had annual sales of $75,000, roughly four times the volume of the typical independent.[17]

Developments in grocery sales demonstrate well the changing relationships between chain stores and independents.[18] In 1900 only 21 chains existed in the grocery trade. By 1920, the number had risen to 180, and by 1929, to 807. In this last year grocery chains operated 54,000 stores, a third of all the chain units in the nation, and accounted for more than a third of the grocery sales in the United States.[19] By 1931, the five largest chains alone—A & P, Kroger, American Stores, Safeway, and First National Stores—made 29 percent of America's grocery sales, up from just 6% 10 years earlier.[20]

What accounted for this dramatic rise of the chains and the equally precipitous decline of the independents? Chain stores possessed numerous advantages. Probably most important, chain stores offered lower prices to consumers—prices one business historian has concluded were "never less than 3 percent and often as much as 10 or 11 percent lower" than those of the independents.[21] Chains could offer lower prices and still earn substantial profits. Often they provided fewer personal services to customers than the independents did, made no deliveries, dealt strictly in cash, and dispensed fewer premiums and trading stamps. More frequently than independents, chains engaged in the most up-to-date business practices: the use of new accounting methods to keep track of inventories; the implementation of new store layouts; and the adoption of new forms of advertising. The scale of operations allowed the chains to pass on savings in costs to their customers. Many chains cut out middlemen in distribution, instead dealing directly with the growers and producers of goods. By 1936, A & P had eliminated many wholesalers through the ownership of 111 warehouses. Chains also engaged in extensive backward vertical integration. A & P possessed subsidiaries that controlled many of its sources of milk, cheese, coffee, canned salmon, and bread. While chain stores still depended on outside providers for most of their goods, by the mid-1930s fully 12% of sales came from goods they themselves manufactured.[22]

Whereas the development of chain stores presented the first challenge to independents in the grocery industry, the growth of supermarkets offered a second one from the 1930s onward, a challenge that chains like A & P also had to meet. Much larger in floor space than the outlets of established chains, the supermarkets, like the chains before them, built up their trade on the basis of low prices. Supermarkets provided even less personal service than most chains. Customers were expected, for the first time, to pick their goods off shelves throughout the stores rather than have them gathered by clerks. Two factors explain the timing of the supermarket challenge. First, Americans' widespread adoption of automobiles meant that supermarkets could locate on the outskirts of town where land was cheap, allowing the construction of large stores with extensive parking lots. Second, supermarkets emphasized sales of nationally known, brand-name goods advertised on the radio—a type of merchandising most Americans found exciting but a type the established chains, tied to private, in-house labels, failed to provide. About 300 supermarkets were in operation in 1935, and within just a year *900* more had opened their doors.[23]

A & P and most of the other national chains that had come into prominence during the 1920s successfully adjusted to the development of supermarkets by closing their small outlets and opening their own supermarkets. A & P, for example, operated 14,926 grocery stores in 1935, but just six years later the number was down to 6,170, of which 1,594 were supermarkets. This transformation made A & P the largest retailer in the world. In 1951 the company boasted sales of nearly $3.2

billion and profits of $32 million, $5 million more than the combined profits of its two nearest rivals, Safeway and Kroger.[24]

Independent retailers responded both politically and economically to the chain store challege and, in the grocery industry, to that of the super-markets. In terms of politics, independent retailers sought the passage of legislation at both the state and the national levels to slow or halt the growth of the chains. On the economic front, many of the surviving independent retailers formed loose associations through which they tried to secure some of the scale benefits accruing to chains, while at the same time preserving their legal independence from one another.

The political campaign against the chains began at the local and state levels with efforts to slow their expansion through taxation. As early as 1923 a tax measure received serious consideration, though not passage, from the Missouri state legislature. Four years later, 13 such bills were introduced into state legislatures, with 4 securing approval. As the Great Depression hurt independents, the movement to limit chains quickened. Between 1930 and 1935, more than 800 chain store taxation measures were considered. By 1941, 27 states had passed anti–chain store tax measures, and despite the repeal of many of these laws, 9 remained effective. Except in a few localities, such as Portland, Oregon, it was less the opposition of independent retailers (who, like most small business people, remained less well organized than their larger counter-parts) and more the spontaneous crusades of politicians that led to the passage of the laws taxing the chains. Especially in the South and the West, the chains were seen as outside, "foreign" interests dominated by Wall Street and sapping local enterprise and initiative. The chains also served as handy targets for state legislatures strapped for tax revenues during the hard times of the 1930s.[25]

The campaign against the chains soon shifted to the national level, where it focused on two measures. The first was the Robinson-Patman Act, a modification of the Clayton Act of 1914. The Robinson-Patman Act ostensibly sought to protect independent retailers from chain store incursions in a number of ways—foremost by prohibiting growers, manufacturers, and wholesalers from giving chains discounts for large-quantity purchases, even though those savings were often passed on to consumers in the form of lower prices. While originally written by officials of the U.S. Wholesale Grocers' Association, whose members disliked giving discounts to the chains, the bill was nonetheless pictured as an aid to small retailers. In a highly charged debate on the bill, preserving economic opportunity and protecting small business people were presented as more important than economic efficiency and lower prices for consumers. As Wright Patman, who sponsored the bill in the

House, put it, "There are a great many people who feel that if we are to preserve democracy in government, in America, we have got to preserve a democracy in business operation." He concluded, "We must make some effort to maintain the *yeomanry* [italics added] in business."[26] Facing little organized opposition—the chains had not yet mastered the art of political lobbying—the bill became law in 1936.

The second national measure to win approval was the Miller-Tydings Act, an amendment to the Sherman Act of 1890, passed by Congress in 1937. Pushed especially hard by independent retail druggists organized in a powerful trade association, the National Association of Retail Druggists (NARD), this act sought to standardize prices charged consumers for goods sold at retail. A retail price maintenance measure, the proposal forbade chain stores from selling their goods at prices below those set by manufacturers. Like the Robinson-Patman Act approved the previous year, the Miller-Tydings Act placed the interests of small business people above those of consumers. And as with the debate on the Robinson-Patman Act, supporters of the Miller-Tydings bill appealed more to emotions than to economics. The measure was needed, its proponents testified, to keep alive an American way of life based on business opportunities for everyone. As the secretary of the American Pharmaceutical Association argued, "The small retail distributors are rapidly approaching the time when they will be forced completely out of an independent business existence. . . . Even if this situation were the outcome of fair methods of competition . . . it would be deplorable. . . . These small businesses have been and are the backbone of the communities of this country. . . . If we ask ourselves honestly, whether we want this country to become a nation of clerks or to remain a nation of opportunity for individual enterprise, there can be only one answer consistent with American ideals."[27]

From these efforts to curb chains through alterations in the nation's antitrust laws, the antichain movement shifted back to an attempt to limit chain growth through taxation. In 1938 Rep. Patman introduced a measure into the House to impose a heavy federal tax on all chains conducting business in more than one state. Quickly dubbed the Death Sentence Tax by its opponents, the measure would have created a tax steeply graduated by the number of units a chain owned (in 1938 the tax on A & P alone would have come to $472 million). Never reported out of committee, this measure failed to win serious consideration after 1940.

The demise of the tax proposal reveals a great deal about the increasing political sophistication of the chains and their growing acceptance by Americans. The chains, especially A & P, became more adept at mustering support for their side of political issues. In 1936 and 1937 representatives of the chains had been ineffective in their opposition to the congressional antichain measures, but they learned from these experiences. In 1938 and 1939 A & P placed in 1,300 newspapers advertisements stressing its low prices and denouncing the proposed tax, and chain spokesmen talked to thousands of women's clubs about Patman's measure. Few consumer groups testified in behalf of the tax. Probably most important in explaining the defeat of the measure, however, was the fact that chains were more fully accepted by most Americans than had been the case just a few years earlier. A & P's recognition of unions and its entrance into collective bargaining did much to defuse earlier labor hostility against the chains, and a host of AF of L unions testified against Patman's proposal. Similarly, farm organizations, led by the American Farm Bureau Federation, recognizing the importance of chains as purchasers of their products, spoke against the tax proposal. Then too, with economic recovery beginning and the growth of the chains at least temporarily slowing in the late 1930s, much of the urgency went out of the antichain campaign.

It is doubtful that any of these laws had much impact on the chains. Few of the state tax laws remained on the books for very long, and the Robinson-Patman and Miller-Tydings acts contained numerous loopholes that allowed chains to continue conducting business with few changes. For instance, the Robinson-Patman Act declared it "unlawful for any person engaged in commerce . . . to discriminate in price between different purchasers of commodities of like grade and quality." Yet because it was often possible to demonstrate that the goods involved in sales to different purchasers varied somewhat, the law was rendered ineffective. Then too, the act never applied to services, only to the sales of goods.[28]

Small retailers also mounted economic responses to the inroads of larger competitors. Like successful small manufacturers, some adopted the strategy of specialization. Mom-and-pop grocery stores continued to attract patronage by offering services, such as home delivery, that no longer were provided by the chains and supermarkets. Or they specialized in terms of the types of goods they carried. In field after field, many small retailers also banded together in associations to secure some of the benefits, especially the discounts won through high-volume purchases, obtained by large-scale enterprises. In the grocery industry, for example, independent retailers formed voluntary groups, such as the Independent Grocers' Association (IGA), and retailer-owned cooperative warehouses. By the 1940s, more than a third of all grocery wholesale sales passed through these institutions. Through them, retail grocers sought to cut their costs of doing business, and were partly successful.[29]

Changes taking place in hardware retailing demonstate well the alterations occurring in retailing across the nation. Like some grocers, some hardware retailers specialized in the goods they handled, and in the postwar years still more joined retailer-owned cooperatives.

Kirk's, a hardware retailer in Muncie, Indiana, typifies how some independents successfully altered their marketing practices.[30] Founded in 1865, Kirk's originally sold hardware, toys, and many other products. As Muncie grew, the store prospered, earning a reputation for reliable goods and services. A major turning point in the store's development occurred in the late 1880s and the early 1890s, when Kirk's began to sell and repair bicycles because the store's owner, Charles B. Kirk, and his wife were cycling enthusiasts. Kirk met Ignatzs Schwinn in Chicago in 1909 and adopted the Schwinn brand as the only make of bicycle his store would carry. Kirk's continued to grow as a family-owned and -operated store in the middle twentieth century, with Charles's three sons and later several grandchildren going into the business. While never abandoning other lines of stock completely, Kirk's placed an increasing emphasis on bicycle and sporting goods sales. These specializations served Kirk's well. Weathering the Great Depression, the firm expanded in the postwar years. Still a family business, Kirk's moved to two new locations in the Muncie area in the 1970s.

Like grocers, many hardware retailers also entered into cooperative arrangements to win some of the rewards of large-scale operations. John Cotter put together one such cooperative as True Value hardware stores.[31] Brought up in the hardware business, Cotter founded True Value in 1948, by which time independent hardware retailers were facing severe competition from chain stores and discount outlets. In this system hundreds of independent retailers came to own Cotter and Company, which in turn acted as their wholesaler. Profits earned at the middleman's sales level were rebated every year to the retailers, which remained independently owned. By the mid-1980s, True Value had 7,000 member stores and 14 major distribution centers, making it the largest hardware distributor in the United States.

How effective were the economic responses of small retailers in blunting the encroachments of their larger competitors? Their effectiveness varied considerably by field. Most small independent retailers failed to adjust to the new way of selling groceries. In this field, in which low prices were of utmost significance, the chains and supermarkets ruled supreme. By 1971, five large supermarket chains dominated food retailing in the United States by emphasizing rapid turnover of stock, high sales per employee, and large store size. In hardware, a field in which individual customer service remained more important, independents working through groups like True Value did better. The number of retail hardware outlets in the United States declined from 35,000 in 1954 to 26,000 in 1972 but stabilized and even rose a bit in the middle and late 1970s.[32]

Services remained the home of small businesses even more than retailing did. Possessing fewer economies of scale, service industries were less conducive to the spread of large firms. As one scholar recently noted, real estate activity continued to be mainly "project based, small scale, and noninstitutional."[33] Most real estate firms were closely tied to their local communities. Only with the development of new communications and computer technologies in the late 1970s and 1980s could local and regional companies like Century 21 and Coldwell Banker grow to become national giants. Small local businesses also dominated the field of law. As in real estate, it required the development of new media and communications techniques for some law firms to grow large, as did Hyatt Legal Services in the 1980s.[34] Still, the power of small companies was eroded in some service industries. With the continued growth of the United States as an urban nation, insurance and banking companies expanded their reach. Although small firms continued to thrive in both these fields, their status was less secure than in earlier times.

Rapid growth characterized the life insurance industry, as the increase in the number of companies greatly outpaced the nation's rise in population. In 1920, 335 companies served 106 million Americans, whereas by 1957, 1,271 firms sold policies to a population of 171 million. The average size of life insurance companies increased. In 1920 life insurance companies had an average of $121 million of policies in force; by 1957, an average of $360 million. Nonetheless, even in the post–World War II period there was plenty of room for new small companies and independent agents. New types of insurance developed, most notably medical insurance. In 1940 only 9% of Americans had hospitalization insurance, but by 1957 some 72% did. While Blue Cross dominated hospitalization insurance, its share of the coverage in this field dropped from about 50% in 1940 to 43% 17 years later. (Not all fields of medical insurance witnessed a broadening of opportunities for new plans and companies, however. Blue Shield increased its share of surgical insurance from 12% in 1941 to 36% by 1957.)[35]

Banking remained dominated by small businesses. The number of commercial banks in the United States fell by half during the depression era and then stabilized at around 15,000 through the 1980s. The average assets of American banks rose substantially. In 1920 average bank assets stood at just $1.7 million; by 1957 the average had risen tenfold to $17 million, and only a fourth of the gain resulted from inflation.[36] In the 1920s and 1930s branch banking came to the United States in a major way. In 1920 less than 5% of banking offices were branches. Only 21 states permitted branch banking at that date, and until the passage of the McFadden Act by Congress in 1927, branch banking was forbidden at the national level. With the liberalization of the laws by the McFadden Act and later legislation, banks with branches came to compose a fifth of the total by 1935, and in 1957 more than half the 13,617 commercial banks had branches. Chain and group banking also developed in the 1920s, only to fall into disrepute because of numerous failures during the depression decade.[37] The coming of federal deposit insurance in 1933 enhanced the safety of small banks and spurred their expansion.

While the closing of very small units was the norm in commercial banking, small investment banking firms could remain prosperous into the postwar years—as shown by the experiences of K. J. Brown, a firm formed in Muncie, Indiana, in 1931 at the nadir of the Great Depression. Run as a family partnership by Kenneth J. Brown and later by his son, the business made money in good times and bad by staying close to its customers through the provision of personal services in its local and later regional market. According to the firm's historian, through "a combination of good management, sound planning, hard work, and maybe even a measure of luck" K. J. Brown grew to become a regional power in investment banking, with, by 1981, branches in Marion, Kokomo, and Richmond, Indiana; in Ottawa, Illinois; and in Lexington, Kentucky.[38]

☐ Small Business in Farming

Of all of the business fields under consideration in this study—manufacturing, sales and services, and agriculture—farming witnessed the most precipitous decline in small businesses during the 50 years following 1920. A scholar examining farming exaggerated when he commented on "the virtual demise of the independent farmer" in 1962, but long-term economic trends did combine with short-term emergencies to favor larger, more mechanized farms over small family holdings.[39] Yet some family farmers continued to do reasonably well—many of them, as in other types of businesses, by specializing in their activities.

Small- and medium-size farms suffered more than larger units during the 1920s and 1930s. Many American farmers had expanded their operations as demand for foodstuffs skyrocketed during World

War I, often using loans backed by mortgages on their farms. When European demand collapsed in the 1920s, many found themselves unable to pay back those loans, went into bankruptcy, and lost their farms. For many farmers, hard times began well before the 1930s. The Great Depression led to a further drop in farm prices and an increase in farm distress across the nation. Most of the New Deal farm programs put funds in the hands of landowners, who often did not pass any of the aid on to their tenants. In the South, units farmed by sharecroppers fell from 776,278 to 541,291 during the depression decade.[40] Despite a recommendation from the Temporary National Economic Committee (TNEC) that "more action" was needed to help the sharecroppers, little was forthcoming.[41]

In the postwar period as before, most federal aid went to sustain landowning farmers. The ending of the farm crises of the 1930s did not bring much relief to family farmers, for they faced long-term problems and, except for brief periods, were rarely prosperous. The basic difficulty was that, as a technological revolution swept through agriculture, farming became increasingly capital-intensive. As relatively small businesses, family farms found it ever harder to raise the funds necessary to prosper. Larger tractors and mechanized equipment, artificial fertilizer (whose use climbed tenfold between 1940 and 1970), and hybrid seeds all cost money. Moreover, as agricultural machinery came into increasing use, the minimum profitable size of farms also grew larger.[42]

Most of the profits in the farm sector derived less from producing foodstuffs than from processing and marketing them, and large vertically integrated agribusinesses came to control certain aspects of the food industry, from growing to marketing, in the postwar years. By 1972, vertically integrated companies accounted for 97% of broiler chicken production, 95% of vegetable processing, 85% of trade in citrus fruits, 70% of potatoes marketed, 54% of turkey production, and 51% of fresh vegetables grown in the United States.[43]

Writing in 1960, the well-known rural sociologist Everett M. Rogers summarized the alterations occurring in agriculture:

1. American farms are increasingly specialized.
2. American farming is . . . also becoming more capitalized.
3. It is characterized by greater efficiency and productivity.
4. American farms are increasing in size. . . .
7. Interdependence between industrial employment and farming is increasing; there is a marked increase in part-time farming. . . .

8. One of the most important changes in the nature of farming is the increasing interdependence of farmers upon agriculture-related industry. . . . A new term—agribusiness—is now applied to the total agricultural economy.[44]

The response of many small farmers was to leave agriculture. Between 1920 and 1945, about 3 million more Americans left farming than entered it. This exodus continued in the postwar years: as between 1945 and 1974, 4.2 million more quit farming than began it. In the 1960s alone, some 600,000 independent family farms disappeared. An ever-smaller proportion of Americans chose farming as their livelihood; whereas in 1920 about 27% of all working Americans were engaged in agriculture, by 1945 the figure was only 14%, and by 1973, just 4.5%.[45]

As more families left agriculture, farming became more concentrated. As early as 1940, the TNEC observed "tendencies . . . toward increasing concentration in the production of food," which it attributed mainly to "the introduction of farm machinery." "Concentration of control," the TNEC reported, "has progressed much further in the processing of agricultural commodities than in any other stage of the agricultural marketing process."[46] Concentration in all aspects of agriculture accelerated after World War II. In 1948 the largest 10% of America's farms produced 24% of the nation's farm output, but by 1968 they accounted for 48%. Meanwhile, the smallest 20% of farms produced just 3% of total output in the 1950s and 1960s. Many small farmers could no longer make a living exclusively by farming, and so they also worked at jobs in nearby towns. By 1960, farms with annual sales of $20,000 or more—just 24% of the nation's farms—accounted for 70% of net farm income. Table 4 illustrates the decline of small-scale farming, which centered on farms consisting of fewer than 260 acres.[47] Average farm size more than doubled from 200 acres in 1950 to 450 acres in 1983.

Some family farmers managed to prosper, however. One success story was the Riggin family, the owners of a dairy near Muncie, Indiana.[48] Rea Riggin, who founded the dairy in 1911, had gained previous experience in specialty garden and flower operations—raising vegetables for sale in the local market and growing roses, carnations, and chrysanthemums for a larger regional market. Riggin also owned a small dairy herd. During the 1920s the Riggins expanded their dairy operations dramatically by specializing in the home delivery of high-quality dairy products. Like most farmers, the Riggins suffered from the Great Depression. By emphasizing their dairy work still more—building new, modern facilities and adding to their line of dairy goods—

Table 4. U.S. Farms by Size, 1920–1954 (in thousands)

	1–49 acres	50–259 acres	260–499 acres	500–999 acres	1,000+ acres
1920	2,300	3,455	476	150	67
1930	2,358	3,239	451	160	81
1940	2,286	3,389	473	167	89
1954	1,696	2,281	482	192	131

U.S. Bureau of the Census, *Historical Statistics of the United States, Colonial Times to 1957* (Washington, D.C.: U.S. Government Printing Office, 1960), 279.

the Riggins were, however, able to recover and expand after World War II. By the 1970s, their business was operating in four counties. Through specialization in one line of goods—for they dropped vegetables and flowers—the Riggins were able to succeed in agriculture.

Occasionally, small businesses also succeeded as specialized vertically integrated food producers, processors, and marketers. Formed right after World War II to catch, process, and sell Alaskan king crabmeat to Americans—an enterprise no other company in the United States was involved in—Wakefield Seafoods both pioneered in the development of a new industry and illustrated how small firms could succeed in modern America.[49]

Lowell Wakefield, who came from a family with experience in Alaska's salmon and herring fisheries, led a group of young men—all of whom knew Lowell and many of whom had been stationed in Alaska with the navy during World War II—in the foundation of Wakefield Seafoods in 1946. Personal ties of acquaintance thus brought together those starting the company. The same ties provided much of the financing for the firm, as Wakefield, together with his family, friends, and business acquaintances, invested personal savings in the enterprise. A quest for adventure mingled with a desire for profits in the minds of those starting the company. All had seen their lives disrupted by the war and, at its conclusion, were, as one explained, "casting about for something to do." They were looking, another later remembered, for "a lot of glamor and excitement" and were eager to be "trying something that had never been done."[50] In addition to private funds, the company depended on government aid to get started. Two-thirds of the funding came from the Reconstruction Finance Corporation (RFC), which, as we saw in chapter 3, was a federal government agency that made loans to small businesses before the formation of the Small Business Administration.

Despite the federal loan, Wakefield Seafoods began its existence on shaky feet. Like most people starting small businesses, those setting up Wakefield Seafoods were overly optimistic about their company's future, expecting to earn large profits within just two or three years. Such was not to be, for the company encountered unexpected difficulties in every stage of its operations. Within a few years the problems were solved, but in the meantime they nearly brought Wakefield Seafoods to its knees. Like most small American businesses, Wakefield Seafoods was underfunded and lacked the financial resources to deal with its difficulties. By the middle of 1948, the company had accumulated liabilities of $400,000 against assets of only $140,000 (and those consisted mainly of an unsold inventory of crabmeat). Wakefield Seafoods was in default of its RFC loan and loans from commercial banks. It could pay neither its fishing crews nor its suppliers of fishing gear. Its officer-investors could take no money out of the company to live on, for the company's cash on hand had dwindled to a paltry $14!

Nonetheless, Wakefield Seafoods remained in operation and emerged as a very successful company in the 1950s. By 1952 the firm had paid off its most pressing debts and within just four more years was paying handsome dividends. No single factor contributed to the firm's step back from the brink of bankruptcy. Rather, several related elements accounted for the success of Wakefield Seafoods. First, the company's officers eagerly embraced technological advances, many of them spin-offs from World War II. Their ship, the *Deep Sea*, was the first to use radar, sonar, and loran (a navigational device) in fishing, and similarly they developed new methods to process, cook, and freeze the crabs they caught. Second, those starting the company were persistent, willing to endure hard times to get their company moving. They refused to give up. When unable to attract fishing and processing crews, the owner-managers manned the nets and processing lines themselves. They operated the company informally—as one later recalled, more as "a gang of friends" than as a group of managers. No managerial hierarchies or clear lines of authority existed. Third, the personal ties that had been so important in starting Wakefield Seafoods also helped account for the firm's survival. Personal friendships between the founders of the company and the heads of the Seattle branch of the RFC, Seattle's commercial banks, and the suppliers of fishing gear were especially important in helping secure extensions on the company's loans. Finally, pure, blind luck—an element often underrated by scholars assessing the success and failure of small businesses— saved Wakefield Seafoods. For no particular reason, the *Deep Sea's* officers in 1949 found twice as many king crabs as they did the previous year.

From these beginnings, Wakefield Seafoods grew in the 1950s and 1960s to become a large company by Alaskan standards. Yet with sales of less than $10 million even in 1967—the year before Norton Simon, a Los Angeles–based conglomerate, acquired it in a friendly takeover—the firm remained small, or at most medium-size, by national standards. As in earlier years, its success derived from numerous factors, but two were central: (a) the initial decision to engage in all the steps necessary to bring a new type of food to the attention of the American public, with much of the profit coming from processing and marketing, and (b) the subsequent move ahead as a niche marketer, its founders seeing an opportunity ignored by larger businesses and taking advantage of it.

□   The Small Business Person

In the middle twentieth century, small business owners differed in several respects from the salaried managers of big businesses. As we have seen, those forming and running small businesses, whether metal-fabricating companies or firms in the seafood industry, had different motivations from those of the typical managers of large corporations. Owning their businesses, small business people identified closely with their enterprises. Far from being "organization men," small business owners were interested in more than merely making money and finding a comfortable plateau or niche within a big business. Explaining his involvement in Wakefield Seafoods, one of the founders simply observed, "If you're going to the moon, everyone wants to crowd on board."[51] In background, too, small business people were different from their counterparts in larger firms. In Lexington, Kentucky, in the 1950s, for example, small business people were generally younger and less well educated than their counterparts in big businesses across the nation, and a higher proportion of small business people came from families with nonbusiness backgrounds. The first regular job of a small business owner was often that of an unskilled or semiskilled worker or clerical worker.[52] These characteristics also typified the small business people in New England's metal-fabricating and machinery-making businesses.

For those who were successful—always a minority of the total who entered small business—involvement in small business ventures offered chances for upward social and economic mobility. As a scholar who studied the situation in Lexington observed, "While in small business younger men can achieve headship of a firm, the leadership of big business is becoming increasingly age-graded."[53] For some minority groups as well, small businesses offered opportunities not found in larger enterprises; however, as in earlier times, those opportunities varied considerably by group and type of enterprise.

As we saw in chapter 2, blacks formed numerous small businesses. In the years before World War II, retail and service businesses attracted most of the blacks engaged in business ownership. Very few owned even small industrial enterprises. At the local level, blacks by the 1920s were especially engaged in the grocery and dry cleaning trades, though in these types of enterprises they faced more competition from whites than other minority groups did. At the regional level, blacks formed banks and insurance companies, nearly all of which remained small when compared with those owned by whites. Many of these ventures perished during the Great Depression, which was even harder on black-owned than white-owned companies. For instance, only 12 of the 134 banks formed by blacks between 1884 and 1935 remained in operation in 1936, leading one scholar to observe at the time, "Notwithstanding the public assertions of many Negro leaders to the contrary, the conviction is growing among them that the future of Negro finance and business is dismal."[54]

This pattern of small business ownership by blacks continued in the postwar years: it remained concentrated in services and sales. In 1969 nearly 60% of minority-owned businesses, with blacks composing 90% of the minority owners, were found in personal services and the retail trades. As before, few black businesses were found in manufacturing. Most black businesses remained small businesses. Only 5% of the minority-owned businesses employed 10 or more persons, compared with 20% for white-owned businesses, and only a third of the minority-owned businesses enjoyed gross receipts of at least $50,000 per year, compared with half of the white-owned businesses. Small businesses did not bring economic advancement to blacks commensurate to their numbers in America's population. In 1969, when blacks made up 11% of the nation's population, they owned just over 2% of the country's businesses.[55]

As before World War II, other minority groups, especially groups of Asian-Americans in large cities, found small business development more rewarding than blacks did. Like Chinese and Japanese immigrants to the United States before them, Koreans coming to America found in small business one road for personal advancement. Moving into Los Angeles in significant numbers during the 1960s and 1970s, many went into service and retail ventures—restaurants, grocery stores, and the like. In part, the Koreans formed small businesses to compensate for the lack of job opportunities with larger enterprises. Racism combined with a lack of language skills and an attachment to Asian customs to prevent their rapid movement into established large businesses. More positively, the possession of enough education and wealth to start new businesses also led them in this direction, as did the existence of support groups, such as clubs and voluntary associations. Many Korean firms even ventured into black neighborhoods lacking basic business services.[56]

Small business owners continued to differ from the executives of large companies in their propensity to join business organizations, especially at the national level. Prizing their independence, small business people were reluctant participants in the growing organizational culture. Small business owners were active in local service clubs, such as the Lions and the Rotary, but paid much less attention to organizational developments at the national level. It required an external event—President Franklin D. Roosevelt's convocation of small business people in Washington, D.C., in 1938—to bring about the creation of the first organization claiming to speak for all types of small business people across the nation, the National Advisory Council of Independent Small Businesses. Other national small business bodies developed in the postwar years, among them the National Federation of Independent Businesses, the National Small Business Men's Association, and the Conference of American Small Business Organizations. Such organizations did not, however, truly represent many small businesses. The bodies had relatively few members—at most 100,000 to 200,000 of the millions of owners in the United States. Neither did the small business organizations accomplish much for their members. Although some did engage in lobbying activities, most were simply fund-raising vehicles for their founders, who ran them as their own private enterprises. Far from being grass-roots groups set up by local small business owners, the bodies were highly centralized organizations supported by very active membership recruiters in the field.[57]

In one area, small business owners were quite similar to most other Americans—in their political views and stances. No distinctly "small business" attitude toward politics existed in America after World War II. Small business owners were no more likely to be Republican or conservative than, for example, salaried Americans who worked as middle-level managers in large firms. In the 1964 presidential election, which pitted a conservative Republican, Barry Goldwater, against a liberal Democrat, Lyndon Johnson, for instance, a majority of small business owners voted Democratic. Neither were small business people more likely than others to be opposed to government aid and welfare programs. By the 1960s, for example, a majority favored a federal government role in guaranteeing medical aid for Americans, since in competitive sectors they needed government compulsion to keep the playing field level. Nor, finally, were they necessarily antilabor in their political and cultural outlooks, unless their firms were actually threatened.[58]

□ Conclusion

As had been true since the Civil War era, America's business system continued to divide into two segments during the 50 years following World War I. Large, capital-intensive "center" firms came to dominate key segments of American industry, crowding out smaller enterprises. Yet smaller firms, sometimes labeled "peripheral" businesses, able to develop special products and niche markets continued to thrive, even in manufacturing. In other parts of the economy—sales and distribution, along with personal and business services—small firms also lost ground to their larger counterparts but generally fared better than in industry. In farming, however, the decline in small business was precipitous. Still, as we saw in chapter 2, it may be simplistic to view the growth of America's business system in strictly dualistic terms—that is, as the development of a system consisting of big business in one sector and small business in the other. In fact, there was a considerable blurring of the line between large and small firms, a blurring that would intensify in the 1970s and 1980s.

A noteworthy example of such blurring was franchising. Although a few industrial companies had used franchising to extend their sales across America during the late nineteenth and early twentieth centuries, franchising truly grew in popularity in the 1920s and 1930s, as oil companies, automobile manufacturers, and restaurants set up nationwide systems of franchised dealers and outlets. Franchising expanded still more rapidly after World War II, until by 1967, sales made through franchised outlets accounted for about 10% of GNP.[59] In franchising, the franchisee remained a legally independent business, most often a small business, separate from the parent company, the franchiser. Many commentators in the 1950s and 1960s praised franchising as a middle way in business, a means by which large companies (the franchisers) and small businesses (the franchisees) could cooperate to their mutual advantage.

To some extent their observations were true. Both could benefit: the franchiser from the rapid development of a national marketing system with relatively little capital investment, the franchisee from the national advertising and business advice provided by the franchiser. Here, it seemed, was an arrangement by which small businesses could maintain their independence while reaping the benefits of belonging to large umbrella organizations. Frequently, however, those hopes proved chimerical. Too often it was the franchiser who gained the most, through various fees and (as in the case of many fast-food operations) the sale of raw materials to its franchisees. Hotly contested legal battles were often required for local franchisees to win even a modicum of rights from the dictates of their powerful franchisers. As in so many other fields, the independence of small business was frequently more apparent than real in franchising.

Despite some efforts at cooperation, tension continued to characterize relations between large and small firms in postwar America. On that score, not much had changed since the rise of big business in the late nineteenth century. Friction would continue into the 1970s and 1980s, but new developments in an increasingly global economy were destined to shift the balance of power a bit more in favor of small firms, particularly those in manufacturing, a field under attack by foreign competitors.

5

Small Business in Modern America, 1972–1990

Writing in 1987, the head of the Small Business Administration (SBA) noted, "Employment growth in industries dominated by small firms continued to outpace the growth in those dominated by large firms," and observed further that for the 1980s "job creation in the economy has been largely an outcome of small business activity, especially activity by firms with fewer than 20 employees."[1] Waxing more eloquent, the *U.S. News and World Report* asserted in late 1989 that "to a far greater extent than most Americans realize, the economy's vitality depends on the fortunes of tiny shops and restaurants, neighborhood services and factories."[2] Small business concerns had in fact penetrated the popular consciousness by this time. In Columbus, Ohio, for example, the automobile bumper sticker "There's no business like a small business AND There's no business like your own business" could be seen on city streets.[3]

As these statements suggest, small businesses have experienced something of a renaissance over the past two decades. The erosion of the General Agreement on Tariffs and Trade and the Bretton Woods Agreement from the early 1970s onward combined with the growth of strong national economies in Japan, West Germany, and several other nations to produce large multinational firms capable of competing with and in some cases surpassing, their American counterparts in mass-production sectors. With the great increase in international competition that occurred in the 1970s and 1980s, many of America's big businesses, especially those in manufacturing, faltered as engines of growth.⁴ Between 1974 and 1984, employment in the Fortune 500 companies declined by 1.5 million. As this situation unfolded, many Americans looked to small firms for economic rejuvenation.

This chapter examines small American businesses in the changing global context of the past two decades. The chapter begins by surveying the status of small firms in modern America sector by sector, revealing a mixed picture of gains and losses. The chapter next examines two inter-related topics of special interest to those who look to small firms to act as the economic salvation of the United States, their performance in pro-moting innovation and creating new jobs. Finally, the chapter closes with a brief investigation of the types of people owning and managing small firms in modern America.

☐ Modern Small Business

As in times past, small firms remained a vital part of America's business system in the 1970s and 1980s. By this date, the SBA was generally defining small businesses as those with fewer than 500 employees.⁵ By this definition, more than 99% of the nation's businesses were classified as small in 1982. Of the 17 million businesses filing federal tax returns in 1986, 13 million had no employees beyond the owner, and only 10,000 firms employed more than 500 workers. Most businesses contin-ued to be run in a highly personal manner, as in colonial days. In 1982, 9.75 million were organized as sole proprietorships and 1.5 million as partnerships, compared with 2.8 million set up as corporations. These small companies accounted for 48% of total nonfarm employment, 42% of private (that is, nongovernmental) sales, and 38% of America's GNP in 1982. Some 27% of the small firms were family farms, and another 27% were in service fields. Most of the rest were in sales, with only a relatively small number in manufacturing.⁶

Reversing their earlier long-term decline relative to big businesses, small firms increased in economic importance. In the decade after 1974, the proportion of full-time, nonagricultural workers who were self-employed rose from 10.7 to 12% for men and from 3.2 to 4.7% for women. Between 1976 and 1984, firms with fewer than 500 workers increased their share of the nation's total employment from 51 to 53%.⁷ Small business development was, by the late 1980s, strong everywhere except New England and the plains states. According to one report, an eighth of all the nation's small businesses were located in California.

An increasing number of small businesses depended at least partly on foreign sales for their livelihood. Once the almost-exclusive domain of big business, overseas markets became more and more important for smaller concerns. Federal government legislation aided in this development. In 1983 Congress enacted a law making it easier to set up export companies, and by early 1989 some 4,180 had been formed, many of them handling the products of small firms. A revolution in transportation and communications based on wide-bodied, jumbo jet airplanes, satellites, and computers allowed small firms to compete on more equal terms with businesses abroad, and by the late 1980s and early 1990s many small firms exported a significant proportion of their output. Of the 243,000 American companies that exported directly through their own sales offices in 1989, 88% had fewer than 500 employees, and fully half the businesses exporting through third parties like brokers and trading companies were small businesses. Altogether, small firms accounted for about 21% of America's manufacturing exports in 1989. A growing number of small businesses also set up their own production facilities overseas, either by themselves or in joint ventures with foreign firms.[8]

While it is beyond the scope of this volume to explain fully the causes for this apparent regeneration of small business—it is still too soon for historians to completely sort matters out—there are several possibilities. Recessions in the 1970s and early 1980s hurt big businesses—especially large firms dependent on world trade—more than smaller companies. Then too, people often form small businesses when they lose their jobs in larger firms. As we have seen, this situation prevailed in the early 1930s, and it may again have been a significant factor in recent years.[9] Structural changes in the nation's and the world's economies, however, have probably done more to further the development of small business. A partial shift in the American economy away from manufacturing, in which big businesses had been most prominent, and to services, which historically had been dominated more by small companies, may have been a factor. In addition, the development of new technologies using computers may have allowed small flexible firms to compete with their larger brethren in a growing number of industrial fields. In the final analysis, no single factor is likely to explain the surge in small business development. A recent study of small manufacturers in Birmingham (England), Boston, and Bologna (Italy) concludes that "no single explanation offers a fully satisfactory explanation of this widespread movement [the growth of small business]."[10] Instead, small businesses rose to prominence in each of those three regions by different paths and for different reasons.

The roles of the federal government in aiding or hindering the recent growth of small businesses were probably less significant than economic factors. Most apparent were the actions of the SBA. Throughout the 1970s and 1980s, the SBA continued to work for small business development through various loan and advisory programs. In 1981 the agency had 500,000 loans, totaling $17 billion, outstanding. Nonetheless, the SBA came under increasing criticism for not adequately meeting the needs of small businesses, especially minority enterprises. A new and unexpected attack on the SBA came from the administration of President Ronald Reagan. Eager to end what he viewed as the federal government's overregulation of the economy, Reagan proposed cutting back or even abolishing the SBA. Thwarted politically on this front, Reagan in 1986 sponsored a White House Conference on Small Business that brought together 1,813 delegates from around the nation to draft recommendations for congressional action. Few of the resulting 60 recommendations received strong presidential backing, however, and fewer still won enactment into law. [11]

One action of the federal government was, however, of some importance, even before Reagan became president. Responding to repeated complaints from small business groups, Congress passed the Regulatory Flexibility Act (RFA) in 1980. This legislation encouraged federal agencies to impose lighter regulatory burdens on smaller businesses than on larger ones—in effect, to create tiers of regulatory burdens according to the size of firms. Even before the passage of the act, however, such tiering was occurring: the Toxic Substances Control Act of 1976 exempted small chemical companies from various testing and reporting requirements; the Office of Federal Contract Compliance exempted businesses with fewer than 50 employees from filing affirmative action plans; and the Occupational Safety and Health Administration exempted firms employing fewer than 20 employees from its regulations. Just how important, then, was the RFA? While of significance in certain fields, its overall importance was limited. The most detailed study yet made of the differential impacts of federal government regulations on large and small firms revealed that, contrary to popular opinion and the outcries of small business people, "regulations have not generally placed smaller businesses at a competitive disadvantage" and concluded that for the most part the RFA was unnecessary. [12]

☐ Small Business by Economic Sector

The field of manufacturing offered the most obvious example of the renewed significance of small businesses. [13] Firms with fewer than 500 employees increased their share of the nation's total manufacturing output from 33 to 37.4% between 1976 and 1986.[14] Even in larger firms, plant size decreased. A study of 410 leading manufacturers revealed that plants constructed before 1970 but still operating nine years later employed an average of 644 workers; for new plants opened in the 1970s, the average number of employees was only 241.[15]

The flexibility that smaller companies and plants had in meeting the challenges of the rapidly changing business environment of the 1970s and 1980s accounted for much of their growing importance in manufacturing. As in earlier times, small firms proved adept at exploiting niche markets with specialized products based on short production runs. By the 1970s and 1980s, however, more was involved. Small businesses' ability to react quickly to alterations in markets and fluctuations in exchange rates in an increasingly unstable economic world helped explain their growing significance. Then too, the use of computers in Computer Aided Design (CAD), Computer Aided Engineering (CAE), and Computer Aided Manufacturing (CAM) allowed small, independent firms to perform tasks that previously only larger businesses could accomplish. Realizing the benefits to be derived from the flexibility inherent in small-size operations, some large companies disintegrated their work, coming to rely more heavily than before on subcontractors for the production of major components for their finished products. What developed in some fields in the 1980s were congeries of small industrial firms, sometimes operating as subcontractors but often also producing on their own. Frequently located near one another in specific regions, the small firms supported one another and in some fields offered a viable alternative to industrial mass production by big businesses.

Nowhere was the growing importance of small industrial businesses more apparent than in America's metalworking (or engineering) industries. Many small companies began operations. Between 1972 and 1982, the average employment in an American metalworking company declined 13%, despite an increase in both employment and real output in the metalworking industries of 11%. How did this situation occur? The introduction, beginning in the 1940s and 1950s, of numerically controlled machine tools permitted small- and medium-size production runs and favored, as one student of the metalworking industry has explained, "the manufacture of complex, non-standardized parts rather than simple, standardized parts in mass-production systems." The result, he noted, "is that restructuring of this sort is likely to lead to the establishment of new plants with more flexibility and lower total employment, at the same time as employment is reduced in older facilities."[16]

Much the same trend developed in the very different industry of moviemaking. From the 1920s into the 1950s, seven major studios dominated moviemaking. Vertically integrated, they owned chains of theaters and, in cities of 100,000 or more, controlled 70% of first-run theater capacity. From the late 1940s onward, the economic situation within the movie industry changed. In 1948 a federal antitrust action forced the studios to divest their theaters, and in the 1950s television introduced a new element of competition. Nonetheless, in the 1950s and 1960s the major studios continued to dominate movie production. In the 1970s and 1980s, however, vertical disintegration occurred, as studios subcontracted more and more of their work and as more independent producers grew up. Literally hundreds of very specialized small production companies, rental studios, editing businesses, lighting firms, and film processing outfits developed in southern California, the heart of the movie industry. This "flexible specialization" of many types of businesses engaged in the various steps of moviemaking offered a workable alternative to big vertically integrated studios and largely replaced them. Located in one area, this agglomeration of small companies allowed producers to reap economies of scale without forming big businesses.[17]

Sales, especially retailing, presented more of a mixed picture for small business people. Challenged by mail-order houses, department stores, and chain stores in earlier years, small retail outlets encountered growing competition from discount stores in the 1970s and 1980s. Suburban shopping malls and later "upscale" downtown malls—both of which grew enormously in popularity—were another threat, for they usually provided little space for small merchants—as one observer noted, just "an odd kiosk or two." One advantage of big businesses lay in the rents they paid. The large "anchor stores," often Sears outlets or nationally known department stores, paid much less rent per square foot of space than their smaller competitors.[18] As a result of these developments, the share of total retail sales made by single-shop stores with 20 or fewer employees dropped from more than 50% in 1958 to just 33% by 1977. By the mid-1980s, the nation's 50 largest retailers accounted for a fourth of America's retail sales.[19] Similarly, the continued development of large supermarkets that often stayed open 24 hours a day further eroded the positions of small mom-and-pop grocery and convenience stores. These developments led one student of distribution trends to conclude, in 1980, "The outlook for small retailing may be described as somewhat discouraging but not totally unnerving."[20]

Services, a fast-growing segment of the American economy, remained a stronghold of small firms. While attracting larger companies and while facing more competition from foreign firms in the 1980s, such fields as banking and insurance were ones in which small businesses increased their shares of both employment and sales from the mid-1970s into the mid-1980s. The United States still possessed, for example, around 15,000 commercial banks in the mid-1980s, about the same number as 50 years earlier. In investment banking a host of discount brokers and hundreds of new mutual funds developed. Ironically, however, the same revolution in communications and computers that permitted the resurgence of small business in manufacturing threatened small firms in some service fields. Large real estate companies, for example, often working through franchise systems, expanded from regional bases to nationwide operations.[21]

In both sales and services, franchising was of increasing importance. As we saw in chapters 2 and 4, franchising came of age in twentieth-century America. The franchise movement boomed in the 1960s, experienced a slowdown in the early 1970s (the result of a recession and of government investigations revealing widespread fraud in certain franchise industries), but picked up steam again in the late 1970s and the 1980s. In 1980, 442,000 franchise outlets made $336 billion in sales in the United States, and by the mid-1980s franchise outlets accounted for more than a third of the total value of the nation's retail sales. As before, Americans viewed franchising as a way to fulfill their dreams of becoming independent business people, while at the same time securing the benefits of belonging to large supportive organizations.[22]

Nonetheless, the independence of the franchisees continued to be more apparent than real, as revealed in growing conflicts between franchisers and their franchisees. Tensions, though existing from the earliest days of franchising, exploded in the late 1980s and early 1990s. On the one hand, franchisers ranging from Kentucky Fried Chicken to Holiday Inn sought to tighten controls over their franchisees, particularly by forcing them to upgrade their often-outmoded facilities. As one franchise consultant noted, "Older franchise companies are facing a threat to their lives [in the form of the more modern facilities of their newer competitors]." "They need," he continued, "to set and maintain new standards. And they need their franchisees to make the necessary investments."[23] Increasingly, however, franchisees rebelled against the demands of their franchisers, often successfully. Burger King franchisees blocked an attempt by Pillsbury to sell off its fast-food subsidiary as part of a defense against a takeover by Grand Metropolitan. Arby's franchisees mounted an attempt to buy the chain when the company took actions they did not like. Franchisees in the Straw Hat Pizza chain purchased the chain's trademark, trade name, and other materials from Marriott when that company tried to sell the chain to

Saga Company; the franchisees then proceeded to form their own co-operative to replace their arrangement with Marriott.[24]

As these examples of franchisee rebellions illustrate, the nature of the franchisee was changing in notable ways. Fewer franchisees were small-scale, mom-and-pop business people operating on a shoestring. As franchising matured as a form of business organization, more franchisees were experienced business people, often ones operating on a large scale. Just how much room was left in franchising for small budding entrepreneurs was problematic as the 1990s opened. An article in the *Wall Street Journal* captured well the changes taking place: "But now the profile of the typical franchise owner is changing. A growing number of cash-rich investors and companies are sinking money into several franchises—or buying rights to an entire state or foreign country. Some big-business executives have turned to franchise ownership after being caught in the corporate-restructuring squeeze. Independent store owners are converting to franchises to gain advertising clout. And experienced franchisees are snapping up franchises in other industries in order to diversify. . . . There has been a marked shift recently toward more-sophisticated buyers with proven business skills and deep pockets."[25]

If sales and services presented mixed pictures to aspiring small business people, agriculture offered less hope. The decline of the family farm that had begun earlier continued unabated through the 1980s. By 1986, only 2.2% of the nation's working population was engaged in agriculture, and by one estimate just 650,000 commercial family farmers remained in the United States. Problems faced by small- and medium-size farmers, already apparent in the 1950s and 1960s, deepened over the next two decades. Temporarily aided by high prices for their crops, many farmers purchased new farmland and equipment in the late 1970s, hoping that crop prices and land values would keep rising. The rosy future hoped for by farmers failed to materialize, however, when foreign markets for American farm products collapsed in the early 1980s. The loss of these markets was catastrophic, for by the 1980s foreign sales took a third of the production of America's farms. Unable to pay the interest on their mortgages, many family farmers lost their land. Some small, marginal farmers were able to hang onto their land by taking part- or full-time jobs in nearby cities, a strategy they had pursued from the 1930s onward. The major winners, to the extent that there were any, were big corporate farmers raising specialty crops. As was already occurring by the 1950s and 1960s, they often operated as parts of large vertically integrated enterprises—agribusinesses—that made their profits more in processing and marketing food than in growing crops.[26]

☐ Innovation and Job Creation

Two closely related topics of particular interest to many Americans but especially to policymakers in the late 1980s and early 1990s were the roles of small businesses in innovation and job creation. As large businesses in the United States seemed to lose their competitive edge to their foreign counterparts in field after field, many Americans came to celebrate small firms for their abilities to make technological breakthroughs and create new jobs. A close examination of the roles of small businesses in these fields reveals, however, a spotty record.

Although big businesses spent much more than small firms on research and development, small businesses remained, as in the past, vital sources of innovation. In the early and middle 1980s, big businesses accounted for about 95% of the corporate-financed research and development conducted in the United States. The 15 largest spenders carried out some 40% of the total. Nonetheless, small firms excelled in conducting research and development projects requiring low amounts of capital and high degrees of specialized knowledge. In the twentieth century, small companies introduced new products as varied as the aerosol can, biosynthetic insulin, double-knit fabrics, quick-frozen food, zippers, and computer software.[27]

Numerous studies have identified small firms as sources of innovations in the nation's business system.[28] One conducted by the U.S. Office of Management and Budget showed that companies employing fewer than 1,000 employees accounted for about half the innovations made by American businesses between 1953 and 1973.[29] Similarly, an examination of product innovations in 121 industries during the 1970s found that 40% were made by firms with no more than 500 employees or by independent inventors.[30] The most recent studies not only show the continuing importance of small firms as sources of innovation but demonstrate as well that they have been more significant in some fields than in others. After examining the sources of 8,074 innovations made by American businesses in 1982, two economists concluded, "Our results are unequivocal—industry innovation tends to decrease as the level of concentration rises."[31] In other words, industries composed of many small businesses (companies with 500 or fewer employees) generated more innovations than those dominated by a few large ones. These economists found, moreover, marked differences in the circumstances under which large and small firms were likely to be innovative: "Industries which are capital-intensive, concentrated, and advertising-intensive tend to promote the innovative advantage in large firms. The small-firm innovative advantage, however, tends to occur in industries in the early stages of the life-cycle, where total innovation and the use of skilled labor play a large role, and where large firms comprise a high share of the market."[32]

Small, flexible companies were also often able to commercialize their findings (or those of other firms) faster than big businesses were. The study of product innovations in 121 industries in the 1970s showed that firms with 500 or fewer employees brought their innovations to market in 2.2 years, considerably faster than the 3.1 years needed by larger companies.[33] In their ability to respond more speedily small firms offer one of their most valuable services to society.

If investigators have established with some certainty the continuing significance of small businesses in the development and commercialization of innovations, they have not yet fully explained these firms' roles in the generation of new jobs. In fact, the question of precisely how important small businesses have been in creating new jobs in modern America is a controversial topic, one rife with significance for government policy decisions.

Much of the controversy has revolved around the work of the scholar and consultant David L. Birch. Like many business writers and economists, Birch has seen in small business the most vibrant engine of growth in the modern American economy. "Galbraith [John Kenneth Galbraith] and others who think that big business is the American economy," Birch has observed, "don't seem to realize that the bubbly, yeasty, creative segment is the small business segment."[34] Birch and scholars like him have characterized big businesses as unexciting, stagnant firms contributing little to the economic growth of the United States. In his initial study of the role of small businesses in generating jobs, Birch claimed that 80% of the new jobs created in America between 1969 and 1976 were in companies employing fewer than 20 workers. Most recently, Birch has backed off from that assertion somewhat, being content to note that "the small-firm share of job creation varies a great deal. The time period and location will affect the outcome dramatically."[35]

Others have disputed Birch's findings. Using much the same type of data that Birch employed, SBA economists found that, for the years 1982 through 1986, companies with fewer than 100 employees accounted for just 52% of America's new private-sector jobs, and that firms with no more than 20 employees were responsible for only 37% of them. Similarly, SBA investigators discovered that, for the years 1985 and 1986, firms with fewer than 100 employees accounted for only 44% of the new jobs created in the United States. "Birch is a chorus of one," concluded Thomas A. Gray, the chief economist for the SBA.[36]

Scholars have also offered thoroughgoing critiques of Birch's work. While most have agreed with his general conclusion—that small firms have been more important than big businesses in the creation of new jobs in recent years—they question exactly how important small businesses have been. The authors of a carefully researched study of job generation by small firms in Europe and the United States concluded that "small firms are net creators of jobs, whereas large firms tend to be net losers of jobs"; however, they found that Birch "probably overestimated employment growth in small firms" and suggested that "revised figures yield a small business share of employment growth of 50 percent."[37] They reached a cautious conclusion about the roles small businesses can be expected to play in global economic growth:

> Whilst it is difficult, because of data problems, to be satisfied that the international comparisons are fully adequate, there appears to be no evidence to support the view that, once the extreme values of the UK and Japan are excluded, countries which have a higher proportion of employment in small firms perform better than those with a low proportion in such firms. There also appears to be no evidence to support the view that those countries in which small firms increased their share of employment most rapidly performed better than other countries. In both cases "performance" is indicated by net employment change and by change in unemployment.
>
> The results tentatively suggest that policies designed to increase the number of small businesses in an economy are unlikely to have a major impact upon either employment creation/unemployment reduction.[38]

How good are the jobs being created by small firms? It is difficult to tell yet, for relatively little research has been done on this topic. It appears that about half these positions have been professional, technical, or managerial; many of the rest have been low-paying, often-dead-end jobs. Average wages in small firms have continued to lag behind those in large companies.[39] Critics have argued that the shift from high-paying manufacturing jobs to lower-paying service jobs represents clear evidence of the decline of the American economy.

☐   The Small Business Person

Despite small business's continuing high mortality rate—in the 1970s and 1980s about half to two-thirds of all newly formed businesses, mainly small firms, failed to reach their fifth birthday, and four-fifths

Table 5. Nonfarm Sole Proprietorships by Gender, 1980–1985

	1980	1985	Percentage Change
Male owned	6,928,659	9,075,651	31.0
Female owned	2,535,240	3,738,107	47.4
Jointly owned	266,120	482,993	81.5
Total	9,730,019	13,296,751	36.7

U.S. Small Business Administration, Office of Advocacy, *Small Business in the American Economy* (Washington, D.C.: U.S. Government Printing Office, 1988), 119.

had disappeared as independent enterprises by their tenth year—the world of small business attracted newcomers in these decades. (Of course, not all those firms failed: some merged with other companies, others voluntarily disbanded, and still others changed their form by adding new partners.) The dreams of independence and profits that had motivated those founding businesses in the past have remained potent in recent decades. Entrepreneurship is alive and well in the United States in the late twentieth century.[40] It is important to realize, however, that many people starting small firms in recent years have not been interested primarily in rapid growth. The vast majority have sought a modicum of independence to do what they want while earning a reasonable income, an income to replace what they left behind in jobs previously held with larger companies. In a sense this approach may be an urban substitute for the old ideal of having a "good" life for one's family on the farm. And indeed it has been this situation of modest success and growth that has developed in most of those small firms which have succeeded. According to one estimate, in the early 1980s "only about 650,000 firms [of some 17 million companies] in the United States qualif[ied] as growing firms and . . . the top 5, 10, and 15 percent of those growth firms create[d] 83, 93, and 98 percent respectively of all gross new jobs."[41]

Small business ownership has offered increasing opportunities for women. Between 1977 and 1983, women formed new businesses, nearly all of which were small, at a rate twice as fast as that of men.[42] The gap between the rates at which men and women started businesses narrowed in the mid-1980s, but women continued to outpace men. As Table 5 shows, between 1980 and 1985 the number of single-owner proprietorships owned by women rose 47%, while the number of those owned by men increased 31%. Businesses owned by women clustered, Figure 2 illustrates, in services and sales, as in previous decades. Nevertheless, as

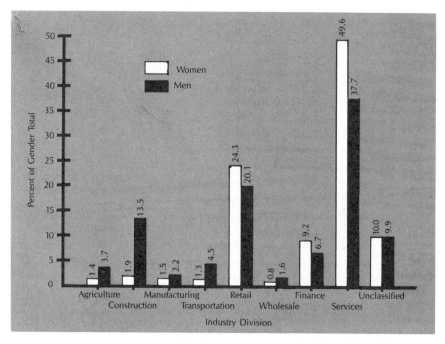

Figure 2. Business Ownership by Gender in 1982. U.S. Small Business Administration, Office of Advocacy, *Small Business in the American Economy* (Washington, D.C.: U.S. Government Printing Office, 1988), 130.

Figure 3 demonstrates, a growing diversity occurred in the types of businesses owned by women. Substantially more, for example, could be found in construction and transportation than in earlier times. As an SBA investigator noted in 1988, "The industry distribution of women-owned nonfarm sole proprietorships is becoming more diverse as women make significant inroads into industries traditionally dominated by men."[43] Even so, women still fell far behind men in the gross sales receipts generated by their companies. In 1988 companies owned by women earned less than 10% of the total business receipts generated in the United States, despite the fact that women owned nearly a third of the nation's businesses.[44]

Because women were relatively new to business ownership, the characteristics of women business owners differed significantly from those of men. While, according to researchers for the SBA, "gender differences in the characteristics of business owners and businesses become less pronounced over time, as women open businesses in a broader

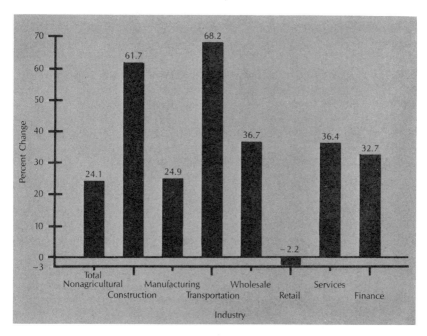

Figure 3. Change in the Number of Self-Employed Women by Industry, 1980–1985. U.S. Small Business Administration, Office of Advocacy, *Small Business in the American Economy* (Washington, D.C.: U.S. Government Printing Office, 1988), 131.

range of industries," important differences remained.[45] Examining information about single-owner proprietorships in 1982, investigators for the SBA found that "compared to businesses owned by men, women-owned businesses tend to be newer and smaller in both employment and receipts size. . . . Women tend to start their businesses with less financial capital than men, and they tend to work fewer hours per week in their ownership roles. Women become business owners with less managerial work experience and are likely to own businesses in the services and retail trade industry divisions."[46]

For minorities, small business ownership offered fewer opportunities than for whites, and the degree of opportunity varied considerably by minority group. The number of minority-owned firms more than doubled between 1972 and 1982. Nonetheless, even in the late 1970s the participation rate of minorities in business ownership was only a fifth that of whites. In 1977, for example, whites owned 63 businesses per 1,000 members of their ethnic group; Asians, 29; Hispanics, 20; and blacks, 9. The variations among the minority groups stemmed mainly from differences in the rates at which their members started new businesses, for the business closure rate for each group was about the same.[47]

What accounted for the varying degrees of business formation by the different minority groups? Probably numerous factors. A recent report by the SBA shows that blacks had less access to financial capital than Asians or Hispanics and that blacks could depend on fewer and less well developed support groups for help in times of need. Black-owned businesses remained clustered primarily in central cities and were particularly hard-hit by the flight of capital to the suburbs, as in the building of suburban malls. More than other groups, blacks also experienced difficulty in finding markets beyond other members of their race—a circumstance that may have retarded business formation and growth, given the relatively limited incomes of most black customers. Difficult to assess but no doubt important in explaining the relative backwardness of blacks in the formation of new businesses have been human elements, such as the lack of role models. When compared with other minority groups, for example, blacks have worked in lower proportions for close relatives who owned businesses.[48]

☐ Conclusion

Small businesses remained very much a part of the American scene as the 1990s opened and, as we have seen, were experiencing a modest revival in some fields, especially manufacturing. While not contributing as much to the nation's employment picture as the rhapsodies of some pundits earlier suggested, small firms did generate a significant share of America's new jobs. As sources of innovation they also remained important, particularly in the commercialization of new processes and products. For those forming new small businesses, the future seemed brighter than it had for many decades, though the outlook varied considerably by ethnic group and field of endeavor. As always, the world of small business remained complex, defying easy generalization.

Conclusion
Future Research Needs

AS I HAVE SUGGESTED IN THIS VOLUME,
scholars today understand much more about the development of small
business in the United States than was the case just a generation ago. The
works of historians, political scientists, economists, sociologists, and others
have begun to illuminate this previously little known field. Despite all that
recent research has accomplished on the history of small business, however,
much remains to be learned. I hope this study has provided a broad survey
of the contours of change in the evolving world of small business, but I
realize that it is far from the last word on the topic. If anything, I hope this
volume stimulates research on the history of small firms and the many
roles they have played in America's development.

Small business development in the United States has been complex, as
has its impact on American politics and culture. That complexity is an
indication of the centrality of small business to American life. From the
founding of the first colonies to the present day, small business has been of
great importance to the majority of Americans: as the dominant form of
business enterprise in their nation and as a symbol for their socioeconomic
aspirations.

The position of small business in America's economy and culture has
changed over time. In the colonial and early national periods—in fact, to
about 1880—few large businesses existed in America, and small firms de-
creed how the nation would develop economically. In these same years a
business ideology based on individual opportunity and grounded in the idea
of small business ownership (with farms thought of, in part, as businesses)

grew up. Challenges arose to small business in manufacturing—and, to a lesser degree, in other fields—with the emergence of large industrial complexes between 1880 and 1920. These challenges intensified during the 50 years following World War I. Small family farms came under increasing pressure from agribusinesses. Retailing, long a stronghold of small business, faced competition from chain stores and other institutions. Despite public attitudes favoring continuance of small business development and sporadic actions by the federal government to give meaning to those attitudes, most forms of small business declined in economic importance relative to big business into the 1970s. Only over the past decade or two have changes in the nation's and the world's economies opened new opportunities for some forms of small businesses, especially those in manufacturing.

Throughout all these changes have also existed elements of continuity in the experiences of small businesses. Those which fared the best—particularly in manufacturing, but often in other fields as well—did so by creating specialized products or services for market niches. In this way, small business owners insulated their firms from direct competition with big businesses. Whether for a small-scale cotton textile manufacturer during the 1880s or for a small producer of computer software a century later, specialization, combined with flexibility, seemed to offer the most fruitful strategy for coexistence with larger concerns. In manufacturing, this strategy often entailed the employment of well-trained and -educated workers able to improve their work processes and the use of the most up-to-date technologies.

Mixed motives lay behind the entrance of Americans into the world of small business. Small business owners have long seen their firms as vehicles for their socioeconomic advancement. Profits and economic growth have been important goals for people starting small businesses in America. Significantly, however, those goals have not been the only, or perhaps even the dominant, ones. Small business owners have also sought independence, combined with a comfortable economic life for their families, as much as they have sought rapid individual economic ascendance. Of course, few attained all they desired. Small businesses have always led perilous lives, with relatively few lasting more than about five years.

Despite the progress recently made in increasing our understanding of the place of small business in American life, scholars need to do still more. We need, I think, both a general reassessment of the evolving place of small firms in America's business system and work on specific aspects of the development of small businesses in the United States. For business and economic historians in particular, the field of small business promises to be a fertile one indeed.[1]

We need to know much more about the historical evolution of small firms and their changing contributions to the economic development of the

United States. The manufacturing sector of our economy has long attracted historians, but relatively few have looked at small industrialists. We need more information about their roles in the industrial growth of the United States. Just how common were small, flexible firms, such as the ones Philip Scranton and John Ingham have recently written about? How did they relate to larger enterprises in their fields? Precisely what roles are small, flexible companies playing in the present-day transformation of American industry, especially the movement away from vertical integration, once a hallmark of American manufacturers? How widespread is this trend? Our lack of knowledge is even more pronounced in the service and sales industries. Broadly defined, service businesses—many of them small firms—now employ about two-thirds of all Americans. Yet we have less knowledge about them than about manufacturing enterprises. Exactly what is happening in the service sector, as the American economy becomes more and more integrated with the global economy? What are the ramifications, for instance, of the recent merger movement among American banks?[2]

More generally, we need to understand better how the management of small firms has been handled in the twentieth century, particularly in the years following World War II. Are most small firms still run as informally as they once were? Or have the demands of the SBA, commercial banks, and other organizations that loan to small businesses perhaps forced the firms to become more bureaucratic? The nature of small businesses may have changed in the 1980s. Proportionally fewer may operate as truly independent enterprises than was the case in earlier times. A larger share may have become subservient to big businesses as subcontractors or as franchise outlets. As one historian has recently suggested, more may have become tied into "technical systems of analysis, bureaucratic values, and reporting required by larger, more powerful organizations."[3] This possible trend deserves a full exploration by scholars.

Closely related to the topic of management style is the issue of innovation. Several recent historical investigations of the sources of innovation in America's business system have focused on big businesses—General Electric, Du Pont, and AT and T.[4] Yet it is unclear just how important big businesses have been in fostering technological innovation in the United States. Much of the early industrial research conducted by large firms aimed mainly at market control. Moreover, as we have seen, in the early 1980s small businesses were the source of innovations in many fields. What of times past? We need to know much more about product and process innovations originating in small and large firms throughout American history before solid conclusions can be reached.

We also need to learn more about how small firms have interacted through their trade associations and other organizations. To what degree have such associations and organizations been important to the evolution of small firms? To what extent have small businesses taken part in the organizational thrust that has swept through much of American society since about 1870? In particular, it would be valuable to learn more about how small companies have banded together to deal with larger firms on something approaching an equal basis. How common, for example, have retailer-owned wholesalers been in America—and how successful?

The entire issue of federal government policy toward small business development deserves careful consideration. Despite all that has been written about, for example, America's antitrust legislation, we still know too little about the evolution of public attitudes and public policies toward small businesses. I think we need especially to learn more fully what occurred with regard to governmental policies and actions in the 1920s, 1930s, and 1940s. We need to understand more completely what lay behind the chain store fight and passage of the Robinson-Patman and Miller-Tydings acts. By the same token, a full-scale history of the formation and work of the SBA would be of great value in illuminating the course of recent events.

Certainly an important policy matter has been the roles of small businesses in the creation of opportunities for business management and ownership among women and minorities. To the extent that they have got ahead in American business at all, women and minorities have, at least until very recently, generally done so in small businesses. Scholars have begun to study this phenomenon, but more remains to be done. It appears that the progress of women into middle- and top-level management ranks in big businesses slowed in the mid-1980s; at the same time, women formed new small businesses at a much faster rate than men did. Perhaps it was precisely because their progress into the middle and upper ranks of management in big businesses was slower than they had anticipated that women left large firms to start their own small businesses. Small companies may also have offered women a better fit with their life-styles, such as the flexibility to balance childbearing and careers, than large businesses did. We need to know more about this situation, as well as the entire topic of the roles small businesses have played for women over time. Similarly, some minorities have advanced through small business opportunities. Yet it is important to recognize, as scholars have recently stressed, that those opportunities have varied considerably by racial and ethnic group and by type of industry.

Beyond these specifics, scholars need to reassess how they have viewed the roles played by small firms in the development of America's business system. As noted earlier, it is important to realize that there have been many types of small businesses in America's past and that, as in the case of their larger counterparts, the nature of these firms has changed over time. The world of small business has not been a static one. It may well be propitious, too, to question the labels often applied to small businesses by scholars and what those labels imply. Should small businesses be called "traditional" businesses, with big businesses pictured as "modern"? Have small businesses composed a "peripheral" segment of the business system of the United States, with larger companies at the "center"? Many recent studies have shown that some small firms may make up the most dynamic part of our modern economy. What, then, of times past? As historians examining industries as diverse as textiles and steel have recently demonstrated, scholars may have long underestimated the significance of small- and medium-size firms in America's economic evolution. A fruitful way to approach a reassessment of small business in America's past might be to take a comparative perspective. With the publication of *Scale and Scope: The Dynamics of Industrial Capitalism,* the business historian Alfred D. Chandler, Jr., has recently shown how valuable this approach can be in studying big businesses across national boundaries.[5] Might not the comparative approach also illuminate the roles small firms have played in business development?[6]

Chronology

1757	Thomas Willing founds the first insurance company in North America.
1781	Robert Morris forms the Bank of North America, the first bank in the United States.
1790s	The Rhode Island merchant Moses Brown and the artisan Samuel Slater start the first successful cotton textile mill in the United States.
1826	The artisan Jonas Chickering sets up a piano-making factory in Boston.
1839	Some 55,565 retail outlets, nearly all small businesses, operate in the United States.
1840	Banks in the United States number 901.
1850	Some 1.5 million farms operate in the United States.
1850s	Railroads develop as the first big businesses in the United States.
1859	The Great Atlantic and Pacific Tea Company (A & P), America's first large retailer, is founded.
1860	Roaming the American backwoods are 16,594 peddlers. Some 30,000 miles of railroad tracks exist in the United States.
1880s	Large manufacturers begin challenging small businesses in many industrial fields.
1890	Congress passes the Sherman (Antitrust) Act. Ten chains of stores provide retail outlets for Americans. Some 170,000 miles of railroad tracks crisscross the nation.

1895–1904	America experiences its first big merger movement.
1900	The United States possesses 500 general insurance companies.
1901	The United States Steel Corporation, America's first billion-dollar company, is formed.
1911	The U.S. Justice Department dissolves the Standard Oil Company and the American Tobacco Company for engaging in unreasonable restraint of trade.
1913	Congress passes the Federal Reserve Act, thereby setting up the Federal Reserve System.
1914	Congress passes the Federal Trade Commission Act and the Clayton (Antitrust) Act in an attempt to make America's business system more competitive.
1915	Retailing goods to Americans are 515 chain stores.
1920	Commercial banks operating in the United States number 30,300. The United States possesses 6.5 million farms.
1925–1931	America experiences its second large merger movement.
1928	Chain stores operating in the United States number 1,718.
1929	Some 168,000 wholesalers and 1.5 million retailers operate in America.
1929–32	A record 110,000 businesses fail in the United States.
1933–42	Congress considers 390 anti–chain store bills.
1936	Congress passes the Robinson-Patman Act to protect small retailers. Some 1,200 supermarkets sell groceries in the United States.
1937	Congress passes the Miller-Tydings Act to protect small businesses.
1938	The Temporary National Economic Committee is set up to investigate the nation's business structure. The first Small Business Conference is held in Washington, D.C.
1940	The Senate Committee on Small Business is established.

1941	The House Committee on Small Business is set up. Twenty-seven states have anti–chain store taxes in effect.
1942	Congress passes the Small Business Act to protect small businesses during World War II.
1950	Congress passes the Cellar-Kefauver Act, which gives the Justice Department more power in anti-trust cases.
1953	Congress creates the Small Business Administration.
1957	Half of America's 13,617 banks operate branches.
1960s	The United States experiences its third big merger movement.
1967	Sales made through franchised outlets compose 10% of America's GNP.
1970s and 1980s	Small businesses adopt flexible manufacturing methods in some fields. America experiences its fourth widespread merger movement.
1980	Franchise outlets account for a third of the retail sales made in the United States.
1986	Only 650,000 commercial family farms remain in America.

NOTES AND REFERENCES

Introduction

1. Phillips Bradley, ed., *Democracy in America*, by Alexis de Tocqueville (New York: Knopf, 1945), 167. I am indebted to George David Smith for this quotation; see his *From Monopoly to Competition: The Transformation of Alcoa, 1888–1986* (Cambridge, England: Cambridge University Press, 1988), 44. Much of this introduction is derived from Mansel G. Blackford, "Small Business in America: An Historiographic Survey," *Business History Review* 65 (Spring 1991).

2. *The State of Small Business: A Report of the President* (Washington: U.S. Government Printing Office, 1988), vii, xi.

3. Ralph Hidy, "Business History: Present Status and Future Needs," *Business History Review* 44 (Winter 1970): 494.

4. Small Business Administration, *Annual Report on Small Business and Competition, 1988* (Washington, D.C.: U.S. Government Printing Office), 19.

5. Harmon Zeigler, *The Politics of Small Business* (Washington, D.C.: Public Affairs Press, 1961), 116.

6. John Bunzel, *The American Small Businessman* (New York: Knopf, 1962), 30.

7. Small Business Administration, *Annual Report, 1988*, 19.

8. Harold G. Vatter, *Small Enterprise and Oligopoly: A Study of the Butter, Flour, Automobile, and Glass Container Industries* (Corvallis: Oregon State University Press, 1955), 109–10.

9. Ross Robertson, "The Small Business Ethic in America," in *The Vital Majority: Small Business in the American Economy,* ed. Deane Carson (Washington, D.C.: Small Business Administration, 1973), 29.

10. Mansel G. Blackford, *Pioneering a Modern Small Business: Wakefield Seafoods and the Alaskan Frontier* (Greenwich, Conn.: JAI Press, 1979), 20.

11. Small businesses are, however, becoming more involved today in foreign markets than in times past. See "The Little Guys Are Making It Big Overseas," *Business Week,* 27 February 1989, 94–96.

12. As a part of this investigation, historians need to explore further the myriad factors that in different eras have conditioned the formation and success or failure of businesses of varied scales. For early works on this topic, see Ruth G. Hutchinson, Arthur R. Hutchinson, and Mabel Newcomer, "A Study in Business Mortality: The Life of Business Enterprises in Poughkeepsie, New York," *American Economic Review* 28 (September 1938): 497–514, and Mabel Newcomer, "The Little Businessman: A Study of Business Proprietors in Poughkeepsie, New York," *Business History Review* 35 (Winter 1961): 477–531. For a more recent study, see Timothy Dunne, "The Measurement and Analysis of Firm Entry and Exit in the United States Manufacturing Sector, 1963–1982," Ph.D. diss., Pennsylvania State University, University Park, 1987.

13. Alfred D. Chandler, Jr., in *The Visible Hand: The Managerial Revolution in American Business* (Cambridge, Mass.: Harvard University Press, 1977), presents a masterly survey of the evolution of America's business system.

14. Small Business Administration, Office of Advocacy, *Small Business in the American Economy* (Washington, D.C.: U.S. Government Printing Office, 1988), v, 41.

15. As quoted in Mansel G. Blackford and K. Austin Kerr, *Business Enterprise in American History* (Boston: Houghton Mifflin, 1990), 1.

16. Rowland Berthoff, "Independence and Enterprise: Small Business in the American Dream," in *Small Business in American Life,* ed. Stuart Bruchey (New York: Columbia University Press, 1980), 29.

17. Bunzel, *The American Small Businessman,* 13.

18. Thomas McCraw, *Prophets of Regulation* (Cambridge, Mass.: Harvard University Press, 1984), chap. 3.

19. Much has been written on the chain store fight. See, especially, David Horowitz, "The Crusade against Chain Stores: Portland's Independent Merchants, 1928–1935," *Oregon Historical Quarterly* 89 (Winter 1988): 341–68, and Carl Ryant, "The South and the Movement against Chain Stores," *Journal of Southern History* 39 (May 1973): 207–22. For an early contemporary account, see Frank Farrington, *Meeting Chain Store Competition* (Chicago: Byxbee, 1922). For an introduction to the politics

involved in the Robinson-Patman Act, see Richard Posner, *The Robinson-Patman Act: Federal Regulation of Price Differences* (Washington, D.C.: American Enterprise Institute for Public Policy Research, 1976).

20. See, for instance, Jim Heath, "American War Mobilization and the Use of Small Manufacturers, 1939–1943," *Business History Review* 46 (Autumn 1972): 295–319; Otto Reichardt, "Industrial Concentration in World War II: The Case of the Aircraft Industry," *Business History Review* 22 (Fall 1975): 129–34; and Harold G. Vatter, *The U.S. Economy in World War II* (New York: Columbia University Press, 1985), chap. 3. And for a different perspective, see Roy Rothwell and Walter Zegveld, *Industrial Innovation and Public Policy: Preparing for the 1980s and the 1990s* (London: Frances Pinter, 1981), especially chap. 10.

21. In "Small Business in America: Two Case Studies" (in *Business and Economic History,* ed. Paul Uselding [Urbana: Bureau of Economic and Business Research, University of Illinois, 1979]), I examine some of the difficulties encountered in doing research on small businesses.

22. Lewis Atherton, "Itinerant Merchandising in the Antebellum South," *Bulletin of the Business Historical Society* 19 (1945): 35–59; "The Pioneer Merchant in Mid-America," *University of Missouri Studies* 14 (1 April 1939); and *The Southern Country Store, 1800–1860* (Baton Rouge: Louisiana State University Press, 1949).

23. Gerald Carson, *The Old Country Store* (New York: Oxford University Press, 1954); Thomas D. Clark, *Pills, Petticoats, and Plows: The Southern Store* (Norman: University of Oklahoma Press, 1944); and Fred Mitchell Jones, "Middlemen in the Domestic Trade of the United States," *Illinois Studies in the Social Sciences* 21 (1937): 1–81, and "Retail Stores in the United States, 1800–1860," *Journal of Marketing* 2 (October 1936): 134–42.

24. Martha Taber, *A History of the Cutlery Industry in the Connecticut Valley* (Northampton, Mass.: Smith College Studies in History, 1955).

25. Theodore Marburg, *Small Business in Brass Manufacturing: The Smith and Griggs Co. of Waterbury* (New York: New York University Press, 1956).

26. James Soltow, "Origins of Small Business: Metal Fabricators and Machinery Makers in New England, 1890–1957," *Transactions of the American Philosophical Society* 55 (December 1965): 1–58.

27. Bruchey, ed., *Small Business in American Life.* See also Vincent Carosso and Stuart Bruchey, eds., *The Survival of Small Business* (New York: Arno Publications, 1979), which reprints several primary and secondary sources on the history of small business.

28. Mansel G. Blackford, *A Portrait Cast in Steel: Buckeye International and Columbus, Ohio, 1881–1980* (Westport, Conn.: Greenwood Press, 1982), and *Pioneering a Modern Small Business.*

29. Steven Fraser, "Combined and Uneven Development in the Men's Clothing Industry," *Business History Review* 57 (Winter 1983): 522–47; Amos Loveday, Jr., *The Rise and Decline of the American Cut Nail Industry: A Study of the Interrelationships of Technology, Business Organization, and Management Techniques* (Westport, Conn.: Greenwood Press, 1983); and Michael Santos, "Laboring on the Periphery: Managers and Workers at the A. M. Byers Company, 1900–1956," *Business History Review* 61 (Spring 1987): 113–33.

30. John N. Ingham, *Making Iron and Steel: Independent Mills in Pittsburgh, 1820–1920* (Columbus: Ohio State University Press, 1991), and Philip Scranton, *Figured Tapestry: Production, Markets, and Power in Philadelphia Textiles, 1885–1941* (Cambridge, England: Cambridge University Press, 1989), and *Proprietary Capitalism: The Textile Manufacture at Philadelphia, 1800–1885* (Cambridge, England: Cambridge University Press, 1983).

31. Thomas Dicke, "Franchising in the American Economy, 1840–1980," Ph.D. diss., Ohio State University, Columbus 1988; this study is a forthcoming publication of the University of North Carolina Press in 1992. On the development of franchising, see also Stan Luxenberg, *Roadside Empires: How the Chains Franchised America* (New York: Viking, 1985), a journalistic account, and Thomas G. Marx, "The Development of the Franchise Distribution System in the U.S. Automobile Industry," *Business History Review* 59 (Autumn 1985): 465–74, a scholarly work.

32. Kurt Mayer, "Small Business as a Social Institution," *Social Research* 14 (March 1947): 349. The question of the socioeconomic backgrounds of small business people and their social mobility has long attracted the attention of scholars; see D. Anderson and P. Davidson, *Occupational Mobility in an American Community* (Stanford, Calif.: Stanford University Press, 1937), and G. F. Lewis, "A Comparison of Some Aspects of the Backgrounds and Careers of Small Businessmen and American Business Leaders," *American Journal of Sociology* 65 (January 1960): 348–55.

33. Joseph Palamountain, Jr., *The Politics of Distribution* (Cambridge, Mass.: Harvard University Press, 1955), 256, 262.

34. Joseph Phillips, *Little Business in the American Economy* (Urbana: University of Illinois Press, 1958), 57, 111.

35. Bunzel, *The American Small Businessman*, and Zeigler, *The Politics of Small Business*.

36. Richard Hamilton, *Restraining Myths: Critical Studies of U.S. Social Structure and Politics* (New York: John Wiley, 1975), 254.

37. Vatter, *Small Enterprise and Oligopoly*, 5.

38. Robert Averitt, *The Dual Economy* (New York: W. W. Norton, 1971); Joseph Bowring, *Competition in the Dual Economy* (Princeton, N.J.: Princeton University Press, 1986), especially chaps. 2 and 3; and

John Kenneth Galbraith, *The Rise of the New Industrial State* (Boston: Houghton Mifflin, 1966).

39.　Jeremy Atack, *Estimations of Economies of Scale in Nineteenth-Century United States Manufacturing* (New York: Garland, 1985); "Firm Size and Industrial Structure in the United States during the Nineteenth Century," *Journal of Economic History* 46 (June 1986): 463–75; and "Industrial Structure and the Emergence of the Modern Industrial Corporation," *Explorations in Economic History* 22 (January 1985): 29–52. But see also John A. James, "Structural Change in American Manufacturing, 1850–1890," *Journal of Economic History* 43 (June 1983): 433–60, and Anthony Patrick O'Brien, "Factory Size, Economies of Scale, and the Great Merger Wave of 1898–1902," *Journal of Economic History* 48 (September 1988): 639–49.

40.　Michael J. Piore and Charles F. Sabel, *The Second Industrial Divide: Possibilities for Prosperity* (New York: Basic Books, 1984), 17. See also Charles F. Sabel and Jonathan Zeitlin, "Historical Alternatives to Mass Production: Politics, Markets, and Technology in Nineteenth-Century Industrialization," *Past and Present* 108 (August 1985): 133–76; this article, dealing mainly with Europe, argues that small industrial firms were able to compete with their larger counterparts until political decisions made in the twentieth century gave an edge to big businesses. For an examination of the continuing importance of small firms as subcontractors, see S. Berger and Michael J. Piore, *Dualism and Discontinuity in Industrial Societies* (Cambridge, England: Cambridge University Press, 1980).

41.　Michael Storper and Susan Christopherson, "Flexible Specialization and Regional Industrial Agglomerations: The Case of the U.S. Motion Picture Company," *Annals of the Association of American Geographers* 77 (March 1987): 104–17; Zoltan J. Acs, "Flexible Specialization Technologies, Innovation, and Small Business," in *Small Business in Regulated Economy*, ed. Richard J. Judd, William T. Greenwood, and Fred W. Becker (Westport, Conn.: Quorum Books, 1988): 41–50; and Bo Carlsson, "The Evolution of Manufacturing Technology and Its Impact on Industrial Structure: An International Study," *Small Business Economics* 1 (1989): 21–37. For more detail on innovation and flexible manufacturing by small firms in the 1970s and 1980s, see Zoltan J. Acs and David B. Audretsch, *Innovation and Small Firms* (Cambridge, Mass.: MIT Press, 1990).

42.　Scranton, *Figured Tapestry*, 3, 6.

43.　See, for example, Steven Soloman, *Small Business USA: The Role of Small Companies in Sparking America's Economic Transformation* (New York: Crown, 1986).

44.　David E. Gumpert, ed., *Growing Concerns: Building and Managing Smaller Businesses* (New York: John Wiley, 1984), 3, 11.

45.　On how scholars have pictured entrepreneurs and entrepreneurship, see Robert F. Hebert and Albert N. Link, *The Entrepreneur:*

Mainstream Views and Radical Critiques (Westport, Conn.: Praeger, 1988). On entrepreneurship and small business, see James Adnor, "The Spirit of Entrepreneurship," *Journal of Small Business Management* 26 (January 1988): 1–4. Historians have also looked at these topics; see, for example, Harold Livesay, "Entrepreneurial Persistence through the Bureaucratic Age," *Business History Review* 51 (Winter 1977): 415–43.

46.   See, for example, Bruce Kirchhoff, Wayne A. Long, W. Ed McMullan, Karl H. Vesper, and William E. Wetzel, Jr., eds., *Frontiers of Entrepreneurship Research* (Wellesley, Mass.: Center for Entrepreneurial Studies, Babson College, 1988).

47.   David Birch, *Job Creation in America: How Our Smallest Companies Put the Most People to Work* (New York: Free Press, 1987).

Chapter 1

1.   Luke Shortfield, *The Western Merchant: A Narrative* (Philadelphia: Grigg, Elliot, 1849), v. Jones used Shortfield as his pen name. A copy of this volume is available in the rare-book room of the Ohio State University library.

2.   Ibid., 25.

3.   For an overview of business development in America to 1850, see Mansel G. Blackford and K. Austin Kerr, *Business Enterprise in American History* (Boston: Houghton Mifflin, 1990), chaps. 1–4.

4.   For an excellent discussion of economic growth in colonial America, see John J. McCusker and Russel R. Menard, *The Economy of British America, 1607–1789* (Chapel Hill: University of North Carolina Press, 1985). See also Edwin Perkins, *The Economy of Colonial America,* 2d ed. (New York: Columbia University Press, 1987), and Gary Walton and James Shepherd, *The Economic Rise of Early America* (Cambridge, England: Cambridge University Press, 1972).

5.   Douglas C. North, in *The Economic Growth of the United States, 1790–1860* (Englewood Cliffs, N.J.: Prentice Hall, 1961), stresses the importance of regional and interregional trade in the development of the United States. Diane Lindstrom, in *Economic Development of the Philadelphia Region, 1810–1850* (New York: Columbia University Press, 1978), emphasizes the significance of local trade between a city and its hinterland. See also Albert Fishlow, *Railroads and the Transformation of the Ante-Bellum Economy* (Cambridge, Mass.: Harvard University Press, 1965); Joseph R. Frese, S. J. Judd, and Jacob Judd, eds., *An Emerging Independent American Economy, 1815–1875* (Tarrytown, N.Y.: Sleepy Hollow Press, 1980); and George Rogers Taylor, *The Transportation Revolution, 1815–1860* (New York: Holt, Rinehart, and Winston, 1951).

6.   Glenn Porter and Harold Livesay, in *Merchants and Manufacturers: Studies in the Changing Structure of Nineteenth-Century Mar-*

keting (Baltimore, Md.: Johns Hopkins University Press, 1971), look at mercantile specialization in the antebellum years.

7. Edwin Perkins, "Who Comprised the 'Business' Sector in Colonial Society? The Foundations of American Entrepreneurship," unpublished paper, 1988. A business historian specializing in the colonial and early national periods, Perkins argues that most colonists were business people and entrepreneurs: "While colonial merchants should clearly be counted among the precursors of subsequent generations of business owners and managers, the singular concentration on this occupational group is too restrictive. As an alternative interpretative approach, I want to advance a much more sweeping proposition—namely that almost every occupational category in colonial society, in fact, qualifies as a legitimate antecedent of the nineteenth-century businessperson. The only notable exceptions were Native Americans, enslaved blacks in rural areas (but not all slaves in urban settings), and the small number of genuinely subsistence farmers in frontier and other remote regions. It follows as a corollary to this general hypothesis that my conception of colonial society reflects a culture permeated with market values and capitalist principles" (5). This paper was subsequently published as Perkins, "The Entrepreneurial Spirit in Colonial America: The Foundations of Modern Business History," *Business History Review* 63 (Spring 1989): 160–86.

8. Alfred D. Chandler, Jr., in *The Visible Hand: The Managerial Revolution in American Business* (Cambridge, Mass.: Harvard University Press, 1977), develops the idea of "throughput" in business.

9. Ibid., chaps. 1 and 2. See also Alfred D. Chandler, Jr., "Anthracite Coal and the Beginnings of the Industrial Revolution in the United States," *Business History Review* 46 (Summer 1972): 141–81.

10. On the business career of Aaron Lopez, see Stanley F. Chyet, *Lopez of Newport: Colonial American Merchant Prince* (Detroit, Mich.: Wayne State University Press, 1970).

11. European trading companies have in fact been seen by some historians as precursors to modern big businesses. See Ann M. Carlos and Stephen Nicholas, " 'Giants of an Earlier Capitalism': The Chartered Trading Companies as Modern Multinationals," *Business History Review* 62 (Autumn 1988): 398–419.

12. Stuart Bruchey, ed., *The Colonial Merchant: Sources and Readings* (New York: Harcourt, Brace, and World, 1966), is a standard work.

13. Fred Mitchell Jones, "Middlemen in the Domestic Trade of the United States, 1800–1860," *Illinois University Studies in the Social Sciences* 21 (1937): 13–15; the quotation is on p. 15.

14. Fred Mitchell Jones, "Retail Stores in the United States, 1800–1860," *Journal of Marketing* 1 (October 1936): 134–42.

15. Jones, "Middlemen in the Domestic Trade," 44.

16. Lewis Atherton, in "The Pioneer Merchant in Mid-

America" (*University of Missouri Studies* 14 [1 April 1939]: 1–135), and
Gerald Carson, in *The Old Country Store* (New York: Oxford University
Press, 1954), offer histories of the country store in America.
    17. John Allen Trimble, "Reminiscences," in John Allen
Trimble Papers (manuscript collection 249, box 7), Ohio Historical Society,
Columbus.
    18. Lewis Atherton, *The Southern Country Store, 1800–1860*
(Baton Rouge: Louisiana State University Press, 1949).
    19. Shortfield, *The Western Merchant*, 62.
    20. Carson, *The Old Country Store*, chap. 5.
    21. *Day Book, General Store, Layfayette, Ohio,* Abraham
Simpson Papers (manuscript collection 713, box 3), Ohio Historical Society,
Columbus.
    22. As quoted in Jones, "Middlemen in the Domestic Trade," 49.
    23. Carson, *The Old Country Store*, chap. 3; Jones, "Middle-
men in the Domestic Trade," 61–63.
    24. Accounts of the history of American agriculture in the
antebellum years include Jeremy Atack and Fred Bateman, *To Their Own
Soil: Agriculture in the Antebellum North* (Ames: Iowa State University
Press, 1987); Clarence Danhof, *Changes in Agriculture: The Northern
United States* (Cambridge, Mass.: Harvard University Press, 1969); and
Paul W. Gates, *The Farmer's Age: Agriculture, 1815–1860* (New York:
Harper and Row, 1960).
    25. McCusker and Menard, *The Economy of British America,*
chap. 14, and Perkins, *The Economy of Colonial America*, chap. 3.
    26. Considerable debate has developed among historians re-
garding just how entrepreneurial and market-oriented colonial and antebellum farmers were or were not. For an introduction to this debate, see
McCusker and Menard, *The Economy of British America*, chap. 14, and
Atack and Bateman, *To Their Own Soil*, chap. 12. For the argument that
most farmers were not primarily market-oriented, see, especially, James A.
Henretta, "Families and Farms: *Mentalite* in Preindustrial America," *Wil-
liam and Mary Quarterly* 35 (January 1978): 3–32, and some of the essays
in Steven Hahn and Jonathan Prude, eds., *The Countryside in the Age of
Capitalist Transformation: Essays in the Social History of Rural America*
(Chapel Hill: University of North Carolina Press, 1985).
    27. T. H. Breen, "Back to Sweat and Toil: Suggestions for the
Study of Agricultural Work in Early America," *Pennsylvania History* 49
(October 1982): 241–58. Breen argues that farmers combined a concern for
profits with membership in their families and communities. Farmers, he
finds, were entrepreneurial in outlook; however, he concludes that their
" 'determined pursuit of profit' occurred within large, extended families. . . . Colonial cultivators tried to obtain the highest possible price when
they sold their produce, and by so doing, they advanced not only their

individual interests and those of their conjugal unit, but also those of future generations that would bear their surnames" (246).

28. Perkins, "Who Comprised the 'Business' Sector in Colonial Society?" 12–16. Percy W. Bidwell and John I. Falconer made much the same argument in their "Pioneering in the Eighteenth Century" (in *History of Agriculture in the United States, 1620–1860* [Washington, D.C.: Carnegie Institution, 1925], 69–83), when they observed, "The pioneer farmer may be compared to a business corporation which pursues a conservative dividend policy. Instead of paying out all of current income to the stockholders, it puts a large share back into the business, thus increasing the value of its capital. The pioneer was engaged in literally 'ploughing in his profits.' The income which he did not take out of his enterprise steadily accrued and was shown in the increased value of his land" (83).

29. Winifred B. Rothenberg, "The Market and Massachusetts Farmers, 1750–1855," *Journal of Economic History* 41 (June 1981): 283–311.

30. Joyce Appleby, "Commercial Farming and the 'Agrarian Myth' in the Early Republic," *Journal of American History* 68 (March 1982): 833–49. On increases in the productivity of American farming in the antebellum years, see the collection of articles in *Agricultural History* 46 (Spring 1972).

31. Atack and Bateman, in *To Their Own Soil*, offer a thorough examination of the economics of northern farming in the late antebellum years; see, especially, chaps. 12–15.

32. Richard D. Heffner, ed., *Democracy in America*, by Alexis de Tocqueville (New York: Mentor, 1956), 216.

33. Appleby, "Commercial Farming." Atack and Bateman in *To Their Own Soil*, make the same point; in fact, on p. 217 they show that in the West, smaller farms produced proportionally more of a surplus than larger farms did.

34. As quoted in Atack and Bateman, *To Their Own Soil*, 204.

35. Danhof, in *Changes in Agriculture*, discusses antebellum farm management in chap. 6. The quotation is from p. 135.

36. Even Atack and Bateman, who argue that American farmers were primarily commercial farmers who were profit-oriented, conclude that nonprofit motives explain some of the actions of the farmers; see their *To Their Own Soil*, 267–74.

37. Daniel Kaufman, *Farm Ledger*, John Kaufman Papers (manuscript collection 737, box 1), Ohio Historical Society, Columbus.

38. On colonial artisans, see Perkins, *The Economy of Colonial America*, chap. 5, and "Who Comprised the 'Business' Sector in Colonial Society?" 10–11.

39. Richard Walsh, "The Revolutionary Charleston Me-

chanic," in *Small Business in American Life,* ed. Stuart Bruchey (New York: Columbia University Press, 1980), 49–80.

40. W. J. Rorabaugh, *The Craft Apprentice: From Franklin to the Machine Age in America* (New York: Oxford University Press, 1986).

41. One exception to this generalization was the production of iron products. Even in the colonial period, large iron "plantations" turned out considerable quantities of iron goods, making colonial America the third-largest producer of iron in the world (after Russia and Sweden) by 1775. See James Mulholland, *A History of Metals in Colonial America* (University: University of Alabama Press, 1981).

42. Thomas C. Cochran, in *Frontiers of Change: Early Industrialism in America* (New York: Oxford University Press, 1981), and David A. Hounshell, in *From the American System to Mass Production: The Development of Manufacturing Technology in the United States* (Baltimore, Md.: Johns Hopkins University Press, 1984), offer different approaches to the Industrial Revolution in America. The figures are in constant dollars.

43. See, especially, Robert Dalzell, Jr., *Enterprising Elite: The Boston Associates and the World They Made* (Cambridge, Mass.: Harvard University Press, 1987). Porter and Livesay, in *Merchants and Manufacturers,* consider the role of merchants in industrialization more generally.

44. Carson, *The Old Country Store,* 23.

45. Gary Kornblith, "The Craftsman as Industrialist: Jonas Chickering and the Transformation of American Piano Making," *Business History Review* 59 (Autumn 1985): 349–68.

46. Martha Taber, "A History of the Cutlery Industry in the Connecticut Valley," *Smith College Studies in History* 41 (1955).

47. Susan E. Hirsch, "From Artisan to Manufacturer: Industrialization and the Small Producer in Newark, 1830–1860," in *Small Business in American Life,* ed. Bruchey, 81–99. For another example of the life and work of artisans in one community, see Steven Joseph Ross, *Workers on the Edge: Work, Leisure, and Politics in Industrializing Cincinnati, 1788–1890* (New York: Columbia University Press, 1985).

48. Jeremy Atack, "Firm Size and Industrial Structure in the United States during the Nineteenth Century," *Journal of Economic History* 46 (June 1986): 463–75. The figures are from p. 470 and are in 1820 dollars.

49. Jeremy Atack, *Estimation of Economies of Scale in Nineteenth Century United States Manufacturing* (New York: Garland, 1985), especially 177–79. See also Kenneth Sokoloff, "Was the Transition from the Artisan Shop to the Non-mechanized Factory Associated with Gains in Efficiency? Evidence from the U.S. Manufacturing Censuses of 1820 and 1850," *Explorations in Economic History* 21 (October 1984): 351–82. Sokoloff estimates that in most antebellum nonmechanized factories, full economies of scale were realized when employment reached about 15 persons per

establishment. In mechanized plants, such as the factories making cotton textiles, scale economies were exhausted when employment reached about 150 persons per plant.

50. Dorothy I. Riddle, in *Service-led Growth: The Role of the Service Sector in World Development* (New York: Praeger, 1986), provides a provocative discussion on the importance of service businessess to economic development. See especially chap. 2.

51. Vincent P. Carosso, in *Investment Banking in America: A History* (Cambridge, Mass.: Harvard University Press, 1970), Benjamin J. Klebaner, in *Commercial Banking in the United States: A History* (Hinsdale, Ill.: Dryden Press, 1974), and Edwin Perkins, in *Financing Anglo-American Trade: The House of Brown, 1800–1880* (Cambridge, Mass.: Harvard University Press, 1975), offer solid introductions to the history of banking in America.

52. Morton Keller, in *The Life Insurance Enterprise, 1885–1910* (Cambridge, Mass.: Harvard University Press, 1963), chap. 1, offers a good introduction to the early history of life insurance in America.

53. James H. Madison, "The Evolution of Credit Reporting Agencies in Nineteenth-Century America," *Business History Review* 48 (Summer 1974): 164–86.

54. Naomi Lamoreaux, "Banks, Kinship, and Economic Development: The New England Case," *Journal of Economic History* 46 (September 1986): 647–67.

55. U.S. Bureau of the Census, *Historical Statistics of the United States, Colonial Times to 1957* (Washington, D.C.: U.S. Government Printing Office, 1960), 624.

56. Richard Hofstadter, *The American Political Tradition* (New York: Knopf, 1948), chap. 3.

57. Heffner, ed., *Democracy in America*, 254–55.

58. Mansel G. Blackford, *The Rise of Modern Business in Great Britain, the United States, and Japan* (Chapel Hill: University of North Carolina Press, 1988), 74, 85.

59. Atherton, "The Pioneer Merchant," 23–30; Carson, *The Old Country Store*, 122–23.

60. Shortfield, *The Western Merchant*, v–vi.

61. For a provocative discussion of the ideology of small business in America, see Rowland Berthoff, "Independence and Enterprise: Small Business in the American Dream," in *Small Business in American Life*, ed. Bruchey, 28–48.

62. Laurel Thatcher Ulrich, *Good Wives: Images and Reality in the Lives of Women in Northern New England, 1650–1750* (New York: Knopf, 1980).

63. Caroline Bird, *Enterprising Women* (New York: W. W. Norton, 1976), chap. 4.

64. Loren Schweninger, "Prosperous Blacks in the South, 1790–1880," *American Historical Review* 95 (February 1990): 31–56, and Juliet E. K. Walker, "Racism, Slavery, and Free Enterprise: Black Entrepreneurship in the United States before the Civil War," *Business History Review* 60 (Autumn 1986): 343–82.
65. Drew McCoy, in *The Elusive Republic: Political Economy in Jeffersonian America* (Chapel Hill: University of North Carolina Press, 1980), explores the relationships between economic growth and the development of ideas in the early United States.
66. Atack and Bateman, in *To Their Own Soil*, chap. 6, offer a detailed discussion of wealth holding in antebellum America.
67. As quoted in McCoy, *The Elusive Republic*, 12.

Chapter 2

1. Marcia Davenport, *The Valley of Decision* (New York: Scribner's, 1942), 20. This quotation was brought to my attention by John I. Ingham, *Making Iron and Steel: Independent Mills in Pittsburgh, 1820–1920* (Columbus: Ohio State University Press, 1991).
2. Spurgeon Bell, *Productivity, Wages, and National Income* (Washington, D.C.: Brookings Institute, 1940), 10. These figures are for gainfully employed workers and exclude self-employed farmers and professionals. Big businesses emerged in railroads even before they did in industry, as early as the 1850s. But because almost no railroads were small businesses, except in the very early days, they are not considered in this study.
3. Samuel P. Hays, in *The Response to Industrialism, 1885–1914* (Chicago: University of Chicago Press, 1957), and Robert H. Wiebe, in *The Search for Order, 1877–1920* (New York: Hill and Wang, 1967), offer solid introductions to the social and economic transformation of the United States. The figures are in constant dollars.
4. Offering different perspectives on the importance of the railroad to nineteenth-century America are Robert William Fogel, *Railroads and American Economic Growth: Essays in Econometric History* (Baltimore, Md.: Johns Hopkins University Press, 1964); Leo Marx, *The Machine in the Garden: Technology and the Pastoral Ideal in America* (New York: Oxford University Press, 1964); and Bruce Mazlish, ed., *The Railroad and the Space Program: An Exploration in Historical Analogy* (Cambridge, Mass.: MIT Press, 1965).
5. David A. Hounshell, *From the American System to Mass Production, 1800–1932: The Development of Manufacturing Technology in the United States* (Baltimore, Md.: Johns Hopkins University Press, 1984), and Howard Mumford Jones, *The Age of Energy: Varieties of American Experience, 1865–1915* (New York: Viking Press, 1970).

6. For an overview of the rise of big business, see Mansel G. Blackford and K. Austin Kerr, *Business Enterprise in American History* (Boston: Houghton Mifflin, 1990), chap. 5. Alfred D. Chandler, Jr.'s *The Visible Hand: The Managerial Revolution in American Business* (Cambridge, Mass.: Harvard University Press, 1877), chap. 8, is the classic statement on these connections. But see also Jeremy Atack, "Industrial Structure and the Emergence of the Modern Industrial Corporation," *Explorations in Economic History* 22 (January 1985): 29–52. Atack shows that these imperatives led to alterations only in certain key industries, the same ones that Chandler argues changed the most. In many fields, Atack illustrates, changes in factory size were not great and were due less to the transportation and technological changes that occurred in the late nineteenth century than to alterations already taking place in America's business environment between 1850 and 1870. "In most industries [those other than the ones Chandler analyzes]," Atack concludes, "the industrial structure which had emerged by 1900 was one which could have resulted from the long-run equilibrium adjustment of plants to conditions which had existed in 1870" (50). John A. James, in "Structural Change in American Manufacturing, 1850–1890" (*Journal of Economic History* 43 [June 1983]: 433–59), while accepting Chandler's major findings, also cautions against drawing too close a connection between technological changes and the rise of big business.

7. On the merger movement, see, especially, Naomi R. Lamoreaux, *The Great Merger Movement in American Business, 1895–1904* (Cambridge, England: Cambridge University Press, 1985), and Anthony Patrick O' Brien, "Factory Size, Economies of Scale, and the Great Merger Wave of 1898–1902," *Journal of Economic History* 48 (September 1988): 639–49.

8. Thomas Navin, "The 500 Largest American Industrials in 1917," *Business History Review* 44 (Autumn 1970): 360–84; Chandler, *The Visible Hand*, 346–47.

9. Bell, *Productivity, Wages, and National Income*, 10.

10. On the development of accounting, see, especially, H. Thomas Johnson and Robert S. Kaplan, *Relevance Lost: The Rise and Fall of Management Accounting* (Boston: Harvard Business School Press, 1987).

11. Ellis W. Hawley, in his conclusion to *The New Deal and the Problem of Monopoly* (Princeton, N.J.: Princeton University Press, 1966), presents a valuable overview of American attitudes toward big business.

12. This account of public attitudes is derived from Louis Galambos (with the assistance of Barbara Barrow Spence), *The Public Image of Big Business in America, 1880–1940* (Baltimore, Md.: Johns Hopkins University Press, 1975), chaps. 3–5. Galambos samples periodicals aimed at professionals (engineers and Protestant clergy), skilled workers, and farmers to derive public attitudes.

13. See Thomas Dicke, "The Public Image of Small Business Portrayed in the American Periodical Press, 1900–1938," master's thesis, Ohio State University, 1983, chap. 1.

14. On law and the rise of big business, see Martin J. Sklar, *The Corporate Reorganization of American Capitalism, 1890–1916: The Market, the Law, and Politics* (New York: Cambridge University Press, 1988), especially chap. 3.

15. Thomas K. McCraw, *Prophets of Regulation* (Cambridge, Mass.: Harvard University Press, 1984), 115.

16. McCraw, *Prophets*, 124–25, and Sklar, *The Corporate Reorganization*, chap. 4.

17. Offering different perspectives on the origins of the Federal Reserve System are James Livingston, *Origins of the Federal Reserve System: Money, Class, and Corporate Capitalism, 1890–1913* (Ithaca, N.Y.: Cornell University Press, 1986); Robert Craig West, *Banking Reform and the Federal Reserve, 1863–1923* (Ithaca, N.Y.: Cornell University Press, 1977); and Eugene Nelson White, *The Regulation and Reform of the American Banking System, 1900–1929* (Princeton, N.J.: Princeton University Press, 1983).

18. Mansel G. Blackford, *The Politics of Business in California, 1890–1920* (Columbus: Ohio State University Press, 1977), chap. 6.

19. James, "Structural Change in American Manufacturing," 433, 435; Harold G. Vatter, "The Position of Small Business in the Structure of American Manufacturing, 1870–1970," in *Small Business in American Life*, ed. Stuart Bruchey (New York: Columbia University Press, 1980), 142–68; and David Brody, "Labor and Small-Scale Enterprise during Industrialization," in *Small Business in American Life*, ed. Bruchey, 263–80.

20. Brody, "Labor and Small-Scale Enterprise," 264.

21. James Soltow, "Structure and Strategy: The Small Manufacturing Enterprise in the Modern Industrial Economy," in *Business and Its Environment: Essays for Thomas C. Cochran*, ed. Harold Isadore Sharlin (Westport, Conn.: Greenwood Press, 1983), 81–99, and Harold G. Vatter, *Small Enterprise and Oligopoly: A Study of the Butter, Flour, Automobile, and Glass Container Industries* (Corvallis: Oregon State University Press, 1955).

22. Vatter, *Small Enterprise and Oligopoly*, chap. 3.

23. Steven Fraser, "Combined and Uneven Development in the Men's Clothing Industry," *Business History Review* 57 (Winter 1983): 522–47.

24. Charles Sabel and Jonathan Zeitlin, in "Historical Alternatives to Mass Production: Politics, Markets, and Technology in Nineteenth-Century Industrialization" (*Past and Present* 108 [August 1985]: 131–76), look mainly at the roles of small business in European industrialization, but the article is suggestive as well about the course of events in the United

States. The authors argue that flexible small businesses generally succeeded in competition with larger manufacturing concerns well into the twentieth century, and that they declined in importance only when political decisions favoring big businesses placed them at an overwhelming disadvantage.

25. This account of the history of the textile industry in the nineteenth century is derived primarily from Philip Scranton, *Proprietary Capitalism: The Textile Manufacture at Philadelphia, 1800–1885* (Cambridge, England: Cambridge University Press, 1983). But see also Robert Dalzell, Jr., *Enterprising Elite: The Boston Associates and the World They Made* (Cambridge, Mass.: Harvard University Press, 1987), and Anthony Wallace, *Rockdale: The Growth of an American Village in the Early Industrial Revolution* (New York: Knopf, 1978).

26. As quoted in Scranton, *Proprietary Capitalism,* 3.

27. This account of the textile industry after the 1880s is derived from Philip Scranton, *Figured Tapestry: Production, Markets, and Power in Philadelphia Textiles, 1885–1941* (Cambridge, England: Cambridge University Press, 1989).

28. The following discussion of the iron and steel industries in Pittsburgh comes from Ingham, *Making Iron and Steel.*

29. The following account of Buckeye Steel's development is taken from Mansel G. Blackford, *A Portrait Cast in Steel: Buckeye International and Columbus, Ohio, 1881–1980* (Westport, Conn.: Greenwood Press, 1982).

30. Mansel G. Blackford, "Scientific Management and Welfare Work in Early Twentieth Century American Business: The Buckeye Steel Castings Company," *Ohio History* 90 (Summer 1981): 239–58.

31. Theodore Marburg, *Small Business in Brass Fabricating: The Smith and Griggs Manufacturing Co. of Waterbury* (New York: New York University Press, 1956).

32. Blackford, *A Portrait Cast in Steel,* 67.

33. Amos J. Loveday, Jr., *The Rise and Decline of the American Cut Nail Industry: A Study of the Interrelationships of Technology, Business Organization, and Management Techniques* (Westport, Conn.: Greenwood Press, 1983).

34. Blackford, *A Portrait Cast in Steel,* 56–57.

35. For another example of this attitude, see Michael W. Santos, "Laboring on the Periphery: Managers and Workers at the A. M. Byers Company, 1900–1956," *Business History Review* 61 (Spring 1987): 113–33.

36. John L. Shover, in *First Majority—Last Minority: The Transforming of Rural Life in America* (De Kalb: Northern Illinois University Press, 1976), chap. 6, offers an excellent explanation of the rise of agribusiness in the United States.

37. Bell, *Productivity, Wages, and National Income,* 10.

38. U.S. Bureau of the Census, *Historical Statistics of the United States, Colonial Times to 1957* (Washington, D.C.: U.S. Government Printing Office, 1960), 278–79. Fred A. Shannon, in *The Farmer's Last Frontier: Agriculture, 1860–1897* (New York: Harper and Row, 1968), chap. 15, offers a solid survey of the changing place of agriculture in the American economy. Allan G. Bogue, in *From Prairie to Cornbelt: Farming on the Illinois and Iowa Prairies in the Nineteenth Century* (Chicago: University of Chicago Press, 1963), presents an excellent regional study. Articles in *Agricultural History* 49 (January 1975) and 51 (January 1977) examine the development, respectively, of farming in the far West and on the Great Plains.

39. As quoted in David B. Danbom, *Resisted Revolution: Urban America and the Industrialization of Agriculture, 1900–1930* (Ames: Iowa State University Press, 1979), 20.

40. U.S. Bureau of the Census, *Historical Statistics*, 281, 285. Shannon, in *Farmer's Last Frontier*, chap. 7, surveys farm mechanization. For more detail, see R. Douglas Hurt, *American Farm Tools: From Hand-Power to Steampower* (Manhattan, Kans.: Sunflower University Press, 1982), and Lester Love, "Empirical Estimates of Technological Change in United States Agriculture, 1850–1958," *Journal of Farm Economics* 44 (November 1962): 941–52.

41. As they became more and more entwined in the market economy, farmers complained of other economic problems. What they perceived to be high and discriminatory railroad rates and elevator charges outraged them, even though the fees were often justified, given the risks involved. Farm mortgage rates also become a burning issue, as a growing proportion of farms carried liens. By 1890, about 30% of the nation's farms were mortgaged, though to only about 35% of their value. For a brief introduction to the changing economic situation of American farmers in the late nineteenth century, see Douglass C. North, *Growth and Welfare in the American Past* (Englewood Cliffs, N.J.: Prentice Hall, 1966), chap. 11. See also H. Peers Brewer, "Eastern Money and Western Mortgages in the 1870s," *Business History Review* 50 (Autumn 1976): 356–80; Gilbert Fite, "Daydreams and Nightmares: The Late Nineteenth Century Agricultural Frontier," *Agricultural History* 40 (October 1966): 285–93; Rodman Paul, "The Wheat Trade between California and the United Kingdom," *Mississippi Valley Historical Review* 45 (December 1958): 391–412; and Morton Rothstein, "America in the International Rivalry for the British Wheat Market, 1860–1914," *Mississippi Valley Historical Review* 47 (December 1960): 401–18.

42. Danbom, in *Resisted Revolution*, chap. 1, presents a compelling picture of agriculture in 1900. Danbom argues, "Despite the changes in land supply, despite commercialization, technological innovation, and industrialism, American rural life in 1900 was in broad outline similar to

what it had always been" (4). Shover, in *First Majority–Last Minority,* makes much the same point, observing, "The traditional ways soil was made to yield up its products for human consumption, either directly, or indirectly through feeding to animals, [were] little different in 1920 than they were in 1820" (115).

43. Shannon, *The Farmer's Last Frontier,* 3–5. Shannon notes that, while willing to work with neighbors on short-term tasks or projects, most farmers were in the end individualists. "But each time an end was gained or definitely lost," Shannon writes, "he [the farmer] slipped back into his wonted habit of dependence on himself and nature" (3–4).

44. As quoted in Danbom, *Resisted Revolution,* 22. On the thought of agriculturalists, see also George McGovern, ed., *Agricultural Thought in the Twentieth Century* (New York: Bobbs-Merrill, 1967).

45. This account of Lewis McMillen's life comes from Wheeler McMillen, *Ohio Farm* (Columbus: Ohio State University Press, 1974). For a similar firsthand account of family farming in western Kansas on the Great Plains, see John Ise, *Sod and Stubble* (Lincoln: University of Nebraska Press, 1936).

46. McMillen, *Ohio Farm,* 117.

47. Ibid., 218.

48. Ibid., 149.

49. Earl W. Hayter, in *The Troubled Farmer, 1850–1900: Rural Adjustment to Industrialism* (De Kalb: Northern Illinois University Press, 1968), presents a fascinating look at farming practices and thoughts. The quotation is from p. 7.

50. Danbom, *Resisted Revolution.*

51. As quoted in Shannon, *The Farmer's Last Frontier,* 158–59.

52. U.S. Bureau of the Census, *Historical Statistics,* 279.

53. Shannon, in *The Farmer's Last Frontier,* chap. 14, offers a concise overview of the origins of the cooperative movement.

54. Blackford, *The Politics of Business in California,* chap. 2. California growers also worked through farm organizations and politics to try to improve the quality of their fruits and vegetables, thus increasing their prices. In these endeavors they were viewed as all too successful by urbanites, who complained vehemently about the high cost of food and who formed their own groups to work through politics to lower food costs in the Golden State.

55. U.S. Bureau of the Census, *Historical Statistics,* 518, 520, 524.

56. Chandler, *The Visible Hand,* chap. 7.

57. U.S. Bureau of the Census, *Historical Statistics,* 523. See also Joseph Cornwall Palamountain, Jr., *The Politics of Distribution* (Cambridge, Mass.: Harvard University Press, 1955), 61.

58. Stanley C. Hollander, "The Effects of Industrialization on

Small Retailing in the United States in the Twentieth Century," in *Small Business in American Life,* ed. Bruchey, 217–18.

59.   Gerald Carson, *The Old Country Store* (New York: Oxford University Press, 1954), 279.

60.   James H. Madison, "The Evolution of Credit Reporting Agencies in Nineteenth-Century America," *Business History Review* 48 (Summer 1974): 182.

61.   U.S. Bureau of the Census, *Historical Statistics,* 672.

62.   H. Roger Grant, *Life Insurance Reform: Consumer Action in the Progressive Era* (Ames: Iowa State University Press, 1979), and Morton Keller, *The Life Insurance Enterprise, 1885–1910* (Cambridge, Mass.: Harvard University Press, 1964).

63.   Benjamin J. Klebaner's *American Commercial Banking* (Boston: Twayne Publishers, 1990), is a short, readable account; see also Richard Sylla, "American Banking and Growth in the Nineteenth Century: A Partial View of the Terrain," *Explorations in Economic History* 9 (Winter 1971–72): 195–227. State studies are Blackford, *The Politics of Business in California,* chap. 6, and Walter L. Buenger and Joseph A. Pratt, *But Also Good Business: Texas Commercial Banks and the Financing of Houston and Texas, 1886–1986* (College Station: Texas A & M Press, 1986).

64.   U.S. Bureau of the Census, *Historical Statistics,* 631.

65.   As quoted in Richard Sylla, "Small-Business Banking in the United States, 1780–1920," in *Small Business in American Life,* ed. Bruchey, 253.

66.   U.S. Bureau of the Census, *Historical Statistics,* 635.

67.   Vincent P. Carosso's *Investment Banking in America: A History* (Cambridge, Mass.: Harvard University Press, 1970), offers an excellent introduction to the history of investment banking in the United States. See also Dolores Greenberg, *Financiers and Railroads, 1869–1889: A Study of Morton, Bliss & Company* (London and Toronto: University of Delaware Press, 1980).

68.   Vincent P. Carosso, in *The Morgans: Private International Bankers* (Cambridge, Mass.: Harvard University Press, 1987), chap. 12, provides a valuable look at the inside workings of the House of Morgan. Carosso concludes that even on the eve of World War I, "at a time when banking, like business generally, was growing rapidly in size and becoming impersonal in character and heavily bureaucratic and hierarchical in structure, the Morgan firms remained loosely organized old-style private banks" (458).

69.   Until quite recently most economists have viewed the development of big businesses as inevitable and as leading to progress. See Joseph A. Schumpeter, *Capitalism, Socialism, and Democracy* (New York: Harper and Brothers, 1942); John Kenneth Galbraith, *The New Industrial State* (Boston: Houghton Mifflin, 1967); Robert Averitt, *The Dual Econ-*

omy (New York: W. W. Norton, 1971); and Joseph Bowring, *Competition in a Dual Economy* (Princeton, N.J.: Princeton University Press, 1986).

70. Chandler, *The Visible Hand,* especially part 5.

71. Another difference between small and large firms may have been in their actions with regard to research and development. Having more resources, large industrial companies were more apt to establish research laboratories. Yet whether these actions meant that the large companies were more innovative than the smaller ones is debatable; large firms often appear to have established the laboratories as a part of their general efforts to control their markets. See, for example, Leonard Reich, *The Making of American Industrial Research: Science and Business at GE and Bell, 1876–1926* (New York: Cambridge University Press, 1985). While no comprehensive studies of innovation at small firms exist for the years 1880–1920, studies of later periods show that small industrial firms have been at least as innovative as larger ones. For an introduction to this topic, see Zoltan J. Acs and David B. Audretsch, "Innovation in Large and Small Firms: An Empirical Analysis," *American Economic Review* 78 (September 1988): 678–90.

72. Chandler, *The Visible Hand,* 371–72.

73. Clyde and Sally Griffen, "Small Business and Occupational Mobility in Mid-Nineteenth-Century Poughkeepsie," in *Small Business in American Life,* ed. Bruchey, 126–27. Of those businesses whose worth was evaluated by the credit reporters, most were small businesses: 42% were worth less than $1000; 38%, between $1001 and $10,000; and 20%, more than $10,000. These mortality rates are comparable to those in later years. Gillette Hutchinson, Arthur R. Hutchinson, and Mabel Newcomer, in "A Study in Business Mortality: The Life of Business Enterprises in Poughkeepsie, New York, 1843–1936" (*American Economic Review* 28 [September 1938]: 497–514), show that over nearly a century, few businesses lasted beyond three years (some of these firms may actually have lasted longer, however—reorganized under new names).

74. Frances W. Gregory and Irene D. Neu, "The American Industrial Elite in the 1870s: Their Social Origins," in *Men in Business,* ed. William Miller (New York: Harper and Row, 1952), 193–211, and William Miller, "The Business Elite in Business Bureaucracies: Careers of Top Executives in the Early Twentieth Century," in *Men in Business,* ed. Miller, 286–305.

75. While a fair amount of research has now been conducted about women's participation in America's labor force during the late nineteenth and early twentieth centuries, relatively little has been done on their roles in business management during this period. But see Caroline Bird, *Enterprising Women* (New York: W. W. Norton, 1976), and Susan Porter Benson, *Counter Cultures: Saleswomen, Managers, and Customers in American Department Stores, 1890–1940* (Urbana: University of Illinois Press, 1986).

76. Ivan H. Light, *Ethnic Enterprise: Business and Welfare among Chinese, Japanese, and Blacks* (Berkeley: University of California Press, 1972). See also Scott Cummings, ed., *Self-Help in Urban America: Patterns of Minority Economic Development* (Port Washington, N.Y.: Kennikat Press, 1980).

77. J. H. Harmon, Jr., Arnett G. Lindsay, and Carter G. Woodson, *The Negro as a Businessman* (College Park, Md.: McGrath, 1929), 29–36.

78. Light, *Ethnic Enterprise*, especially chaps. 3 and 8. On blacks in business during the late nineteenth and early twentieth centuries, see also Harmon, Lindsay, and Woodson, *The Negro as Business Man;* Abram Harris, *The Negro as Capitalist: A Study of Banking and Business among American Negroes* (New York: Negro Universities Press, 1936); Alexa Benson Henderson, "Herman E. Perry and Black Enterprise in Atlanta, 1908–1925," *Business History Review* 61 (Summer 1987): 216–42; and Walter Weare, *Black Business in the New South: A Social History of the North Carolina Mutual Insurance Company* (Urbana: University of Illinois Press, 1973).

79. Thomas S. Dicke, "Franchising in the American Economy, 1840–1980," Ph.D. diss., Ohio State University, Columbus, 1988, chap. 2 (a forthcoming publication of the University of North Carolina Press in 1992).

80. Robert Wiebe's *Search For Order* (New York: Hill and Wang, 1967) provides a classic analysis of this transformation.

81. Louis Galambos, "The Emerging Organizational Synthesis in Modern American History," *Business History Review* 44 (Autumn 1970): 279–90, and "Technology, Political Economy, and Professionalization: Central Themes of the Organizational Synthesis," *Business History Review* 57 (Winter 1983): 471–93.

82. James H. Soltow, "Small City Industrialists in the Age of Organization," *Business History Review* 33 (Summer 1959): 178–89.

83. Blackford, *The Politics of Business in California*.

84. Palamountain, *The Politics of Distribution*, 94.

Chapter 3

1. John H. Bunzel, in *The American Small Businessman* (New York: Knopf, 1962), 3–8, presents a vivid account of the conference. See also Harmon Zeigler, *The Politics of Small Business* (Washington, D.C.: Public Affairs Press, 1961), 17.

2. Louis Galambos (with the assistance of Barbara Barrow Spence), *The Public Image of Big Business in America, 1880–1940* (Baltimore, Md.: Johns Hopkins University Press, 1975), chaps. 7–9. Surveying American attitudes in the late 1930s, Galambos concludes: "The values and

attitudes of the new culture clearly emerged intact from the 1930s. By that time most Americans saw antitrust as a dead or dying issue. They were coming to accept—in varying degrees—a different outlook embodying modern organizational norms and a new image of the large corporation. . . . By 1940 the corporate culture had largely supplanted the individualistic-egalitarian outlook characteristic of the nineteenth century. The era of the organization man had begun" (249).

3. As quoted in Richard Hofstadter, "What Happened to the Antitrust Movement?" in *The Paranoid Style in American Politics and Other Essays*, ed. Hofstadter (New York: Knopf, 1966), 222.

4. Ibid., 213.

5. William H. Whyte, Jr., *The Organization Man* (New York: Simon and Schuster, 1956), 130.

6. Thomas Dicke, "The Public Image of Small Business Portrayed in the American Periodical Press, 1900–1938," master's thesis, Ohio State University, Columbus, 1983, chaps. 2–3.

7. Bunzel, *The American Small Businessman*, vii, 127.

8. *Colliers*, 20 July 1938, 58, as quoted in Dicke, "The Public Image of Small Business," 73–74.

9. Daniel Beaver, "Newton Baker and the Genesis of the War Industries Board, 1917–1918," *Journal of American History*, 52 (June 1965): 43–58, and Robert D. Cuff, *The War Industries Board: Business-Government Relations during World War I* (Baltimore, Md.: Johns Hopkins University Press, 1973).

10. Robert D. Cuff and Melvin Urofsky, "The Steel Industry and Price-Fixing during World War I," *Business History Review* 44 (Autumn 1970): 291–306; Robert H. Himmelberg, "The War Industries Board and the Anti-Trust Question in November, 1918," *Journal of American History* 52 (June 1965): 59–74; and Melvin Urofsky, *Big Steel and the Wilson Administration: A Study in Business-Government Relations* (Columbus: Ohio State University Press, 1969).

11. See, for instance, K. Austin Kerr, *American Railroad Politics, 1914–1920: Rates, Wages, and Efficiency* (Pittsburgh: University of Pittsburgh Press, 1968).

12. Guy Alchon, *The Invisible Hand of Planning: Capitalism, Social Science, and the State in the 1920s* (Princeton, N.J.: Princeton University Press, 1985); William Barber, *From New Era to New Deal: Herbert Hoover, the Economists, and American Economic Policy, 1921–1933* (Cambridge, England: Cambridge University Press, 1989); Ellis Hawley, "Herbert Hoover, the Commerce Secretariat, and the Vision of an Associative State, 1921–1928," *Journal of American History* 61 (June 1974): 116–40; Robert H. Himmelberg, *The Origins of the National Recovery Administration: Business, Government, and the Trade Association Issue, 1921–1933* (New York: Fordam University Press, 1976); and Evan Metcalf, "Secretary

Hoover and the Emergence of Macroeconomic Management," *Business History Review* 49 (Spring 1975): 60–80.

13. M. Browning Carrott, "The Supreme Court and American Trade Associations, 1921–1925," *Business History Review* 44 (Autumn 1970): 320–38, and William G. Robbins, "Voluntary Cooperation vs. Regulatory Paternalism: The Lumber Trade in the 1920s," *Business History Review* 56 (Autumn 1982): 358–79.

14. Spurgeon Bell, *Productivity, Wages, and National Income* (Washington, D.C.: Brookings Institute, 1940), 10, and Joseph D. Phillips, *Little Business in the American Economy* (Urbana: University of Illinois Press, 1958), 4–5.

15. Ellis Hawley, "Three Facets of Hooverian Associationalism: Lumber, Aviation, and Movies, 1921–1930," in *Regulation in Perspective*, ed. Thomas K. McCraw (Cambridge, Mass.: Harvard University Press, 1981), 95–123, and David Lee, "Herbert Hoover and the Development of Commercial Aviation, 1921–1926," *Business History Review* 58 (Spring 1984): 78–102.

16. Mansel G. Blackford and K. Austin Kerr, *Business Enterprise in American History* (Boston: Houghton Mifflin, 1990), 321. Peter Fearon, in *War, Prosperity, and Depression: The U.S. Economy, 1917–45* (Lawrence: University of Kansas Press, 1987), chaps. 5–15, offers an excellent economic analysis of the Great Depression. See also Michael Bernstein, *The Great Depression: Delayed Recovery and Economic Change in America, 1929–1939* (Cambridge, England: Cambridge University Press, 1987).

17. Gerald Nash, "Experiments in Industrial Mobilization: WIB and NRA," *Mid-America* 45 (July 1963): 157–76.

18. Ellis Hawley's *The New Deal and the Problem of Monopoly* (Princeton, N.J.: Princeton University Press, 1966), part 1, is the standard history of the NRA.

19. But see Donald R. Brand, *Corporatism and the Rule of Law: A Study of the National Recovery Administration* (Ithaca, N.Y.: Cornell University Press, 1988), for a more positive assessment. The NRA dealt mainly with the industrial and service sectors of the nation's economy. Congress passed the Agricultural Adjustment Act (AAA) in 1933 to help farmers. As with the NIRA, the benefits of the AAA flowed primarily to the better established business people—in this case, landowning farmers. Tenant farmers, especially if they were members of minority groups, benefited little from the AAA or other federal farm policies in the 1930s.

20. U.S. Temporary National Economic Committee (TNEC), "Problems of Small Business," monograph no. 17 (Washington, D.C.: U.S. Government Printing Office, 1941), 342–43. See also Phillips, *Little Business*, 101–3. Of the $450 million in loans authorized by the RFC between 1932 and 1939, less than 4% were for loans of under $10,000 and only about 30% were for loans of under $100,000.

21. U.S. TNEC, "Problems of Small Business," 139.

22. Robert M. Collins, in *The Business Response to Keynes, 1929–1964* (New York: Columbia University Press, 1981), chaps. 2–3, provides an excellent analysis of changes in government-business relations. Roosevelt never gave up completely on big business. For instance, in 1933, at the instigation of his Department of Commerce, a group of big business leaders formed the Business Council, an organization that played important roles in business legislation throughout the 1930s and beyond. See also Kim McQuaid, *Big Business and Presidential Power: From FDR to Reagan* (New York: Morrow, 1982), chap. 1.

23. Gene Gressley, "Thurmond Arnold, Antitrust, and the New Deal," *Business History Review* 38 (Summer 1964): 214–31, and Wilson Miscamble, "Thurmond Arnold Goes to Washington: A Look at Antitrust Policy in the Later New Deal," *Business History Review* 56 (Spring 1982): 1–15.

24. Zeigler, *The Politics of Small Business,* 81.

25. As quoted in Bunzel, *The American Small Businessman,* 65.

26. Phillips, *Little Business,* 4.

27. Ibid., 57.

28. U.S. TNEC, "Problems of Small Business," 66.

29. Joseph Steindle, "Small and Big Business: Economic Problems of the Size of Firms," in *The Survival of Small Business,* ed. Vincent P. Carosso and Stuart Bruchey (New York: Arno Press, 1979), 40. Many small businesses—those not organized as corporations—are omitted from these figures, but the study reported by Steindle is nonetheless highly suggestive of the problems small firms faced.

30. U.S. TNEC, "Problems of Small Business," 7.

31. Ibid., chaps. 2–3 summarize the studies in detail.

32. Ibid., xix.

33. Harold G. Vatter, *The U.S. Economy in World War II* (New York: Columbia University Press, 1985), chap. 3; the quotation is from p. 58. See also Jim F. Heath, "American War Mobilization and the Use of Small Manufacturers, 1939–1943," *Business History Review* 46 (Autumn, 1972): 295–319. Heath observes, "In sum, the Roosevelt administration's policy for the use of small business during World War II paralleled the position occupied by small business in America at the time. Big business, because of its know-how and resources, was essential for winning the war. But small business was symbolically important and could not be completely ignored" (318).

34. As quoted in Heath, "American War Mobilization," 298. The SWPC was somewhat more successful than the SWPD in aiding small businesses. By the end of 1944, the SWPC had approved 3,174 loan applications, totaling $256 million. Of these loans, however, only 427 were for $5,000 or less—just 14% of the total. While these loans helped, they were

still inadequate in meeting the needs of small business owners. On the loans, see Phillips, *Little Business*, 105.

35. Vatter, *The U.S. Economy*, 60.

36. As quoted in Zeigler, *The Politics of Small Business*, 96.

37. Vatter, *The U.S. Economy*, 67.

38. Ibid., 61. See also Harold G. Vatter, "The Position of Small Business in the Structure of American Manufacturing, 1870–1970," in *Small Business in American Life*, ed. Stuart Bruchey (New York: Columbia University Press, 1980), 155, and Steindle, "Small and Big Business," 48–49. Of course, some successful small firms were also growing in size and, as time progressed, showing up in the statistics as big businesses. Whatever the reason, America increasingly became the home of big business. Yet not all industrial fields experienced increased concentration. In aircraft manufacturing, for instance, there was little change in the relationship between small and big businesses during the war. See Otto H. Reichardt, "Industrial Concentration and World War II: A Note on the Aircraft Industry," *Business History Review* 49 (Winter 1975): 498–503.

39. Vatter, *The U.S. Economy*, 66, and "The Position of Small Business," 155.

40. U.S. TNEC, "Problems of Small Business," 241.

41. For a summary of the changes occurring in America's postwar economy, see Blackford and Kerr, *Business Enterprise in American History*, chaps. 10–11.

42. On American business in the postwar global marketplace, see Mansel G. Blackford, *The Rise of Modern Business in Great Britain, the United States, and Japan* (Chapel Hill: University of North Carolina Press, 1988), chaps. 7–8.

43. As quoted in Blackford and Kerr, *Business Enterprise in American History*, 393. For a case study, however, see Donald J. Mrozek, "The Truman Administration and the Enlistment of the Aviation Industry in Postwar Defense," *Business History Review* 48 (Spring 1974): 73–94. Mrozek shows that smaller firms were among the most vocal advocates of government spending for the aerospace industry: "Local interest groups and smaller businessmen, who were vastly less concerned [than their larger competitors] with theories of national security and whose financial expectations were less sanguine than those of the major aircraft industrialists, contributed significantly to the achievement of Truman's defense objectives" (88).

44. James L. Clayton, ed., *The Economic Impact of the Cold War: Sources and Readings* (New York: Harcourt, Brace, and World, 1970), 138–39. In the same year, 370 large businesses (each employing more than 1,000 workers) received all but $190 million of the $5.1 billion in contracts.

45. Mark H. Rose, *Interstate: Express Highway Politics, 1941–1956* (Lawrence: Regents Press of Kansas, 1979).

46. Hofstadter, "What Happened to the Antitrust Movement?" 188.

47. Ibid., and Philip Kovaleff, *Business and Government during the Eisenhower Administration: A Study of the Antitrust Policy of the Antitrust Division of the Justice Department* (Athens: Ohio University Press, 1980).

48. Addison W. Parris's *The Small Business Administration* (New York: Praeger, 1968) is the standard history of the founding and early years of the SBA. See also Zeigler, *The Politics of Small Business*, chap. 7.

49. The SDPA's efforts were, however, largely ineffective. The SDPA had no power to acquire production facilities and then sell or lease them to small businesses, as had the SWPC in World War II. Neither could the SDPA make loans to small businesses. The SDPA could make recommendations on loans to the RFC, but the RFC was under no obligation to follow those recommendations. As in World War II, the federal government favored big businesses in its defense spending for the Korean War. See Zeigler, *The Politics of Small Business*, 102–4.

50. Parris, *The Small Business Administration*, chap. 1.

51. Zeigler, *The Politics of Small Business*, 106.

52. As quoted in Parris, *The Small Business Administration*, 23.

53. Ibid., chaps. 1–2; the quotations are from pp. 3 and 27, respectively.

54. Ibid., chap. 3. The types of loans granted small businesses by the SBA included regular business loans, economic opportunity loans, disaster loans, and development company loans. At the close of 1965, the SBA had outstanding $725 million in regular business loans, $5 million in economic opportunity loans, $230 million in disaster loans, and $60 million in development company loans.

55. Ibid., chap. 11; the quotations are from pp. 233–34.

56. As quoted in Zeigler, *The Politics of Small Business*, 111.

57. Roy Ash and Harry Gray, "How Litton Keeps It Up," *Fortune*, September 1966, 39.

58. Blackford and Kerr, in *Business Enterprise in American History*, 353–61, examine the formation of conglomerates and the merger movement. On American business strategy and the development of conglomerates, see Jon Didrichsen, "The Development of Diversified and Conglomerate Firms in the United States, 1920–1970," *Business History Review* 46 (Summer 1972): 202–19.

59. Blackford and Kerr, *Business Enterprise in American History*, 367. John Kenneth Galbraith, in *The New Industrial State* (Boston: Houghton Mifflin, 1967), provides a vivid account of the development of big business in the United States during the 1950s and 1960s.

60. Kurt Mayer, "Small Business as a Social Institution," *Social Research* 14 (March 1947): 332.

61. Bunzel, *The American Small Businessman*, 59.

62. William A. Brock and David S. Evans, *The Economics of Small Business: Their Role and Regulation in the U.S. Economy* (New York: Holmes and Meier, 1987), 15.

Chapter 4

1. As quoted in James H. Soltow, "Origins of Small Business: Metal Fabricators and Machinery Makers in New England, 1890–1957," *Transactions of the American Philosophical Society* 55 (December 1965): 11.

2. Harold G. Vatter, "The Position of Small Business in the Structure of American Manufacturing, 1870–1970," in *Small Business in American Life*, ed. Stuart Bruchey (New York: Columbia University Press, 1980), 160.

3. David C. Mowery, "Industrial Research and Firm Size, Survival, and Growth in American Manufacturing, 1921–1946: An Assessment," *Journal of Economic History* 43 (December 1983): 953–80.

4. Vatter, "The Position of Small Business," 160.

5. W. Arnold Hosmer, "Small Manufacturing Enterprises," *Harvard Business Review* 35 (November–December 1957): 111–22; the quotation is from p. 118.

6. Ibid., 119.

7. The discussion of this industry is derived from Soltow, "Origins of Small Business." See also Wayne G. Broehl, Jr., *Precision Valley: The Machine Tool Companies of Springfield, Vermont* (Englewood Cliffs, N.J.: Prentice Hall, 1959).

8. Soltow, "Origins of Small Business," 48.

9. Ibid., 11.

10. Max Holland's *When the Machine Stopped: A Cautionary Tale from Industrial America* (Boston: Harvard Business School Press, 1989) is the source of my information on the history of Burg Tool.

11. For case studies of two other successful small industrial companies in the early and middle periods of twentieth-century America, see Paula Petrik, "The House that Parcheesi Built: Selchow and Righter Company," *Business History Review* 60 (Autumn 1986): 410–38, and Michael W. Santos, "Laboring on the Periphery: Managers and Workers at the A. M. Byers Company, 1900–1956," *Business History Review* 61 (Spring 1987): 113–33. Both firms—one in the iron industry, the other in toy making—succeeded as family businesses employing traditional methods of management.

12. As quoted in Richard S. Tedlow, *New and Improved: The Story of Mass Marketing in America* (New York: Basic Books, 1990), 188. Tedlow's study provides an excellent analysis of changes occurring in Amer-

ica's marketing institutions in the twentieth century. Chap. 4 of *New and Improved*, on which parts of this chapter are based, examines the rise of chain stores and supermarkets in the grocery industry.

13. U.S. Bureau of the Census, *Historical Statistics of the United States, Colonial Times to 1957* (Washington, D.C.: U.S. Government Printing Office, 1960), 523.

14. Mansel G. Blackford and K. Austin Kerr, in *Business Enterprise in American History* (Boston: Houghton Mifflin, 1990), 271–74, discuss the rise of chains.

15. U.S. Temporary National Economic Committee (TNEC), "Problems of Small Business," monograph no. 17 (Washington, D.C.: U.S. Government Printing Office, 1941), 176–77.

16. Ibid., Carl G. Ryant, "The South and the Movement against Chain Stores," *Journal of Southern History* 39 (May 1973): 219; and Joseph Cornwall Palamountain, Jr., *The Politics of Distribution* (Cambridge, Mass.: Harvard University Press, 1955), 7.

17. Ibid.

18. The growth of chain stores was also particularly pronounced in pharmaceuticals. By 1935, chain drugstores were making 26% of all drug sales.

19. U.S. Bureau of the Census, *Historical Statistics,* 523.

20. Tedlow, *New and Improved,* 197.

21. Ibid., 198. Tedlow concludes that "the grocery revolution in the interwar years was based predominantly but not solely on price" (197).

22. Ibid., 199–214.

23. Ibid., 238–46.

24. A & P's success was, however, only temporary. Poor managerial decisions led the company into decline from the late 1950s on. See Tedlow, *New and Improved,* 241–54.

25. Palamountain, *The Politics of Distribution,* chap. 6, and Ryant, "The South and the Movement against Chain Stores," 205–22. See also David Horowitz, "The Crusade against Chain Stores: Portland's Independent Merchants, 1928–1935," *Oregon Historical Quarterly* 89 (Winter 1988): 341–68. Tedlow, in *New and Improved,* 214–26, offers a concise summary of the anti–chain store fight.

26. As quoted in Palamountain, *The Politics of Distribution,* 211.

27. Ibid., 245.

28. On the Robinson-Patman Act, see Richard A. Posner, *The Robinson-Patman Act: Federal Regulation of Price Differences* (Washington, D.C.: American Enterprise Institute for Public Policy Research, 1976). While ideologically motivated, this study offers a fairly balanced assessment of the consequences of the measure.

29. Palamountain, *The Politics of Distribution,* 79–81.

30. E. Bruce Geelhoed, "Business and the American Family: A Local View," *Indiana Social Studies Quarterly* 33 (Autumn 1980): 58–67.

31. Edward R. Kantowicz, *John Cotter: 70 Years of Hardware* (Chicago: Regnery Books, 1986). See also Eugene F. Grape, "Retailer-owned Cooperative Wholesaling in the Hardware Trade," Ph.D. diss., Ohio State University, Columbus, 1966.

32. Conversely, as independent retailers formed new types of purchasing arrangements, the number of full-line hardware wholesalers in the United States plummeted from 460 in 1963 to just 210 by 1984. See Kantowicz, *John Cotter,* chap. 14.

33. Marc A. Weiss, in "Real Estate History: An Overview and Research Agenda," *Business History Review* 63 (Summer 1989): 241–82, provides a valuable historiographic review; the quotation is from p. 260. Articles by Christine Meisner Rosen, William B. Friedricks, and Patricia Burgess Stach in the same issue of the journal offer insights into the evolution of different segments of the real estate field.

34. Some large law firms did develop earlier. By the 1950s, Sullivan and Cromwell, a corporate law firm based in New York, had major legal departments in securities, real estate, taxes, antitrust, and litigation. Each department was headed by a senior partner, and a central committee of seven senior partners coordinated the work of the departments. See Nancy Lisagor and Frank Lipsius, *A Law unto Itself: The Untold Story of the Law Firm Sullivan and Cromwell* (New York: Morrow, 1988).

35. U.S. Bureau of the Census, *Historical Statistics,* 7, 672, 677.

36. Ibid., 623–24.

37. Ibid., 631, 635. For a discussion of changes in banking legislation, see Sue Carol Patrick, "Reform of the Federal Reserve System in the Early 1930s: The Politics of Money and Banking," Ph.D. diss., Indiana University, Bloomington, 1988. For more information on the changing structure of American banking, see Gerald C. Fischer, *American Banking Structure* (New York: Columbia University Press, 1968).

38. Bruce Geelhoed, *Bringing Wall Street to Main Street: The Story of K. J. Brown and Company, Inc., 1931–1981* (Muncie, Ind.: Ball State University Business History Series, 1981), vii.

39. John H. Bunzel, *The American Small Businessman* (New York: Knopf, 1962), 28.

40. Much has been written about farm problems in America during the 1920s and 1930s. See, especially, Jerold Auerback, "Southern Tenant Farmers: Socialist Critics of the New Deal," *Labor History* 7 (Winter 1966): 3–18; Gilbert C. Fite, *George N. Peek and the Fight for Farm Parity* (Norman: University of Oklahoma Press, 1954); Van L. Perkins, *Crisis in Agriculture: the Agriculture Adjustment Administration and the New Deal, 1933* (Berkeley: University of California Press, 1969); Theodore Saloutos, "New Deal Agricultural Policy: An Evaluation," *Journal of Ameri-*

can History 61 (September 1974): 394–416; and James H. Shideler, *Farm Crisis, 1919–1923* (Berkeley: University of California Press, 1957).

41. U.S. TNEC, "Agriculture and the National Economy," monograph no. 23 (Washington, D.C.: U.S. Government Printing Office, 1940), 15.

42. Blackford and Kerr, in *Business Enterprise in American History*, 277, 368–70, summarize the major problems American farmers faced. For more detail, see John Shover, *First Majority—Last Minority: The Transforming of Rural Life in America* (De Kalb: Northern Illinois University Press, 1976), and Jay Staten, *The Embattled Farmer* (Golden, Colo.: Fulcrum, 1987).

43. Shover, *First Majority—Last Minority*, 180.

44. As quoted in ibid., 148.

45. Shover, *First Majority—Last Minority*, and Staten, *The Embattled Farmer.*

46. U.S. TNEC, "Agriculture and the National Economy," 9, 13, 23.

47. U.S. Bureau of the Census, *Historical Statistics*, 279.

48. Geelhoeld, "Business and the American Family," 58–67.

49. My *Pioneering a Modern Small Business: Wakefield Seafood and the Alaskan Frontier* (Greenwich, Conn.: JAI Press, 1979), provides a detailed look at the evolution of this company as a successful small business.

50. Ibid., 9–10.

51. Ibid., 21.

52. Gordon Lewis, "A Comparison of Some Aspects of the Backgrounds and Careers of Small Businessmen and American Business Leaders," *American Journal of Sociology* 65 (January 1960): 348–55.

53. Ibid., 352.

54. Abram L. Harris, *The Negro as Capitalist: A Study of Banking and Business among American Negroes* (New York: Negro Universities Press, 1936), 177. See also J. H. Harmon, Jr., Arnett G. Lindsay, and Carter Woodson, *The Negro as Businessman* (College Park, Md.: McGrath, 1929), and Ivan H. Light, *Ethnic Enterprise in America: Business and Welfare among Chinese, Japanese, and Blacks* (Berkeley: University of California Press, 1972).

55. Ronald W. Bailey, ed., *Black Business Enterprise: Historical and Contemporary Perspectives* (New York: Basic Books, 1971), 8–11.

56. Ivan Light, "Asian Enterprise in America," in *Self-Help in Urban America: Patterns of Minority Business Enterprise*, ed. Scott Cummings (Port Washington, N.Y.: Kennikat Press, 1980), 33–57. As Light notes, "The foreign born have been persistently overrepresented in the U.S. business population in this century" (33). For more detail, see Ivan Light and Edna Bonachich, *Immigrant Entrepreneurs: Koreans in Los Angeles, 1965–1982* (Berkeley: University of California Press, 1988).

57. Offering penetrating analyses of these organizations are Richard Hamilton, *Restraining Myths: Critical Studies of U.S. Social Structure and Politics* (New York: John Wiley, 1975), chap. 7, and Harmon Zeigler, *The Politics of Small Business* (Washington, D.C.: Public Affairs Press, 1961), chap. 3.

58. Hamilton, *Restraining Myths*, chap. 2. Hamilton successfully refutes the findings of earlier studies that small business people were more conservative than other Americans (most earlier studies were based on analyses of the rhetoric of the officers of small business organizations, rhetoric that did not accurately represent what most small business people thought). From analyses of voting records, Hamilton concludes: "Small businessmen do not form a conservative monolith. They are not conservative absolutely, or, in comparison with managers or more affluent independents, relatively. . . . The political reality, in short, is just the opposite of what has been claimed. . . . In summary . . . these lines of investigation showed no support for the assumption of special conservatism among marginal businessmen" (67).

59. Blackford and Kerr, in *Business Enterprise in American History*, 370–73, sketch the development of franchising in the United States. The seminal history of franchising is Thomas Dicke, "Franchising in the American Economy, 1840–1980," Ph.D. diss., Ohio State University, Columbus, 1988, forthcoming as a book published by the University of North Carolina Press, 1992.

Chapter 5

1. Small Business Administration, *Annual Report on Small Business and Competition* (Washington, D.C.: U.S. Government Printing Office, 1988), xv–xvi.

2. *U.S. News and World Report*, 23 October 1989, 71.

3. Author's observation, 11 July 1989.

4. On the growth of global competition in manufacturing, see, especially, Alfred D. Chandler, Jr., *Scale and Scope: The Dynamics of Industrial Capitalism* (Cambridge, Mass.: Harvard University Press, 1990), 605–21.

5. Small Business Administration, *Annual Report, 1988*, 19. A more detailed breakdown of the SBA's definitions was under 20 employees, very small; 20–99, small; 100–499, medium-size; and over 500, large.

6. Offering valuable surveys of small business in the modern American economy are Steven Soloman, *Small Business USA: The Role of Small Companies in Sparking America's Economic Transformation* (New York: Crown, 1986), chap. 2, and James H. Thompson and Dennis R. Leyden, "The United States of America," in *The Small Firm: An International Survey*, ed. David J. Storey (New York: St. Martin's Press, 1983).

See also William A. Brock and David S. Evans, "Small Business Economics," *Small Business Economics* 1 (1989): 7–20.

7. Brock and Evans, "Small Business Economics," 7.

8. *Business Week,* 27 February 1989, 94–95; *New York Times,* 27 November 1989; and *USA Today,* 7 May 1990.

9. See, especially, "Eye on the Future: Fear of Layoff Spurs Employees to Launch Part-Time Businesses," *Wall Street Journal,* 25 May 1990, 1.

10. David Storey and S. Johnson, *Job Generation and Labour Market Change* (London: Macmillan, 1987), 125. There are still other possible reasons for the resurgence of small business. New communication technologies have allowed people to run small businesses, such as mail-order enterprises, out of their homes. Some people who came of age in the 1960s may have preferred not "to sell out to the establishment" but to start alternative small businesses instead. Finally, as we shall see in more detail later in this chapter, women have gone into small business ownership when blocked from advancement in large enterprises. I am indebted to Caroline Chin of Twayne Publishers for these thoughts.

11. For an account of the 1986 conference, see "A Tribute to Small Business: America's Growth Industry," a 72-page pamphlet published jointly by the SBA and Pacific Bell in 1987. See also *Wall Street Journal,* 18 August 1986.

12. William A. Brock and David S. Evans, *The Economics of Small Businesses: Their Role and Regulation in the U.S. Economy* (New York: Holmes and Meier, 1986), 184. See also Richard J. Judd, William T. Greenwood, and Fred W. Becker, eds., *Small Business in a Regulated Economy: Issues and Policy Implications* (Westport, Conn.: Quorum Books, 1988).

13. For an overview of the growing importance of small industrial companies worldwide, see Michael J. Piore and Charles F. Sabel, *The Second Industrial Divide: Possibilities for Prosperity* (New York: Basic Books, 1984).

14. Small Business Administration, Office of Advocacy, *Small Business in the American Economy* (Washington, D.C.: U.S. Government Printing Office, 1988), 41, 46–47. Still other statistics illustrate the same trend. For instance, between 1980 and 1985 the share of America's manufacturing shipments accounted for by Fortune 500 companies declined from 89 to 77%. See Bo Carlsson, "The Evolution of Manufacturing Technology and Its Impact on Industrial Structure: An International Study," *Small Business Economics* 1 (1989): 21–37.

15. Soloman, *Small Business USA,* 29.

16. Carlsson, "The Evolution of Manufacturing Technology," 34–35.

17. Michael Storper and Susan Christopher, "Flexible Special-

ization and Regional Industrial Agglomerations: The Case of the U.S. Motion Picture Industry," *Annals of the Association of American Geographers* 71 (March 1987): 104–17.

18. Stanley C. Hollander, "The Effects of Industrialization on Small Retailing in the Twentieth Century," in *Small Business in American Life*, ed. Stuart Bruchey (New York: Columbia University Press, 1980), 219.

19. Soloman, *Small Business USA*, 26.

20. Hollander, "The Effects of Industrialization," 233.

21. Soloman, *Small Business USA*, 27–28.

22. For a survey of franchising in the 1970s and 1980s, see Mansel G. Blackford and K. Austin Kerr, *Business Enterprise in American History* (Boston: Houghton Mifflin, 1990), 372; for more detail, see Thomas S. Dicke, "Franchising in the American Economy, 1840–1980," Ph.D. diss., Ohio State University, Columbus, 1988, chap. 5.

23. *Wall Street Journal*, 15 January 1990.

24. *Wall Street Journal*, 13 September 1989, and *Business Week*, 13 November 1989, 85.

25. *Wall Street Journal* 29 August 1988. See also *Wall Street Journal* 30 December 1988.

26. Blackford and Kerr, in *Business Enterprise in American History*, 368–70, offer a survey of the economic problems family farmers faced in the 1980s; for more detail, see Jay Staten, *The Embattled Farmer* (Golden, Colo.: Fulcrum, 1987). There were exceptions to this generally dismal picture of family farms in decline. By renouncing capital-intensive farming methods (such as the heavy use of artificial fertilizer) and by specializing in the crops they produced, some family farmers continued to succeed. Just how far this "alternative farming" movement would go remains a question in the 1990s. See Jeanne McDermott, "Some Heartland Farmers Just Say No to Chemicals," *Smithsonian*, April 1990, 114–27.

27. Soloman, in *Small Business USA*, chap. 4., offers a valuable survey of innovations made by small businesses.

28. Ray Oakley, Roy Rothwell, and Sarah Cooper's *Management of Innovation in High Technology Small Firms* (Westport, Conn.: Quorum Books, 1988) offers a fascinating comparison of small, high-technology firms in California, southeastern England, and part of Scotland.

29. Thompson and Leyden, "The United States of America," 23.

30. Soloman, *Small Business USA*, 123–24.

31. Zoltan J. Acs and David B. Audretsch, "Innovation in Large and Small Firms: An Empirical Analysis," *American Economic Review* 78 (September 1988): 688.

32. Zoltan J. Acs and David B. Audretsch, "Innovation, Market Structure, and Firm Size," *Review of Economics and Statistics* 69 (No-

vember 1987): 573. For more detail, see Acs and Audretsch, *Innovation and Small Firms* (Cambridge, Mass.: MIT Press, 1990).

33. Soloman, *Small Business USA*, 123.

34. David L. Birch, *Job Creation in America: How Our Smallest Companies Put the Most People to Work* (New York: Free Press, 1987), 9.

35. *Wall Street Journal*, letter to editor, 21 November 1988.

36. *Wall Street Journal*, 8 November 1988. See also *Wall Street Journal*, 12 January 1989 and 13 March 1990 and *New York Times*, 1 May 1988.

37. Storey and Johnson, *Job Generation and Labour Market Change*, 66, 119.

38. Ibid., 3; for a critique of Storey and Johnson, see Felix R. FitzRoy, "Firm Size, Efficiency, and Employment," *Small Business Economics* 1 (1989): 75–80.

39. Soloman, *Small Business USA*, 65–66. For a more optimistic assessment, see Small Business Administration, *Small Business in the American Economy*, 193–97.

40. For an introduction to the nature of entrepreneurs in modern American, see Bruce Kirchhoff, Wayne A. Long, W. Ed McMullan, Karl H. Vesper, William E. Wetzel, Jr., eds., *Frontiers of Entrepreneurship Research* (Wellesley, Mass.: Center for Entrepreneurial Studies, Babson College, 1988). On entrepreneurship in small business, see James Adnor, "The Spirit of Entrepreneurship," *Journal of Small Business Management* 26 (January 1988): 1–4.

41. Donald L. Sexton and Nancy Bowman-Upton, "A Growth Model of New Venture Development," unpublished paper, November 1987. Birch has recently estimated that 18% of America's businesses account for 86% of the new jobs created in the nation; see Birch, *Job Creation in America*, 37–38.

42. "What Do Women Want? A Company They Can Call Their Own," *Business Week*, 22 December 1986, 60–61.

43. Small Business Administration, *Small Business in the American Economy*, 117. Chap. 4 of this report offers a wealth of detailed information about businesses owned by women.

44. "What Do Women Want?" 60–61.

45. Small Business Administration, *Small Business in the American Economy*, 118.

46. Ibid., 117.

47. Ibid., 165–67.

48. Ibid., 165–91. See also *New York Times*, 5 July 1987, and *Wall Street Journal*, 16 May 1986; 20 April, 17 May, and 7 December 1987; and 11 May 1988.

Conclusion

1. Much of this conclusion is derived from Mansel G. Blackford, "Small Business in America: An Historiographic Survey," forthcoming in *Business History Review* 65 (Spring 1991).

2. For an introduction to the development of America's service industries, see Dorothy I. Riddle, *Service-led Growth: The Role of the Service Sector in World Development* (New York: Praeger, 1986).

3. K. Austin Kerr, "Small Business in the United States during the Twentieth Century" (paper presented at the conference on "Comparative Enterprise Management: The Lessons of Business History," Budapest, 13–15 June 1989), 1.

4. David Hounshell and John Smith, Jr., *Science and Corporate Strategy: Du Pont R & D, 1902–1980* (Cambridge, England: Cambridge University Press, 1988), and Leonard S. Reich, *The Making of American Industrial Research: Science and Business at GE and Bell, 1876–1926* (Cambridge, England: Cambridge University Press, 1985).

5. Alfred D. Chandler, Jr., *Scale and Scope: The Dynamics of Industrial Capitalism* (Cambridge, Mass.: Harvard University Press, 1990).

6. Several scholars have compared individual aspects of small business development across national boundaries, but no comprehensive historical account exists. See, for example, Ray Oakley, Roy Rothwell, and Sarah Cooper, *Management of Innovation in High Technology Small Firms* (New York: Quorum Books, 1988), and David Storey, ed., *The Small Firm: An International Survey* (London: Croom Helm, 1983).

SELECTED
BIBLIOGRAPHY

General

Averitt, Robert. *The Dual Economy.* New York: W. W. Norton, 1971.

Blackford, Mansel G. "Small Business in America." In *Business and Economic History,* edited by Paul Uselding, 9–15. Urbana: University of Illinois Press, 1979.

———. "Small Business in America: An Historiographic Essay." *Business History Review* 65 (Spring 1991).

Bowring, Joseph. *Competition in a Dual Economy.* Princeton, N.J.: Princeton University Press, 1986.

Brown, Paul. "The Economics of Small Business Enterprise." Ph.D. diss., Ohio State University, Columbus, 1941.

Bruchey, Stuart, ed. *Small Business in American Life.* New York: Columbia University Press, 1980.

Bunzel, John. *The American Small Businessman.* Salt Lake City: University of Utah Press, 1956.

Carosso, Vincent, and Stuart Bruchey, eds. *The Survival of Small Business.* New York: Arno Press, 1979.

Carson, Deane, ed. *The Vital Majority: Small Business in the American Economy.* Washington, D.C.: Small Business Administration, 1973.

Dicke, Thomas. "The Public Image of Small Business Portrayed in the American Periodical Press, 1900–1938." Master's thesis, Ohio State University, Columbus, 1983.

Galambos, Louis. *The Public Image of Big Business in America, 1880–1940.* Baltimore, Md.: Johns Hopkins University Press, 1975.

Geelhoed, E. Bruce. "Business and the American Family: A Local View." *Indiana Social Studies Quarterly* 33 (Autumn 1980): 58–67.

Hamilton, Richard. *Restraining Myths: Critical Studies of U.S. Social Structure and Politics.* New York: John Wiley, 1975.

Hawley, Ellis. *The New Deal and the Problem of Monopoly.* Princeton, N.J.: Princeton University Press, 1966.

Hutchinson, R. G., A. R. Hutchinson, and Mabel Newcomer. "Study in Business Mortality." *American Economic Review* 28 (September 1938): 497–514.

Kerr, K. Austin. "Small Business in the United States during the Twentieth Century." Paper presented at the conference on "Comparative Enterprise Management: The Lessons of Business History," Budapest, 13–15 June 1989.

Lewis, Gordon. "A Comparison of Some Aspects of the Backgrounds and Careers of Small Businessmen and American Business Leaders." *American Journal of Sociology* 65 (January 1960): 348–55.

Livesay, Harold. "Entrepreneurial Dominance in Businesses Large and Small, Past and Present." *Business History Review* 63 (Spring 1989): 1–21.

———. "Entrepreneurial Persistence through the Bureaucratic Age." *Business History Review* 51 (Winter 1977): 415–43.

Mayer, Kurt. "Small Business as a Social Institution." *Social Research* 14 (March 1947): 332–49.

Newcomer, Mabel. "The Little Businessman: A Study of Business Proprietors in Poughkeepsie, New York." *Business History Review* 35 (Winter 1961): 447–531.

Parris, Addison. *The Small Business Administration.* New York: Praeger, 1968.

Perkins, Edwin. "The Entrepreneurial Spirit of Colonial America: The Foundations of Modern Business History." *Business History Review* 63 (Spring 1989): 160–85.

Phillips, Joseph D. *Little Business in the American Economy.* Urbana: University of Illinois Press, 1958.

Zeigler, Harmon. *The Politics of Small Business.* Washington, D.C.: Public Affairs Press, 1961.

Farming

Appleby, Joyce. "Commercial Farming and the 'Agrarian Myth' in the Early Republic." *Journal of American History* 68 (March 1982): 833–49.

Atack, Jeremy, and Fred Bateman. *To Their Own Soil: Agriculture in the Antebellum North.* Ames: Iowa State University Press, 1987.

Cochrane, Willard, and Mary Ryan. *American Farm Policy, 1948–1973.* Minneapolis: University of Minnesota Press, 1976.

Danbom, David. *The Resisted Revolution: Urban America and the Industrialization of Agriculture, 1900–1930.* Ames: Iowa State University Press, 1979.

Danhof, Clarence. *Changes in Agriculture: The Northern United States, 1820–1870.* Cambridge, Mass.: Harvard University Press, 1969.

Friedberger, Mark. *Farm Families and Change in Twentieth-Century America.* Lexington: University Press of Kentucky, 1988.

Gallman, Robert. "Changes in Total U.S. Agricultural Factor Productivity in the Nineteenth Century." *Agricultural History* 46 (January 1972): 191–210.

Gates, Paul. *The Farmers Age: Agriculture, 1815–1860.* New York: Harper and Row, 1960.

Govan, Thomas. "Agrarian and Agrarianism: A Study in the Use and Abuse of Words." *Journal of Southern History* 30 (February 1964): 35–47.

Hahn, Steven, and Jonathan Prude, eds. *The Countryside in the Age of Capitalist Transformation: Essays in the Social History of Rural America.* Chapel Hill: University of North Carolina Press, 1985.

Hurt, R. Douglas. *American Farm Tools: From Hand-Power to Steam-Power.* Manhattan, Kans.: Sunflower University Press, 1982.

Love, Lester. "Empirical Estimates of Technological Change in U.S. Agriculture, 1850–1958." *Journal of Farm Economics* 44 (November 1962): 941–52.

McConnell, Grant. *The Decline of Agrarian Democracy.* Berkeley: University of California Press, 1959.

McMillen, Wheeler. *Ohio Farm.* Columbus: Ohio State University Press, 1974.

Opie, John. *The Law of the Land: Two Hundred Years of American Farmland Policy.* Lincoln: University of Nebraska Press, 1987.

Pisani, Donald J. *From the Family Farm to Agribusiness: The Irrigation Crusade in California and the West, 1850–1931.* Berkeley: University of California Press, 1989.

Shannon, Fred. *The Farmer's Last Frontier: Agriculture, 1860–1897.* New York: Harper and Row, 1945.

Shover, John. *First Majority—Last Minority: The Transformation of Rural Life in America.* De Kalb: Northern Illinois University Press, 1976.

Staten, John. *The Embattled Farmer.* Golden, Colo.: Fulcrum, 1987.

Manufacturing

Atack, Jeremy. "Firm Size and Industrial Structure in the United States during the Nineteenth Century." *Journal of Economic History* 46 (June 1986): 463–75.

———. "Industrial Structure and the Emergence of the Modern Industrial Corporation." *Explorations in Economic History* 22 (January 1985): 29–52.

Blackford, Mansel G. *Pioneering a Modern Small Business: Wakefield Seafoods and the Alaskan Frontier.* Greenwich, Conn.: JAI Press, 1979.

―――. *A Portrait Cast in Steel: Buckeye International and Columbus, Ohio, 1881–1980.* Westport, Conn.: Greenwood Press, 1982.

Broehl, Wayne G., Jr. *Precision Valley: The Machine Tool Companies of Springfield, Vermont.* Englewood Cliffs, N.J.: Prentice Hall, 1959.

Dicke, Thomas. "The Small Firm and the Associationalist Model: Federal Glass, 1900–1958." In *Essays in Economic and Business History,* edited by Edwin Perkins, 149–61. Los Angeles: University of Southern California Press, 1986.

Dunne, Timothy. "The Measurement and Analysis of Firm Entry and Exit in the United States Manufacturing Sector, 1963–1982." Ph.D. diss., Pennsylvania State University, University Park, 1987.

Fraser, Steven. "Combined and Uneven Development in the Men's Clothing Industry," *Business History Review* 57 (Winter 1983): 522–47.

Heath, Jim. "American War Mobilization and the Use of Small Manufacturers, 1939–1943." *Business History Review* 46 (Autumn 1972): 295–319.

Hosmer, W. Arnold. "Small Manufacturing Enterprises." *Business History Review* 35 (November–December 1957): 111–22.

Ingham, John N. *Making Iron and Steel: Independent Mills in Pittsburgh, 1820–1920* Columbus: Ohio State University Press, 1991.

James, John. "Structural Change in American Manufacturing." *Journal of Economic History* 43 (June 1983): 433–60.

Kornblith, Gary. "The Craftsman as Industrialist: Jonas Chickering and the Transformation of American Piano Making." *Business History Review* 59 (Autumn 1985): 349–68.

Loveday, Amos, Jr. *The Rise and Decline of the American Cut Nail Industry.* Westport, Conn.: Greenwood Press, 1983.

Marburg, Theodore F. *Small Business in Brass Fabricating: The Smith and Griggs Manufacturing Company at Waterbury.* New York: New York University Press, 1956.

Mowery, David C. "Industrial Research and Firm Size, Survival, and Growth in American Manufacturing, 1921–1946: An Assessment." *Journal of Economic History* 43 (December 1983): 953–80.

O'Brien, Patrick. "Factory Size, Economies of Scale, and the Great Merger Wave of 1898–1902." *Journal of Economic History* 48 (September 1988): 639–49.

Petrik, Paula. "The House That Parcheesi Built: Selchow and Richter Company." *Business History Review* 60 (Autumn 1986): 410–37.

Sabel, Charles, and Jonathan Zeitlin. "Historical Alternatives to Mass Production: Politics, Markets, and Technology in Nineteenth Century Industrialization." *Past and Present* 108 (August 1985): 133–76.

Santos, Michael. "Laboring on the Periphery: Managers and Workers at the A. M. Byers Company, 1900–1956." *Business History Review* 61 (Spring 1987): 113–33.

Scranton, Philip. *Figured Tapestry: Production, Markets, and Power in Philadelphia Textiles, 1885–1941.* Cambridge, England: Cambridge University Press, 1989.

———. *Proprietary Capitalism: The Textile Manufacture at Philadelphia, 1800–1885.* Cambridge, England: Cambridge University Press, 1983.

Sokoloff, Kenneth L. "Was the Transition from Artisanal Shop to the Nonmechanized Factory Associated with Gains in Efficiency? Evidence from the U.S. Manufacturing Censuses of 1820 and 1850." *Explorations in Economic History* 20 (October 1984): 351–82.

Soltow, James. "Origins of Small Business: Metal Fabricators and Machinery Makers in New England, 1890–1957." *Transactions of the American Philosophical Society* 55 (December 1965): 1–58.

———. "Small City Industrialists in the Age of Organization: A Case Study of the Manufacturers' Association of Montgomery County, Pennsylvania, 1908–1958." *Business History Review* 33 (Summer 1959): 178–89.

Taber, Martha. *A History of the Cutlery Industry in the Connecticut Valley.* Northampton, Mass.: Smith College Studies in History, 1955.

Vatter, Harold. *Small Enterprise and Oligopoly: A Study of the Butter, Flour, Automobile, and Glass Container Industries.* Corvallis: Oregon State University Press, 1955.

———. *The U.S. Economy in World War II.* New York: Columbia University Press, 1985.

Distribution and Services

Adelman, Morris. *A & P: A Study in Price-Cost Behavior and Public Policy.* Cambridge, Mass.: Harvard University Press, 1959.

Atherton, Lewis. "Itinerant Merchandising in the Antebellum South." *Bulletin of the Business Historical Society* 19 (1945): 35–59.

———. *The Pioneer Merchant in Mid-America.* Columbia: University of Missouri Studies, 1939.

———. *The Southern Country Store, 1800–1860.* Baton Rouge: Louisiana State University Press, 1949.

Carson, Gerald. *The Old Country Store.* New York: Oxford University Press, 1954.

Charvat, Frank. "The Development of the Supermarket Industry through 1950 with Emphasis on Concomitant Changes in the Food Store Sales Pattern." Ph.D. diss., Northwestern University, Evanston, Illinois, 1954.

Clark, Thomas D. *Pills, Petticoats, and Plows: The Southern Store.* Norman: University of Oklahoma Press, 1944.

Dart, Jack. "Power, Conflict, and Satisfaction: Perceptions of Shopping Center–Based Small Retailers." *American Journal of Small Business* 12 (Winter 1988): 35–44.

Dicke, Thomas. "A History of Franchising in America, 1840–1978." Ph.D. diss., Ohio State University, Columbus, 1988; publication forthcoming by the University of North Carolina Press in 1992.

Geelhoeld, Bruce. *Bringing Wall Street to Main Street: The Story of K. J. Brown and Company, Inc.* Muncie, Ind.: Ball State University Publications, 1981.

German, Gene Arlin. "The Dynamics of Food Retailing, 1900–1975." Ph.D. diss., Cornell University, Ithaca, New York, 1978.

Grape, Eugene F. "Retailer-owned Wholesaling in the Hardware Trade." Ph.D. diss., Ohio State University, Columbus, 1966.

Hollander, S. C. *Restraints upon Retail Competition.* East Lansing: Michigan State University Press, 1965.

Horowitz, David. "The Crusade against Chain Stores: Portland's Independent Merchants, 1928–1935." *Oregon Historical Quarterly* 89 (Winter 1988): 341–68.

Howard, Marshall. "The Marketing of Petroleum Products: A Study in the Relations between Large and Small Business." Ph.D. diss., Cornell University, Ithaca, New York, 1951.

Jones, Fred Mitchell. "Middlemen in the Domestic Trade of the United States." *Illinois Studies in the Social Sciences* 21 (1937): 1–81.

——. "Retail Stores in the United States, 1800–1860." *Journal of Marketing* 1 (October 1936): 134–42.

Kantowicz, Edward. *John Cotton: 70 Years of Hardware.* Chicago: Regnery, 1986.

Madison, James B. "Changing Patterns of Urban Retailing in the 1920s." In *Business and Economic History,* edited by Paul Uselding, 102–11. Urbana: University of Illinois Press, 1976.

——. "The Evolution of Commercial Credit Reporting Agencies in Nineteenth-Century America." *Business History Review* 48 (Summer 1974): 164–86.

Marx, Thomas. "The Development of the Franchise Distribution System in the U.S. Automobile Industry." *Business History Review* 59 (Autumn 1985): 465–74.

Merwin, Charles. *Financing Small Corporations in Five Manufacturing Industries, 1926–1936.* New York: Arno Press, 1942.

Palamountain, Joseph, Jr. *The Politics of Distribution.* Cambridge, Mass.: Harvard University Press, 1955.

Richards, Max. "Intermediate and Long-Term Credit for Small Corporations." Ph.D. diss., University of Illinois, Urbana, 1955.

Riddle, Dorothy. *Service-led Growth: The Role of the Service Sector in World Development.* New York: Praeger, 1986.

Rowe, Frederick. *Price Discrimination under the Robinson-Patman Act.* Boston: Little, Brown, 1962.

Ryant, Carl. "The South and the Movement against Chain Stores." *Journal of Southern History* 39 (May 1973): 207–22.

Zimmerman, M. M. *The Super Market: A Revolution in Distribution.* New York: Mass Distribution Services, 1959.

Modern-Day America

Acs, Zoltan J., and David B. Audretsch. "Innovation in Large and Small Firms: An Empirical Analysis." *American Economic Review* 78 (September 1988): 678–90.

———. "Innovation, Market Structure, and Firm Size." *Review of Economics and Statistics* 69 (November 1987): 567–74.

———. *Innovation and Small Firms.* Cambridge, Mass.: MIT Press, 1990.

Birch, David. *Job Creation in America: How Our Smallest Companies Put the Most People to Work.* New York: Free Press, 1987.

Brock, William A., and David S. Evans. *The Economics of Small Business: Their Role and Regulation in the U.S. Economy.* New York: Holmes and Meier, 1986.

Carlsson, Bo. "The Evolution of Manufacturing Technology and Its Impact on Industrial Structure." *Small Business Economics* 1 (1989): 21–38.

Fitzroy, Felix R. "Firm Size, Efficiency, and Employment." *Small Business Economics* 1 (1989): 75–80.

Frontiers of Entrepreneurship Research. Various editors. Wellesley, Mass.: Babson College, 1981–88.

Gumpert, David, ed. *Growing Concerns: Building and Managing the Smaller Business.* New York: John Wiley, 1984.

Hollander, Edward. *The Future of Small Business.* New York: Praeger, 1967.

Judd, Richard J., William T. Greenwood, and Fred W. Becker. *Small Business in a Regulated Economy: Issues and Policy Implications.* Westport, Conn.: Quorum Books, 1988.

Oakey, Ray, Roy Rothwell, and Sarah Cooper. *Management of Innovation in High Technology Small Firms.* Westport, Conn.: Greenwood Press, 1988.

Rothwell, Roy, and Walter Zegveld. *Industrial Innovation and Public Policy: *Preparing for the 1980s and 1990s.* London: Frances Pinter, 1981.

Soloman, Steven. *Small Business USA: The Role of Small Companies in Sparking America's Economic Transformation.* New York: Crown, 1986.

Storper, M., and Susan Christopher. "Flexible Specialization and Regional Agglomerations: The Case of the U.S. Motion Picture Industry." *Annals of the Association of American Geography 77* (March 1987): 104–17.

Small Business Abroad

Bannock, Graham. *The Economics of Small Firms: Return from the Wilderness.* Oxford, England: Basil Blackwell, 1981.

Benson, John. *The Penny Capitalists: A Study of Nineteenth-Century Working-Class Entrepreneurs.* New Brunswick, N.J.: Rutgers University Press, 1983.

Blim, Michael L. *Made in Italy: Small Scale Industrialization and Its Consequences.* New York: Praeger, 1990.

Boswell, Jonathan. *The Rise and Decline of Small Firms.* London: George Allen and Unwin, 1973.

Burns, Paul, and Jim Dewhurst, eds. *Small Business in Europe.* London: Macmillan, 1986.

Curran, James, John Stanworth, and David Watkins, eds. *The Survival of the Small Firm.* 2 vols. Brookfield, Vt.: Gower, 1986.

Gill, John. *Factors Affecting the Survival and Growth of the Smaller Company.* Brookfield, Vt.: Gower, 1985.

Koshiba, Tesshu. "Intra-Industry Trade in the Manufacturing Industries of Japan." Paper presented at the Japan Association for Planning Administration, Tohoku University, 9–10 November 1985.

Okochi, Akio, and Shigeaki Yasuoka, eds. *Family Business in the Era of Industrial Growth.* Tokyo: University of Tokyo Press, n.d.

Pelzel, John. "The Small Industrialist in Japan." *Explorations in Entrepreneurial History 7* (1954): 79–93.

Piore, Michael, and Charles Sabel. *The Second Industrial Divide.* New York: Basic Books, 1984.

Rose, Mary B. *The Gregs of Quarry Bank Mill: The Rise and Decline of a Family Firm, 1750–1914.* New York: Cambridge University Press, 1986.

Soltow, James. "Entrepreneurial Strategy in Small Industry: Belgian Metal Fabricators." *Proceedings of the American Philosophical Society 115* (January 1971): 32–64.

Steindl, Joseph. *Small and Big Business.* Oxford, England: Basil Blackwell, 1947.

Storey, David. *Entrepreneurship and the New Firm*. London: Croom Helm, 1982.

———. *The Small Firm: An International Survey*. New York: St. Martin's Press, 1983.

Storey, David, and Steven Johnson. *Job Generation and Labour Market Change*. New York: Macmillan, 1987.

Winstanley, Michael. *The Shopkeeper's World, 1830–1914*. Manchester, England: Manchester University Press, 1983.

Yasuoka, Shigeaki. "Ownership and Management of Family Businesses: An International Comparison." Paper published by United Nations University, 1982.

INDEX

accounting practices, 6, 9, 30–31, 46
Acs, Zoltan J., xix
agribusiness, 47–48, 97–98, 113
agriculture, in colonial and antebellum
    America, 3, 11–15; and the family
    farm, 12–13, 49–51, 98–99, 113;
    in 1880–1920, 47–53; in 1921–71,
    96–101; since 1971, 113
American Association of Small Busi-
    ness, 78
American Stores, 89
American Tobacco Company, 32
apprenticeship system, 16–17
Arnold, Thurmond, 71
associationalism, 68
artisans, 3, 15–20
Atack, Jeremy, xix
Atherton, Lewis, xvi
Atlantic Fruit and Sugar Company, 30
Averitt, Robert, xviii

Bank of North America, 21
banking, 21–23, 55–59, 95–96, 112
Banks of the United States, 22–23, 55
Baruch, Bernard, 67
Berthoff, Rowland, xiv
Birch, David, xx, 115–16
Blackford, Mansel, xvii
Blue Cross, 95
Blue Shield, 95
Boston Associates, 17, 38
Bowring, Joseph, xviii
Bradstreet Company, 55

brass-making, xvi, 44–45
Bretton Woods Agreement, 76, 106
Brown, Moses, 17
Bruchey, Stuart, xvi, xviii
Buckeye Steel Castings Company, 43–
    47, 59, 68
Bunzel, John, xiv
Burg Tool Company, 86–88

Carlsson, Bo, xix
Carnegie Steel Company, 27–28, 41–
    42 See also: United States Steel
    Corporation
Cellar-Kefauver Act, 77
Century 21, 95
chain stores, 53–54, 70, 89–93 See
    also: Robertson-Patman Act and
    Miller-Tydings Act
Chandler, Alfred D., Jr., xiii, 4, 124
Chickering, Jonas, 18
Christopher, Susan, xix
Clayton Act, xv, 33, 91
Coldwell Banker, 95
Conference of American Small Business
    Organizations, 78, 103
conglomerates, 80
Cotter, John, 94
country stores, xvi, 1–2, 6–10, 24, 54
Courtauld, Samuel, 23
credit-rating industry, 22, 55
Crugar, Henry, 5
cutlery-making, xvi, 19

Davenport, Marcia, 27
defense spending, 67–68, 74–77
definitions of small business, xi–xiii, 107
department stores, 10–11, 53, 89
Dicke, Thomas, xvii
dual economy, xviii, 57–60, 104–105, 124
Dunn and Bradstreet Company, 55, 57

Elkins Act, 34
Eisenhower, Dwight D., 77–78

Federal Reserve Act, 34
Federal Reserve System, 34, 70
Federal Trade Commission, 33
First National Stores, 89
flexible production, xix, 19, 39–40, 57, 84, 109–111, 122
foreign trade, 4, 49, 76, 107–108
franchising, xvii, 59–60, 104–105, 112–13
Fraser, Stephen, xvii

Galbraith, John Kenneth, xviii, 115
General Agreement on Tariffs and Trade, 76, 106
Goodspeed, Wilbur, 43–44
Great Atlantic and Pacific Tea Company (A & P), 53–54, 89–93
grocery industry, 89–93
Grund, Francis, xiv
Gumpert, David, xix

Hamilton, Richard, xviii
Hancock, Thomas, 5, 24
hardware industry, 94–95
Hepburn Act, 34
Hidy, Ralph, xi
Hoover, Herbert, 68–69
House of Morgan, 56–57
Humphry, George M., 78
Hyatt Legal Services, 95

ideology of small business, 23–24, 60–61, 101–104, 116–20, 122 *See also*: public attitudes

Independent Grocers' Association, 93
industrialization, 17, 28 *See also*: manufacturing
Ingham, John, xvii, xix, 123
insurance industry, 22, 55, 58–59, 95
Interstate Commerce Commission, 34

J.C. Penny Company, 89
Jackson, Andrew, 8, 22
Jefferson, Thomas, 25
job creation, 106–107, 114–16
Jones, John Beauchamp, 1–2, 9

K.J. Brown Company, 96
Kaufman, Daniel, 14–15
Kirk, Charles, 94
Kroger Company, 89

Lopez, Aaron, 5–6
Loveday, Amos, xvii
Lowell, Francis Cabot, 17
Lukens, Rebecca, 25

machine-making, xvi, 84–88, 109–110
Mann-Elkins Act, 34
Manufacturer's Association of Montgomery County, Massachusetts, 60–61
manufacturing, xvi–xviii; in the colonial and antebellum years, 3, 15–20; in 1880–1920, 27–29, 35–47; in 1921–71, 74–76, 83–88; since 1971, 109–111
Marburg, Theodore, xvi
Mayer, Kurt, xvii
McFadden Act, 96
McMillen, Lewis D., 50–51
Meat Inspection Act, 34
merchants, 1–11, 17
mergers, 29–30, 68, 80;
metal-working *See* machine-making
Miller-Tydings Act, xv, 70, 92–93, 124
minorities, 25, 58–59, 102–103, 119–20, 124
Morgan, J.P., 56
Morris, Robert, 21

mortality rates, 58, 73–74, 116–17
moviemaking, xix, 111

National Advisory Council of Independent Small Businesses, 103
National Association of Manufacturers, 47, 61
National Association of Retail Druggists, 61, 92
National Federation of Independent Businesses, 78, 103
National Industrial Recovery Act, 69
National Recovery Administration, 69
National Small Business Men's Association, 78, 103
New Deal, 69–74

Palamountain, Joseph, xvii–xviii
Parry, David, 61
Patman, Wright, 91–92
peddlers, 5, 11
Phillips, Joseph, xviii
Piore, Michael J., xix
public attitudes toward small business, 31–35, 64–67
Pure Food and Drug Act, 34

R.G. Dunn Company, 55
Reagan, Ronald, xi, 109
real estate industry, 95, 112
Reconstruction Finance Corporation, 69–70, 77–78, 99–100
Regulatory Fexibility Act, xv, 109
research and development, 83, 114–15, 123
retailing, xviii; by country stores, xvi, 6–10; specialization in, 10–11, in 1880–1920, 53–54; in 1921–71, 88–95; since 1971, 111
Riggin, Rea, 98–99
Robertson, Ross, xii
Robinson-Patman Act, xv, 70, 91–93, 124
Rogers, Everett M., 97
Roosevelt, Franklin D., 63, 69–71, 103

Sabel, Charles F., xix
Santos, Michael, xvii

Scovil Company, 11
Scranton, Philip, xvii, xix, 123
Service Corps of Retired Executives, 79
service industries, in colonial and antebellum America, 20–23; in 1880–1920, 54–57; in 1921–1971, 95–96; since 1971, 111–12
Sherman Act, xv, 32–33, 92
Simpson, Abraham, 9
Slater, Samuel, 17
Small Business Administration, 106, 115, 118–19; creation of, xv, 77–78; and definitions of small business, xii–xiii, 78–79, 107; work of, 78–80, 109
Small Business Conference (1938), 63, 78
Small Defense Plants Administration, 77
Smaller War Plants Corporation, 74–75, 77
Smaller War Plants Division, 74–75, 77
Smith and Griggs Company, xvi, 44–45
Soltow, James, xvi–xvii
Standard Oil Company, 32, 44
steel-making, xvii, 27–28, 41–44, 68, 84 *See also* machine-making
Stewart, Alexander T., 53
Storper, Michael, xix
supermarkets, 90–91, 94–95

Taber, Martha, xvi
Temporary National Economic Committee, 71, 73–74, 76, 81, 97–98
textile-making, xvii, 17, 20, 38–41, 47, 84
Tocqueville, Alexis de, xi, 13, 23
Toxic Substances Control Act, 109
Trimble, John Allen, 7
True Value Hardware, 94–95

United Fruit Company, 30
United States Steel Corporation, 28, 41

Vatter, Harold, xviii

Wakefield, Lowell, 99
Wakefield Seafoods, 99–101

War Industries Board, 67–68
White House Conference on Small Business (1986), 109
wholesaling, 6, 53–54
Willing, Thomas, 22

Wilson, Woodrow, 67
women, 25, 58, 117–19, 124
Woolworths, 89

Zeigler, Harmon, xviii

THE AUTHOR

Mansel G. Blackford is a professor at The Ohio State University, where he teaches business history. He has published *Politics of Business in California, Pioneering a Modern Small Business, A Portrait Cast in Steel, Business Enterprise in American History* (with K. Austin Kerr), *The Rise of Modern Business in Great Britain, the United States, and Japan,* and *Local Businesses: Exploring their History* (with K. Austin Kerr and Amos Loveday). He has served as the president of the Economic and Business Historical Society and as a trustee of the Business History Society. He has taught for two years as a Senior Fulbright Lecturer to Japan.